What Government Does:
How Political Executives Manage

Also by Paul R. Lawrence and Mark A. Abramson

Paths to Making a Difference: Leading in Government

Learning the Ropes: Insights for Political Appointees

Transforming Organizations

What Government Does:
How Political Executives Manage

Paul R. Lawrence
Ernst & Young LLP

Mark A. Abramson
Leadership Inc.

ROWMAN & LITTLEFIELD PUBLISHERS, INC.
Lanham • Boulder • New York • Toronto • Plymouth, UK

ROWMAN & LITTLEFIELD PUBLISHERS, INC.

Published in the United States of America
by Rowman & Littlefield Publishers, Inc.
A wholly owned subsidiary of The Rowman & Littlefield Publishing Group, Inc.
4501 Forbes Boulevard, Suite 200, Lanham, Maryland 20706
http://www.rowmanlittlefield.com

Estover Road, Plymouth PL6 7PY, United Kingdom

British Library Cataloguing in Publication Information Available

Library of Congress Cataloging-in-Publication Data

Lawrence, Paul R., 1956-
What government does : how political executives manage / [edited by] Paul R. Lawrence
and Mark A. Abramson.
    p. cm.
    Includes bibliographical references.
    ISBN 978-1-4422-3242-6 (cloth : alk. paper)—ISBN 978-1-4422-3244-0 (ebook)
    ISBN 978-1-4422-3243-3 (paper : alk. paper): 1. Government executives—United
    States. 2. Political leadership—United States. : I. Title.
    JK723.E9 P39 2014
    352.60973—dc23

                                                                    2011034368

Printed in the United States of America

♾™ The paper used in this publication meets the minimum requirements of American
National Standard for Information Sciences—Permanence of Paper for Printed Library
Materials, ANSI/NISO Z39.48-1992.

To

*Allison Paige Lawrence and
Gregory James Lawrence*

Dylan, Olivia, and Otis Abramson

Benjamin Koen

Contents

Acknowledgments

In undertaking a four-year project, there are numerous people to thank for their valuable assistance over the project's length. We want to first thank the Ernst & Young LLP professionals who participated. We want to thank Marc Andersen, Werner Lippuner, Aloha McBride, Kevin Nagel, Rollie Quinn, Robert Shope, and Linda Springer for their support and valuable assistance.

We want to thank the support team that assisted us in the production of the book series. We want to thank Lucia Barzellato, Lori Bin, Les Brorsen, Mark Bushell, Cheryl Overby, Stephen Seliskar, Eboni Thomas, Lauren Verdery, and Karon Walker from Ernst & Young LLP. Special thanks to Uschi Schreiber, Ernst & Young Global Government and Public Sector Leader.

We want to thank Philip Kent and Suzanne Glassman for their work on many of the photographs that appear throughout the book. We were ably assisted by Sean Heffernan, who worked closely with us on the preparation of the book series. We received invaluable assistance from Linnae Vaughn throughout the entire project.

The book series could not have been completed without our top-notch production team at FIREBRAND. We want to thank Sandy Jones, Effie Metropoulos, and Scott Rodgerson for their hard work on this four-year project. We want to especially thank Sandy Jones for making numerous revisions throughout the layout and editing stages of the production process for all three books in the series. We want to thank Effie Metropoulos for her excellent editing skills and for achieving the difficult goal of consistency throughout the book series.

We want to thank Jon Sisk and Benjamin Verdi at Rowman & Littlefield for their valuable assistance. We have enjoyed working with Jon over the years on numerous books.

Chapter Two is adapted from Chapters 2–4, Paul R. Lawrence and Mark A. Abramson, *Paths to Making a Difference: Leading in Government, Revised Edition* (Lanham: Rowman & Littlefield Publishers, Inc., 2011). Part of Chapter Two is based on material that was originally published in *The Public Manager*, Summer 2012, and is used with permission from *The Public Manager*. The essays on pages 25–32 were adapted from the AOL Government website. Aloha McBride and Marc Andersen assisted in the preparation of the essays.

Last but certainly not least are the 42 individuals who agreed to be featured in this book and who gave us a substantial amount of their time. It is a true understatement to say that there would have been no book series without their participation. In addition, we want to thank their staffs for working closely with us in scheduling our interviews and reviewing our final product.

We learned that each of the participants is ably supported by thoughtful and energetic staff members who assist them in accomplishing their organization's mission: Rebecca Adelman, Tammi Adair, James Anderson, Janet Arneson, Jennifer Arvantis, Michael Barre, Christopher Bentley, Andrea Bleistein, Terrence Bogans, Linda Bonney, Marcy Brodsky, Yvonne Brown, Miles Brundage, Megan Byrnes, Jeff Carter, Debbie Crump, Marcia Davies, Karen Duncan, Stephen Dunwoody, Catherine Early, Brenda Faas, Stephanie Fine, Paige Fitzgerald, Warren Flatau, Betty Garrison, Catina Gibbs, William Glavin, Andrew Gumbiner, Marla Hendriksson, Angela Hogue, Denise Herbert, Linda Holland, Thomas Irwin, Charlyn Isaac, Beth Jones, Dennis Jones, Bartel Kendrick, Dottie Lee, Jennifer Lee, Thomas Lillie, Debra Livramento, Rose Lusi, Amit Magdieli, Chad Maisel, Brittney Manchester, Charles McLeod, Dawn Mimes, Dixi Moody, V. Gabriela Morales, Mary O'Driscoll, Patty Pace, Kelly Palmer, Peter Pappas, Naureen Rahman, Grace Ramdat, Jennifer Rankin Byrne, Belinda Rawls, Gareth Rees, Lucy Salah, Emily Schwartz, Melissa Schwartz, Roslyn Sellars, Yolanda Sharpe, Nadia Shepherd, Alexandra Sova, Joel Spangenberg, Garth Spencer, Ben Stein, Jen Stutsman, Carol Thomas, Maria Thomas, Laura Thrower, Lucas Tickner, Lynda Tran, Sedelta Verble, Krishanti Vignarajah, Cheryl Walker, Matthew Warshaw, Lily West, Deidre Wilkinson, Demetriss Williams, Maureen Wood, and Katie Yocum.

Chapter One

Introduction

Introduction

What This Book Is About

In the spring of 2009, we launched an ambitious project. Would 42 top political executives in the Obama Administration be willing to meet with us regularly for interviews to discuss their experience managing in government? Our initial goal was to track their learning curve and understand more about their journeys as political executives.

We wanted to capture the experience of political executives in real time while it was still fresh. There is a clear need to better understand the experience of political executives so that lessons can be learned and shared. We wanted to document their insights as reported to us, so that they might be shared with future political executives.

In addition to learning about the management experiences of the political executives we interviewed (Chapter Two), we also learned much about what government does. While it was not a surprise, the dramatic range in government activities impressed us. This book is also about the wide range of activities undertaken by the federal government. Several of the agencies date their origin back to the Constitution of the United States. The National Institute of Standards and Technology and the United States Patent and Trademark Office proudly point to their constitutional origins.

From our research, we developed a typology based on what government actually does. While the public may perceive government as all about policy, the bulk of government work is about delivering specific services either directly to the American public or conducting activities on behalf of the nation. Based on our research, we devote chapters to leaders of government agencies whose jobs we have organized as follows:

- **The Deputy Secretaries:** Federal Cabinet Departments are run by their Chief Operating Officer, the Deputy Secretary. Based on interviews with 11 Deputy Secretaries, we describe insights about managing federal Cabinet Departments to produce results.
- **The Producers:** Based on interviews with nine producers, this chapter describes agencies that have clear deliverables to the public, such as providing student loans, veterans benefits, and transportation security.
- **The Regulators:** Based on interviews with seven regulators, this chapter describes agencies that regulate the nation's safety, such as the Food and Drug Administration and the Consumer Product Safety Commission.
- **The Infrastructors:** Based on interviews with four infrastructors, this chapter describes federal agencies responsible for the nation's infrastructure, such as the Federal Highway Administration and the Federal Railroad Administration.

- **The Scientists:** Based on interviews with five science executives, this chapter describes the nation's top science organizations, responsible for delivering first-rate research and development; they include the U.S. Geological Survey and the National Institute of Standards and Technology.
- **The Collaborators:** Based on interviews with six collaborators, this chapter describes the challenge of leading small agencies in which the political executive must forge partnerships and alliances with other federal agencies and the private and non-profit sectors.

Another goal of this book is to provide useful insights to the White House Office of Presidential Personnel (OPP). The job of the OPP is to select the nation's top political executives—a crucial task. This book offers OPP a way to think about the political positions it is filling. Traditionally, presidential appointee positions are organized by Department or around policy clusters (health, defense, natural resources). As noted above, we offer a framework organized around the activities conducted by government. The job "specs" for a producer (Chapter Four), a regulator (Chapter Five), or a Deputy Secretary (Chapter Three) are dramatically different. The desired professional backgrounds and other requirements for each type of position are discussed in each chapter.

To appreciate this alternative framework, consider the following pages, in which we present a list of the 42 political executives we interviewed over a four-year period from 2009 to 2013. This presentation lists the executives interviewed by Department. In contrast, the Table of Contents of this book lists the individuals interviewed by type of agency. We believe that this framework better reflects the reality of what government does and offers a framework in which to assess the desired skillsets for each type of agency.

What We Would Like the Office of Presidential Personnel to Know About Different Types of Jobs

Based on our interviews, we believe that the following insights will be useful to the Office of Presidential Personnel in selecting political executives. While the lessons below might be self-evident, we believe it is helpful to restate them and reiterate their importance.

Insight One: All jobs are not the same. Throughout this book, we cluster the positions studied around the type of functions to be performed in the position. While it may be readily apparent that being a government scientist is different from being a regulator, which is different from being a producer, we continue to find many examples of the presumption that all jobs are the same and that any smart person can fill any of them. This is not the case.

Specifically, this book makes an important distinction between "policy" jobs and "management" jobs. All the positions described in this book are management positions. While many come to Washington to "do policy," much of the work of

List of Political Executives Interviewed by Organization

Consumer Product Safety Commission
Inez Moore Tenenbaum, Chairman

Department of Agriculture
Jonathan S. Adelstein, Administrator, Rural Utilities Service
Kathleen A. Merrigan, Deputy Secretary

Department of Commerce
Rebecca M. Blank, Under Secretary for Economic Affairs, Economics and Statistics
    Administration
Patrick D. Gallagher, Director, National Institute of Standards and Technology and
    Under Secretary of Commerce for Standards and Technology
Dennis F. Hightower, Deputy Secretary
David A. Hinson, National Director, Minority Business Development Agency
David J. Kappos, Under Secretary of Commerce for Intellectual Property and
    Director, United States Patent and Trademark Office
Kathryn D. Sullivan, Deputy Administrator, National Oceanic and Atmospheric
    Administration

Department of Education
Anthony W. Miller, Deputy Secretary
James W. Runcie, Chief Operating Officer, Office of Federal Student Aid
William J. Taggart, former Chief Operating Officer, Office of Federal Student Aid

Department of Energy
Arun Majumdar, Director, Advanced Research Projects Agency-Energy
Richard G. Newell, Administrator, U.S. Energy Information Administration
Daniel B. Poneman, Deputy Secretary

Department of Health and Human Services
William V. Corr, Deputy Secretary
Margaret A. Hamburg, Commissioner, Food and Drug Administration
Pamela S. Hyde, Administrator, Substance Abuse and Mental Health Services
    Administration,
Mary K. Wakefield, Administrator, Health Resources and Services Administration

Department of Homeland Security
Rafael Borras, Under Secretary for Management
Alejandro Mayorkas, Director, U.S. Citizenship and Immigration Services
John T. Morton, Director, United States Immigration and Customs Enforcement
John S. Pistole, Administrator, Transportation Security Administration

Department of Housing and Urban Development
Maurice Jones, Deputy Secretary
David H. Stevens, Assistant Secretary for Housing and Commissioner,
    Federal Housing Administration

Department of Labor
Seth D. Harris, Deputy Secretary
Raymond M. Jefferson, Assistant Secretary of the Veterans' Employment and
    Training Service
Joseph A. Main, Assistant Secretary of Labor for Mine Safety and Health

Department of State
Thomas R. Nides, Deputy Secretary for Management and Resources

Department of the Interior
Daniel M. Ashe, Director, U.S. Fish and Wildlife Service
Michael R. Bromwich, Director, Bureau of Ocean Energy Management, Regulation
    and Enforcement
David J. Hayes, Deputy Secretary
Marcia K. McNutt, Director, U.S. Geological Survey

Department of Transportation
Victor M. Mendez, Administrator, Federal Highway Administration
David L. Strickland, Administrator, National Highway Traffic Safety Administration
Joseph C. Szabo, Administrator, Federal Railroad Administration

Department of Veterans Affairs
W. Scott Gould, Deputy Secretary
Allison A. Hickey, Under Secretary for Benefits
Robert A. Petzel, Under Secretary for Health

Federal Energy Regulatory Commission
Jon Wellinghoff, Chairman

Office of Personnel Management
John Berry, Director

United States Nuclear Regulatory Commission
Allison M. Macfarlane, Chairman

agencies is about executing—not making—policy. This book does not include policy jobs, such as the Assistant Secretary for Policy and Planning position.

The concepts of a policy person and a managerial person are archetypes that can be used in sorting candidates for the right job. A policy person is clearly appropriate for the position of Assistant Secretary for Planning and Evaluation (ASPE) in the Department of Health and Human Services. Based on observations over the years and research conducted for this book, a managerial person faces a high probability of being frustrated by the "lack of action" and "all that talking and debating" when placed in a policy job. Conversely, a policy person may find a managerial position frustrating. In the case of the producers, they find great satisfaction in serving in agencies where there are clear objectives and performance data. As Bill Taggart tells us, "There are two separate sets of skills—the implementers are not the policy folks and the policy makers are not implementers."

Insight Two: Identify the right set of experiences for the job. To us, the most compelling part of OPP's job is deciding upon the set of experiences most needed in a specific position at a specific point in time. There is no doubt that nearly everyone on the long list for a Presidential appointment is clearly qualified, in the sense of having a distinguished professional career and impressive educational credentials. But the key question is whether the person has the right set of experiences for a specific job at the point in time when she or he is selected.

An example of changing the desired set of experiences for a job is the White House decision in 1998 to seek a "manager" as the head of the Internal Revenue Service (IRS). Throughout its history, the IRS had always had a distinguished tax lawyer as its head. In 1998, a decision was made to look for a business executive who would be able to manage the information technology challenges then facing IRS. Charles Rossotti was selected. The right set of experiences had changed for IRS. In 2013, President Obama nominated another individual with extensive business experience, John Koskinen, to serve as IRS Commissioner.

In this book, another example of the White House deciding on a new set of desired experiences for a position is the selection of Michael Bromwich to take over the Minerals Management Service (MMS) in the Department of the Interior in the aftermath of the Deep Horizon crisis in the Gulf of Mexico. Instead of seeking an individual with the traditional set of energy and natural resources experience for MMS, a decision was made to recruit an executive with crisis management and turnaround skills. In addition, at that point in the history of MMS, it was appropriate (and perhaps necessary) to select an individual who had *not* had previous experience with the energy industry.

Insight Three: Experience matters for each job. After coming to agreement on the right set of experiences, realizing the importance of experience cannot ever be overestimated. A key job facing OPP is determining the right set of experiences for a specific moment in an organization's history. After that determination is made, finding people with the right set of experiences is crucial.

An additional challenge for the OPP is anticipating problems ahead of time and making selections partly based on the question, "What type of individual and what type of experience would be necessary if the agency faced a major crisis?" In the case of the Mine Safety and Health Administration, Administrator Joe Main had the experience to deal with the Upper Big Branch mine explosion. Main recalls, "I've lived through these experiences before, so I knew what to expect … My experiences earlier in my career were crucial."

Chapter Two

The Job of the Political Executive:
Running an Agency

The Job of the Political Executive: Running an Agency

What do political executives do? How do they spend their time? What do they leave behind after their tenure? To answer these questions, we interviewed 42 top political executives in the Obama Administration (as described in Chapter One).

Our interviews focused on how each of the 42 executives spent their time and energy. We found that they spent much of their time on management. The box below lists seven key activities of political executives.

The subtitle of this chapter is "Running an Agency." Sometimes to their surprise, the executives we interviewed spent a large part of their job managing the organization to which they were appointed. Political executives often come to Washington initially to make policy but soon find out that their role in policy may, in fact, be somewhat limited for a variety of reasons. Indeed, they spend much of their time making sure the agency runs right. This phenomenon is described by Sheila Bair, former Chairman of the Federal Deposit Insurance Corporation, in her memoir: "As it turned out, though I took the FDIC job because of my love for financial policy issues, I found that a substantial part of my time was spent dealing with management problems" (Bair).

Like Bair, Mary Wakefield came to Washington to work on health policy. While Wakefield knew that she would be spending time working with HRSA's network of grantees and implementing the Affordable Care Act, she was surprised at the time required to work on strengthening the agency itself. Wakefield recalls, "I had to look at the infrastructure of our organization and how well it supported meeting our mission to improve access to quality health care. This involved carefully reviewing and adjusting our deployment of people and resources, from realigning the agency's organizational structure to investing in training and information technology. For example, too often we were still processing paperwork the old way and agency hiring was slow."

In reflecting on her accomplishments at HRSA, Wakefield says, "I think one of my major accomplishments is strengthening the organization. We now have a much stronger organization. I must admit, this took far more of my time than I

Key Activities of Political Executives

- Assessing the organization
- Strengthening the organization
- Obtaining mission alignment
- Developing strong processes
- Mastering metrics and measuring progress
- Building relationships
- Enhancing credibility and visibility
- Fostering innovation

anticipated but meeting program and policy expectations is contingent on a high performing organization."

Assessing the Organization

Political executives face their initial management challenge when they arrive at their office on their first day. They must decide how quickly they want to move on assessing their organization. The dilemma is described by David Kappos, former Director of the United States Patent and Trademark Office: "I knew the issues facing the USPTO, so I wanted to get off to a fast start. I know you only have a certain period of time in these jobs so I didn't want to waste a single day. I wanted to get a running start and hit the ground running, but I didn't want to jump out of the chopper shooting."

Nearly all of the political executives interviewed wisely avoided the tendency to jump out of the chopper shooting. David Stevens, former Commissioner of the Federal Housing Administration (FHA), describes his deliberative pace in assessing his organization. Stevens recalls, "I spent my first days at FHA assessing the organization. I would go out into the field and talk with our staff. We held large staff meetings and an offsite planning retreat. I wanted to better understand the major issues facing the Department. I focused on what I thought I could accomplish and what would make a real difference."

During his initial assessment, Stevens says, "It became obvious to me that we needed to better manage risk. We needed a risk office and a chief risk officer. I felt FHA needed to go outside of the organization to recruit some top-notch Deputy Assistant Secretaries. We needed to recruit people with experience in credit risk, credit policy, and lending." Unlike several of the executives profiled here, Stevens concluded during his assessment of the organization that reorganization was not needed. "I decided," recalls Stevens, "that I didn't want to reorganize. So I put my efforts into assessing the talent already in the organization."

Assessments of the organization are especially crucial when a political executive arrives to find the agency in a firestorm of negative publicity. David Strickland, Administrator of the National Highway Traffic Safety Administration (NHTSA), found himself in that situation when he arrived at NHTSA in the midst of the furor over the Toyota automobile recall. "When I got here in January (2010), there had already been a significant amount of work in progress on Toyota," recounts Strickland. "There was much work underway, including a study by the National Academy of Sciences and a research initiative with the National Aeronautics and Space Administration. My first task was to determine whether NHTSA was broken. Some people were saying that we had a broken culture here. I decided that they were wrong and that NHTSA was not broken. That decision was a risk I had to take, but I believed it. It turns out that I was right. The final analysis showed that NHTSA had done a fantastic job on the Toyota recall."

In some cases, problems find the new political executive without having to look very hard. Jonathan Adelstein, former Administrator, Rural Utilities Services (RUS), recalls, "When I got here, I quickly found that we had a crisis in management regarding the information technology system we were using to accept applications for broadband projects. The process was in meltdown due to the unprecedented number of applications for loans and grants. RUS was working with another agency on application intake and it just wasn't working. It was a stressful situation in the beginning."

Assessing the organization by visiting field organizations is an effective tool for learning about the agency. Like David Stevens, Allison Hickey's early days at the Veterans Benefits Administration (VBA) in the Department of Veterans Affairs (VA) consisted of visits to employees in VBA regional offices. "I wanted to learn the VBA business and understand the process," recalls Under Secretary Hickey. "I wanted to see what they were doing and experience firsthand our claims processes and challenges. I did this for all lines of business. I wanted to understand our businesses."

Because of his career-long interest in human resources, former Deputy Secretary Scott Gould spent part of his first several months assessing the VA workforce. Gould concluded that the workforce needed strengthening. "I found a different style and culture in the Department than I had anticipated," recalls Gould. "We had to keep asking people, 'What do you think?' and 'How will this serve veterans?' They often had a hard time answering. The career team was not as willing to question assumptions as I had anticipated. We concluded that we had to build the analytical and core skills of the organization, as well as create a culture of advocacy where they feel confident to speak their minds."

Strengthening the Organization

After their assessment of the organization was completed, the executives we interviewed quickly moved to strengthening organizational capabilities. After her arrival as Commissioner of the Food and Drug Administration (FDA), Margaret Hamburg concluded that strengthening the institution would be a major priority for her during her tenure as Commissioner. Hamburg recalls, "I found that I had to focus on positioning FDA for the future. I wanted the agency to be as effective as it could be. This required a whole new level of engagement with the agency. The agency depends on trust and confidence. I wanted to strengthen the quality of the work to be done … There was no beginning and end to this initiative. If we didn't address this issue, we would be losing critical ground. We have gotten some increases in our budget. We need to forge stronger working relations with many groups. We have gone up in public approval of the agency."

Another consistent theme from our interviews is the importance of getting the right people into the organization and improving the organization's internal operations. While it has become a cliché in recent years, people are the organization's most important asset. According to all the executives interviewed, this is especially true in government where "knowledge work" and "knowledge workers" are the norm. The federal government is widely credited with having the most educated workforce in the nation.

Daniel Poneman, Deputy Secretary of the Department of Energy, describes the importance of people in his organization. "The Department is all about its people. It's a great organization that depends on a good esprit de corps," he explains. "The people I work with are glad to be here. They have engaging work."

Because of the importance of people to the successful accomplishment of the Department's mission, Poneman devotes a significant amount of his time to people issues facing the Department. "I've worked on ensuring that we have a process for getting good people into the Department and then retaining them once they are hired and are here," says Poneman.

According to Poneman, hiring is only one part of the personnel challenge. "[Hiring] is just the front edge," he explains. "Our mission is evolving, and we need to continue to provide career paths that are exciting so we not only attract but retain talent."

Government science executives also emphasized in our interviews the importance of people. "The Energy Information Administration (EIA) is all about its people—federal employees and contractors," says Richard Newell, former Administrator of EIA. "It is a people organization. We have 370 federal employees with about 200 contractors. We need to keep them and attract new people. I'm pleased that people in our community are asking me about whether there are any new positions at EIA."

Patrick Gallagher, Director of the National Institute of Standards and Technology (NIST), is very clear about his deep commitment to the institution. "I want to create an environment conducive for our scientists," he says. "We have world-class scientists here. Our job is all about attracting people—hiring and then retaining them. Retaining people is always a challenge because they can make three or four times more money anywhere else, either in the academic community or [private] industry. Not only am I impressed that NIST has three Nobel Prize winners here, I'm more impressed that all three have stayed."

During his confirmation hearings, Arun Majumdar, the first Director of the Advanced Research Projects Agency-Energy (ARPA-E), told Senate committee members that people were one of the five core values instrumental to ARPA-E. In describing his early days at ARPA-E, Majumdar tells us, "I started recruiting people. I wanted to get the right people. Putting together your team is critical. As a new agency with special hiring authorities, we had the flexibility to recruit outside of the civil service system. People didn't have to wait for six months to be hired. We have proved that good people will come here. We were able to get nearly all the people we wanted."

Nearly all those interviewed are very aware of the need to prepare for the forthcoming retirement wave among their civil servants. William Taggart, former

Chief Operating Officer (COO) of the Office of Federal Student Aid (FSA) in the Department of Education, tells us, "Nearly 20 percent of [our employees] will be eligible to retire in the next five years. We had only 975 people, with headcount falling, while our workloads were up 200 percent in some cases. It was clear that we needed to hire more staff to perform tasks that were deemed as 'inherently governmental.' We needed to hire the right people, with the right competencies, who knew how to work in a team-based environment."

Reflecting on his experience at the Department of Labor, Seth Harris, Deputy Secretary, says, "Improving management in the Department is a real challenge. We needed to improve the Senior Executive Service (SES) and develop an ever-stronger corps of SES members. We needed to define what it means to be an elite manager in the SES and what skills they need. We needed to do more skill development. I'm not just talking about training, I mean skill development. We also worked on individual performance measures and better SES evaluations."

A key part of building organizational capacity is changing the culture of the organization. Rafael Borras, Under Secretary for Management at the Department of Homeland Security (DHS), describes this challenge. "There is the cultural part of my job which is less about policies," says Borras. "Culture and priorities interact with each other. We have many agencies (in DHS) which have their own history. We needed to get them to interact with each other and interact differently with each other. We want to change people's DNA, not just to change their minds."

Inez Tenenbaum, Chairman of the Consumer Product Safety Commission, also recognizes the importance of cultural change as part of building organizational capacity. Tenenbaum says, "We are trying to create a new culture here and get people to change the way they are doing business. We want to create a culture of excellence. We want to bring in new talent and get new people."

Obtaining Mission Alignment

Based on their assessment of the organization, political executives frequently find that their organization is not aligned to meet their current mission. The misalignment is often reflected in the organizational structure of the agency. Patrick Gallagher at NIST concluded that reorganization was necessary for his organization to achieve greater alignment between organizational units. From Gallagher's perspective, the reorganization of NIST was not an end in itself, but a crucial element of his strategy to change NIST's culture and to strengthen the organization to survive the fast pace of change in the 21st century. "The reorganization was never just about organizational structure or who reports to whom. It wasn't about boxes," he says. "It was about getting the organization better aligned. We wanted to get the right people and align them in the new organization. Alignment was our larger goal. We need to reset the agency."

Gallagher's management agenda was to move NIST away from an activity-based structure for the agency's laboratories, which were organized like a university. "In that structure, our managers acted much like chairs of academic departments," Gallagher recalls. "We wanted to move toward a mission approach."

The mission focus and reorganization were also part of Gallagher's goal to make NIST a better workplace and to enhance the agency's image among federal agencies and the research community. "NIST is a very special place," he says. "Researchers at NIST like their work and their mission. I wanted to restore the old sense of mission that [NIST's predecessor] the National Bureau of Standards had. Our efforts have brought more visibility to the organization."

Pamela Hyde, Administrator of the Substance Abuse and Mental Health Administration (SAMHSA), Department of Health and Human Services, also concluded that a reorganization was necessary as part of agency mission alignment. Hyde recalls, "I found that policy was everyplace. We had some policy in the budget office. There were also policy people in the office of Administrator. The Centers within SAMHSA were very siloed. Policy was very diffuse in the agency, so we created a new policy office. We have about 50 people all together … We also moved grants management into finance, so that we had all the money functions in the same place. We still have activities spread out all over the agency. We have homeless programs in all three centers. We are not organized for the 21st century. We had to push through the organizational realignment. It has not quite materialized into the vision we had. It is still in process."

David Hinson, National Director of the Minority Business Development Agency (MBDA), Department of Commerce, realized that organizational alignment would be a major priority for him. He recalls, "We tended to work in silos before I arrived … I tried to get the agency more focused. I wanted to begin to quantify the results of the agency. I wanted to change the tone of the organization. I've been trying to get all of us to work together."

Developing Strong Processes

Along with building organizational capability, the executives we interviewed also focused on the internal operations and work processes performed in their organizations. We learned that developing strong processes was important not only to the producers discussed in Chapter 4, but to many of the political executives we interviewed. Seth Harris faced both people and process issues in his role as Deputy Secretary of Labor. "We had to improve the business practices of the Department," asserts Harris. He concluded that the Department needed to launch a new strategic planning process.

In some cases, a political executive is hired specifically to improve the processes of his organization. Referring to his discussions with Secretary Shaun Donovan about his position as Deputy Secretary at the Department of Housing and Urban Development (HUD), Maurice Jones recalls, "It was clear that I was going to focus on operational excellence … I have been focusing on human capital and financial processes. You can have the greatest, most innovative policies, but without execution, these policies can't succeed." Jones also notes his concern about the health of the organization. "I want to leave the Department a better place. I would say the long term health of the organization is at risk … We need to focus on people, processes, and priorities."

There are many examples of political executives focusing on improving processes. A backlog problem faced Allison Hickey, Under Secretary for Benefits in the Department of Veterans Affairs. Much of the growth in backlog was due to an increase in both the number of claims and complexity of the claims. In order to improve the process, the Veterans Benefit Administration (VBA) began to treat less complex claims differently than more complicated claims. VBA created "express lanes" for certain claims. "We are able to push these less complicated claims through at a faster pace," describes Hickey. "If we can do this, there will be less work on the front end. We can get less complicated claims through which will then allow us to spend more time on tougher, more complicated claims. We are trying to manage our throughputs."

An emphasis on improving processes is seen at the Transportation Security Administration under Administrator John Pistole. After his arrival in June 2010, Pistole quickly came to the conclusion that his agency needed to change the way it was operating. "We had been using a one-size-fits-all approach," says Pistole. "But I knew it didn't have to be this way. As an FBI agent, I would get on a plane with special treatment. So I knew we were already treating people differently. I knew that there were many possibilities of doing things differently."

While clarifying the decision-making process at the Department of Education, Secretary Duncan and Deputy Secretary Anthony Miller's team also worked to set clear expectations and explicit goals. "We developed an operational plan and shared it with staff throughout the Department," says Miller. "It's important to let people know what is expected of their operating units. As leaders, we must be clearer and more transparent communicating performance expectations. This is basic management—setting forth your goals. We also started to link the planning process in the Department with the budget process and get alignment. We have over 150 discretionary programs in the Department, which were not well aligned."

Based on his previous experience in government, Seth Harris says, "I realize how short the time you have in government really is when you're a political appointee. The challenge is whether you are going to leave 'footprints in concrete' or 'footprints in the snow.' There are so many things that can be undone after you leave or an Administration changes. This time around, I came to a better understanding of how to succeed here. You have to change the processes and make it the new way of doing business. You need to implement repetitive processes. While it is difficult to do, you can do it. You can give people a new set of tools. You can start them using program evaluation and developing operating plans. I've learned that you need to engage the civil service to change the DNA of the organization.

You can get the Department to start using new procedures which will be the way they do business in the future by building on and adapting existing procedures that they have used for years. Mixing the new with the old seemed to be a recipe for successful change. You have to get into the systems of government. You can change government, but it takes time."

Mastering Metrics and Measuring Progress

In addition to improving processes, an important common theme among the political executives profiled in this book is the importance of numbers and metrics. David Kappos, former Director of the United States Patent and Trademark Office (USPTO), says, "We understand our inputs and outputs at USPTO." In attacking the challenge of reducing the paperwork backlog at USPTO, Kappos knew it was important to track the agency's progress—both to provide transparency to the public and to use it as a management tool inside the organization.

"The USPTO has a critical role to play in our economic recovery," Kappos told us in 2010. "That's why people really care about the backlog, which hinders innovation and economic growth. In response, we set specific targets. Our goal is to get the backlog under 700,000. We haven't been under that figure for many years. The goal is to get it down to a backlog of 325,000. That would be about 70 dockets per examiner, which is about right … we set 699,000 for FY 2011. Getting under 700,000 would be a major accomplishment."

Kappos accomplished the goal in July 2011 when patents pending fell to 689,226. Since then, they have continued to fall and reached an all-time low in August 2012 when patents pending dipped to 623,168. Kappos created the PTO Dashboard, which is updated monthly on the agency's website to track progress on key performance indicators such as patents pending.

A similar situation faced Allison Hickey during her first year at VBA. One of the items she quickly identified as a major challenge to the agency was the lack of metrics to measure success. Hickey faced a large inventory of claims and a backlog. On top of the existing claims inventory and backlog of regular claims she found upon arrival, there were new Agent Orange claims to settle which required reallocating staff from processing other claims to complete the Agent Orange backlog. Over a two-year period, VA received 260,000 claims from three new Agent Orange conditions, which required a surge of over 37 percent of VBA's workforce to work on adjudicating these claims.

Metrics are now clearly high on the radar screen at the Veterans Benefits Administration. In September 2012, VA announced that VBA had processed over one million claims for the third year in a row. In August 2012, VBA had its most productive claims processing period in history, completing a record 107,462 claims, which surpassed the previous monthly record of 103,296 set in 2010. Hickey comments that the reduction is a testament to the dedication of VBA to meet the increasing needs of veterans. In the summer of 2012, VBA had 870,000 claims in its inventory. The claims backlog is defined as those claims that have been pending longer than the goal of 125 days.

For many executives, the key challenge is to decide on the metrics by which to assess their organization. Alejandro Mayorkas, Director of U.S. Citizenship and Immigration Services, recounts: "A key challenge is metrics. What is the appropriate metric for admitting people to the United States?" Traditionally, agencies have measured production in terms of how quickly they can complete a certain number of cases. Mayorkas recounts, "Given our responsibility to combat fraud and help safeguard our nation's security, a metric of production does not fairly address how we are executing on our mission."

Deputy Secretary Seth Harris at the Department of Labor realized that, together with the strategic planning process, the Department needed new performance measures. "The Department was measuring the wrong things," says Harris. "The measures were typically internal, and we were not measuring outcomes. The Department had focused on outputs and process measures previously. We realized that measuring outcomes is incredibly hard, but absolutely essential."

Building Relationships

For the political executives interviewed, building relationships means reaching out to key stakeholders and partners both inside and outside of Washington, D.C. David Hinson, National Director of the Minority Business Development Agency (MBDA) in the Department of Commerce, and Ray Jefferson, former Assistant Secretary at the Veterans' Employment and Training Services (VETS) in the Department of Labor, adopted similar external strategies to achieve their missions.

"I spent a lot of time during my first year on the road building relationships," Hinson recalls. "You need to build good relationships with corporate America. Building these relationships is crucial."

In describing his strategy for VETS, Jefferson explains, "We want to create partnerships ... to find employment opportunities for veterans."

Both Hinson and Jefferson developed working relationships with the Chamber of Commerce, among many other organizations, in support of their different missions: assisting minority businesses and assisting veterans to find employment opportunities.

In addition to their work with the private sector and non-profit organizations, David Hinson and Ray Jefferson spent a significant amount of time working with other government agencies. Both MBDA and VETS were created to serve as "spurs" and leaders in government for their respective missions. Hinson and Jefferson had to carve out roles and activities in which their agencies could contribute in a crowded field of numerous agencies, all of whom have some piece of the action in their policy area.

Building relationships also includes enhancing relationships with an organization's own employees. Bill Taggart made employee engagement one of his top priorities. "Many of the staff worked at FSA an average of 18 years but did not feel valued by senior management," Taggart says. "I held several town hall meetings to get the employees' unfiltered feedback. They had a lot on their minds and were very vocal. That meant to me that they cared about the organization. It would have been much worse if I had been met with silence. It was essential for me to help the employees to feel better about the organization. I decided to get them involved in developing a new vision, mission, and core values for the organization. More than 200 employees participated in the process and helped to develop a new working relationship between the FSA employees and the COO."

Jonathan Adelstein, former Administrator of the Rural Utilities Service in the Department of Agriculture, also emphasizes employee engagement. "I worked closely with the career staff here to make revisions in [procedures for] our second funding round. I wanted their buy-in and inspiration," he explains. "I wanted to know their ideas. We shared ideas and got different opinions on various options for round two. I believe in listening to staff. We had a very collegial relationship; it was not top-down. We had an ongoing dialogue."

The desire for openness with employees prompted Robert Mendez, Administrator of the Federal Highway Administration, to use a variety of outreach tools. "When I first got here, I drafted a message to employees," says Mendez. "We have done webinars and teleconferences to employees. We also have two annual meetings with all of our divisional managers and office managers. It is important for me to communicate with people and get out and mingle. I also follow up with employees via e-mail." The emphasis on communication was crucial to Mendez. "It may not be a great insight," says Mendez, "but I found communication to be very important. You need to repeat information to people and tell them what you are doing. You have to keep employees informed on the importance of issues and you have to work to develop your message to them."

All those interviewed also recognize that building relationships with members of Congress and their staffs is crucial. In explaining his strategy, Arun Majumdar says, "I tell them what I do. I like to explain our agency in layman's terms. I try to make it easy for them to understand and talk to them in terms of impact and savings, while giving them the big picture. It's been a pleasant and enjoyable experience to work so closely with Congress. I'm from California and have never worked with Congress before. You need to spend time with them. They need to trust you. That takes time and you have to devote ongoing meetings to them."

Equally important to those interviewed is fostering relationships with the White House and the Office of Management and Budget (OMB). Former OPM Director John Berry says, "I wanted to develop a good relationship with OMB, which I have done. I work closely with OMB on all our initiatives. I've also engaged the White House on many initiatives, such as our activities on improving work life and veterans' hiring. We worked hard on building our relationship with the White House."

While it is easy to focus on external stakeholders, Congress, and the Office of Management and Budget, Linda Springer, former Director of the Office of Personnel Management, recommends that political executives also spend time with key colleagues in their own Department. She strongly recommends that political executives spend time and get to know their Inspector General, Chief Financial Officer, and staff in agency field offices (Springer).

Enhancing Credibility and Visibility

Many of the executives we interviewed place great emphasis on enhancing the credibility and visibility of their agency. Government agencies need to maintain a good reputation with Congress in order to receive their annual appropriations. But the leaders we interviewed also stress internal reasons for enhancing the agency's credibility and visibility.

John Morton, former Director, United States Immigration and Customs Enforcement, Department of Homeland Security, describes this challenge: "The agency needed a champion. We were doing fantastic work. The agency felt under-appreciated. I felt that the men and women of this agency should get the recognition they deserved. It was the most misunderstood agency in government. I wanted to reshape the perception of the agency … I wanted to promote and champion our investigative work. I want the agency to be recognized for its strong investigative arm. I wanted to tell people what we do."

Many executives were surprised by the low visibility of their agencies. As Under Secretary for Economic Affairs in the Department of Commerce, Rebecca Blank worked to boost visibility by finding opportunities in which economic analysis could contribute to policy making in the Administration.

"We increased the visibility of the Economics and Statistics Administration in the White House," Blank says. "We are now getting more requests to do studies. The staff here is available to do this work and is enjoying getting involved in current issues and doing deep analysis. They like having new products and reports. These reports have generated requests from other parts of government to do similar studies."

When she arrived at the Consumer Product Safety Commission, Inez Tenenbaum also found an organization with very poor internal communications—including among Commissioners—and a visible lack of transparency. "I tried to open up the agency," says Tenenbaum. "I started to meet with all my key managers about how we were going to operate. I started weekly meetings with the other Commissioners. I also started holding votes at our meetings and broadcasting those meetings on the Web. Previously, the Commission did its voting by ballot, with no meetings. I quickly changed that. I wanted people to be able to see what we are doing."

There was also a clear need to find more effective ways to communicate with the public. During her first year at the agency, Tenenbaum pushed for expansion of the agency's social media use. The resulting initiative, CPSC 2.0, included the creation of an OnSafety blog, the @OnSafety Twitter, a YouTube Channel, a recall widget, and a Flickr page.

Another way in which leaders and organizations can enhance credibility is an effective response to well-known external events. The U.S. Geological Survey (USGS) faced a series of natural disasters in a two-year period, including the Haiti earthquake in January 2010, the Iceland volcano in March 2010, and the Japanese earthquake of March 2011. USGS's effective response to the increased number of natural disasters had positive impacts inside the agency, as well as outside the organization. Marcia McNutt, former Director of the U.S. Geological Survey, states, "I think we increased the stature of the agency, increased our visibility and our name recognition. We received much attention in 2010 and were on the front pages of many newspapers. We made a contribution in 2010. We were involved in responses to the earthquakes and volcanoes. It showed our diverse expertise in many areas. I think all the increased attention also helped inside the agency. It showed the relevance of the agency and it started people within the agency to think about things that we can do that they never imagined before."

Enhancing an organization's credibility is especially critical when an executive takes over an agency that has recently faced a crisis or a scandal. In taking on the position of Director of the Minerals Management Service in the Department of the Interior in the aftermath of the Gulf Oil Spill in 2010, Michael Bromwich found a negative culture.

"The agency was suffering from years of negative publicity. There had been instances of corruption that had happened several years before … There was massive media attention given to the agency and many negative stories … We were the most heavily criticized agency in government when I started in June 2010, which did create a crisis mentality in the agency and in the Department of the Interior generally. We were being criticized in the media every day—every media outlet felt obliged to publish numerous critical pieces about the agency.

"Morale was as low as I've ever seen it in any organization," he continues. "There was a lot of tension in the agency, and a stream of negative commentary about it, including from inside the government. There was no end in sight to the negative publicity. I was very careful not to reinforce all this negative feedback by jumping on the bandwagon of criticism, but on the other hand I could not defend past acts of misconduct or lack of competence."

David Hinson links improvements in the internal operations of his agency to its image both inside and outside the Department of Commerce. "I had to build credibility for the agency," Hinson says. "I wanted to show people what we were capable of doing. This required that we improve the skillsets of the agency. We had to make clear our expectations on training. I looked at everybody in the agency and decided what new capabilities we needed."

When Rafael Borras arrived at the Department of Homeland Security, the Department had been on the Government Accountability Office's High Risk List since 2003. Hence, one of the major challenges facing Borras was enhancing the Department's reputation and evaluations with its oversight organizations. Rafael Borras says, "Our efforts have helped enhance our conversations with the Government Accountability Office and other oversight groups. We come back with a plan now when we have a problem we are trying to solve, and a way to measure our progress."

Fostering Innovation

The political executives we interviewed are all proud of their innovations. Examples of the innovations are presented on page 27.

We found that innovation in government can most effectively be discussed by making the following distinction between types of government innovation:

- **Innovation from inside government,** when government employees seek to find new solutions and improvements in the delivery of traditional government activities
- **Innovation engaging the private sector in problem solution**

Innovation from Inside Government

This type of innovation has received the most attention over the years. Since 1985, the John F. Kennedy School of Government's Innovations in American Government program has recognized nearly 500 innovation initiatives in federal, state, and local government. The Innovations awards program was created to foster increased attention in government to finding new ways to deliver services that address the nation's most pressing issues, and to reward and recognize those organizations that undertake new initiatives.

The challenge facing government has been in finding ways to institutionalize the quest for innovation. The bureaucracy has historically excelled at developing routines that can be repeated and duplicated. Thus, finding new routines (or new ways of doing business) has not traditionally been encouraged. During our interviews for this book, we found an increasing number of examples of the federal government's actively institutionalizing innovation.

At the Department of Veterans Affairs, an Employee Innovation Competition was created as part of the Department's Innovation Initiative (VAi2). The VAi2 program is significant because it created an ongoing process which could tap into the experience and expertise of its employees. Historically, employees have always had the opportunity to volunteer ideas (e.g., the 20th century's employee suggestion box). What is different about the VAi2 program is that it organizes employee participation by identifying specific topics to improve care quality, access, and transparency in the delivery of programs to the nation's veterans (see *Innovation Initiative:*

The Department of Veterans Affairs on page 27 for a further discussion of this innovation initiative).

At the Department of Agriculture, innovation took the form of delivering a new program—Know Your Farmer, Know Your Food (KYF2). Instead of creating a new office, the Department organized an initiative through a cross-department task force, with every Agriculture agency represented. The concept was to involve the entire Department with participation from the many Agricultural components rather than locating the KYF2 program in a single office (see *The Know Your Farmer, Know Your Food Program: The Department of Agriculture* on page 29 for a further discussion of this innovation initiative).

At the Department of Education, a new twist was developed on an old tool of government—the traditional grant. Instead of creating a formula grant program (in which every state receives funds), the Department used the grant instrument to create a nationwide competition in which only a limited number of states would receive funding based on the quality of their proposals to reform education in their states (see *The Race To The Top Program: The Department of Education* on page 31 for a further discussion of this innovation initiative).

Engaging the Private Sector in Problem Solution

Innovation that engages the private sector appears to be expanding throughout the government.

Government is increasingly recognizing that in many cases, it does not have the solution to a problem that it is trying to solve or a product it is trying to develop. Thus, government is developing new ways to engage citizens, universities, corporations, and non-profits in problem-solving. During our interviews, we saw this approach in the following initiatives:

- The Challenge.gov website was created to be an online platform which government agencies can use to bring the "best ideas and top talent to bear on our nation's most pressing challenges." Since 2010, the website has run nearly 300 competitions, many of which include monetary rewards.
- Similar to Challenge.gov, the VAi2 program ran an Industry Innovation Competition in which it sought ideas in response to the Department's specified list of topics on which it was seeking innovation solutions.
- At the Department of Transportation, the Federal Highway Administration created its Every Day Counts program. FHWA is seeking to engage industry in finding new ways to accelerate technology and innovation deployment, as well as to shorten project delivery time (see *The Every Day Counts Program: The Department of Transportation* on page 33 for a further discussion on this innovation initiative).
- At the Department of Energy, the Advanced Research Projects Agency-Energy (ARPA-E) was built on the model developed by the Defense Advanced Research Projects Agency (DARPA). ARPA-E is now engaging the private sector by soliciting concept papers in specified areas which are then reviewed,

with full proposals requested for those who pass the initial review. Based on the full proposals, awards are made to develop technologies that are too risky for private-sector investment, but have the potential to identify disruptive energy technologies that can make current technologies obsolete.

In all of our interviews, we found government political executives wanting to ingrain the quest for innovation in their organizations—both for innovation driven within government and innovation engaging the private sector. In both quests for innovation, competition, recognition, and rewards are being used to solicit ideas.

Some leaders recognize that innovation is more than tactics. Arun Majumdar, former Director of ARPA-E, sums this up nicely when he tells us, "I want innovation to be the DNA of ARPA-E. It is part of our core strategy. Once you get people here, you have to give them the freedom to solve problems. So the key elements to creating a culture are getting talent, creating an open dialogue, and allowing people to realize their potential."

Innovation in Action

Innovation Initiative: The Department of Veterans Affairs

Organizations, both in the public and private sector, have come a long way since the employee suggestion box of the 20th century. For much of the last century, the suggestion box was the major vehicle for soliciting input from within organizations. Other than receiving mail and perhaps conducting focus groups, organizations were also limited in the ways that they received information and ideas from outside their organization.

Twenty-first-century organizations have a variety of powerful tools to obtain new ideas from both inside and outside their organizations. In the federal government today, the Department of Veterans Affairs has become a leader in implementing new ways to innovate. The VA Innovation Initiative (VAi2) was launched in 2010 as part of the Department-wide transformation effort led by Secretary Eric K. Shinseki, Deputy Secretary W. Scott Gould, and Chief of Staff John R. Gingrich.

"We launched the VA Innovation Initiative with the purpose of designing and managing a structured process for innovating at VA," says former Deputy Secretary Gould, who also served as chair of the Executive Selection Board of the Department of Veterans Affairs Innovation Initiative.

In describing the creation of the program, Jonah J. Czerwinski, Director of VAi2, recalls, "We had a venture capital mindset, but not exactly the venture capital toolset. We needed to use the tools that existed in government to bring about innovation, without making direct financial investments in companies."

In creating the program, Czerwinski and his team created a four-pronged approach:

Industry innovation competitions. "We launched with the Industry Innovation Competition in June 2010," recounts Czerwinski. "The goal of the program is to get the best thinking from the private sector to solve the Department's most pressing problems." As an outgrowth of a brainstorming session with VA colleagues, the VAi2 team determined that the Broad Agency Announcement (BAA) was the best tool to specify broad areas of high interest to the Department (such as redesigning the PTSD treatment experience or creating a mobile application for streamlined veterans benefits). While rarely used by VA, the BAA procurement vehicle was key for innovations because it permitted a more open engagement with industry and a more flexible process that included the ability to select more than one approach to a problem.

Since the creation of the program, over 600 ideas in 11 topic areas have been submitted to the Department. Based on the review of those ideas, a total of 37 pilot projects were selected for award and funding. So far, funding for the pilot projects ranges from a few hundred thousand dollars to $9 million. Pilot projects are designed to deliver results within 24 months. At the end of the project, the pilot is evaluated and a decision made as to whether a full and open competition will be pursued to implement the tested concept.

The competitions have been successful. Former Deputy Secretary Gould reports, "We have seen several promising innovations fielded. For example, one provides VA clinicians with secure mobile access to patient electronic health records and another puts EKGs on mobile devices, allowing cardiologists to review and respond to critical time-sensitive information from anywhere for the first time."

Employee competitions. "These competitions are similar to our industry competitions but are designed to draw on our own employees within VA to tap into their experience and expertise," says Czerwinski. "Employees submit ideas, which are subsequently crowdsourced to help us manage the inflow. We then select pilot projects which are implemented by VA employees."

Over 15,000 ideas from employees have been submitted to date. The VAi2 program invests in the internal pilot, such as software development to test an idea. No money is awarded directly to employees.

Prize contests. "We used the new authorities in the America COMPETES Reauthorization Act of 2010 to conduct prize competitions," recounts Czerwinski. VAi2 sponsored a challenge competition on the Challenge.gov website that sought the development of an app that provides immediate access to resources that the homeless need. Volunteers and outreach workers would be able to use the winning app to look up the location and availability of shelters, free clinics, and other social services, and instantaneously be able to share this information with those in need. The challenge awarded $10,000 to five finalists, with an additional $25,000 being awarded to the Grand Prize winner.

One of the outcomes of that effort led to rock star Jon Bon Jovi joining forces with the VA in an effort to challenge software developers to create mobile apps that can help homeless vets connect with services they need in real time and nearby.

Special projects. "When an emergent opportunity arises," says Czerwinski, "we may conduct a special project to generate rapid innovation." To date, VAi2 has managed two special projects: the Agent Orange Fast Track system and the Open Source Electronic Health Record project.

Innovation projects are supported on both the health side and benefits side of VA. Former Deputy Secretary Gould explains, "VA innovations cover more than health care. The first business incubator for veteran entrepreneurs was launched under VAi2 and now more than 200 veteran-owned ventures are thriving in the VETransfer pipeline less than a year since its launch."

A clear goal of the initiative has been to avoid becoming just another management fad to be tried and subsequently discarded. In order to institutionalize innovation at VA, the Department is in the process of transitioning VAi2 into a new Center for Innovation at VA. The Department of Veterans Affairs clearly offers a model for other Departments and agencies to follow in fostering innovation, both from within and outside their organizations.

The Know Your Farmer, Know Your Food Program: The Department of Agriculture

Historically, a major criticism of government has been that it consists of individual government agencies (often called stovepipes or silos) which tend not to work very well with other agencies, even those within their own Department.

When she arrived at the Department of Agriculture (USDA), former Deputy Secretary Kathleen Merrigan found some truth in this criticism of government. Many agencies within USDA viewed themselves as somewhat independent of the Office of the Secretary.

"Historically, the power in the bureaucracy has been in the hands of agency administrators," says Merrigan, once an agency administrator herself. "Administrators run their own budget, Congressional outreach, and public affairs offices."

A major stumbling block to innovation in government has been this tendency for each government unit to do "its own thing," independently of the others. Thus, while these units could achieve their individual missions, they often had difficulty in achieving cross-departmental goals or missions.

To achieve departmental missions, it is necessary to create new mechanisms which cut across agency boundaries. One such mechanism is cross-cutting departmental (or government-wide) initiatives to achieve a specific mission.

During the Obama Administration, the Department of Agriculture has been seen as a leader in developing and fostering such initiatives. At Agriculture, leading such initiatives became a significant component of the job of former Deputy Secretary Merrigan. In addition to her ongoing budget and management responsibilities, Merrigan played leadership roles in two major departmental initiatives: the Healthy Kids Initiative and the Know Your Farmer, Know Your Food initiative.

In describing the Healthy Kids Initiative, Merrigan says, "This was a USDA-driven and White House-orchestrated interdepartmental effort to improve the health of children by combating both obesity and hunger. The First Lady's Let's Move! campaign and passage of the Healthy Hunger-Free Kids

Act in December 2010 are direct results of this early effort. Major reforms are now underway that will improve school meals and increase the availability of healthy food options in neighborhoods. We are all working with the First Lady to achieve the Administration's goal of ending childhood obesity in a generation."

The second of the Department's major initiatives is Know Your Farmer, Know Your Food (KYF2), which highlights the critical connection between farmers and consumers. Launched in September 2009, this department-wide initiative is aimed at carrying out the President's commitment to locally grown food by strengthening local and regional food systems. "The initiative enabled us to reach out to different constituents and it has taken off like wildfire," says Merrigan.

An innovative feature of this initiative is that it has no office, budget, or staff dedicated to it. The initiative was created to coordinate the Department's vast resources and expertise on local and regional food systems across its 17 agencies.

Instead of creating a new office, Merrigan organized the initiative through a cross-department task force, with every USDA agency represented on it. Merrigan chairs the task force, which meets every two weeks and is made up of career mid-level managers who voluntarily add the KYF2 work to their regular work assignments. The task force is charged with breaking down bureaucratic silos, developing common-sense solutions for communities and farmers, and fostering new partnerships inside USDA and across the nation.

"This initiative, fostering local and regional food systems, will live beyond me and this particular Administration because we created cross-agency energy and engaged and empowered staff. People tell me that this management effort has been transformative and that they are enjoying their jobs now more than they have in years, even though in total, they are being asked to do more."

Since its creation, the initiative has continued to expand. On February 29, 2012, Agriculture Secretary Tom Vilsack and former Deputy Secretary Merrigan unveiled the Know Your Farmer, Know Your Food Compass. The KYF2 Compass is an interactive web-based tool which highlights departmental support for local and regional food projects and successful producer, business, and community case studies. The Compass includes an interactive U.S. map which shows local and regional food projects in all 50 states, with accompanying case studies, photos, and video content.

In launching the Compass, former Deputy Secretary Merrigan says, "By encouraging all Americans to know their farmer, USDA is helping consumers learn more about agriculture and people producing your food. The KYF2 initiative helps farmers and ranchers tap into a vibrant, growing market opportunity. And it's also stimulating a broader national conversation about where our food comes from and how important agriculture is to our country."

As a follow-up to the February 2012 launch of the Compass, Deputy Secretary Merrigan conducted a virtual town hall meeting in March to further publicize the KYF2 initiative. The meeting was streamed live at www.whitehouse.gov, with questions coming from virtual participants via Twitter. Participants could also watch the town meeting on Facebook and submit comments.

As government continues to search for ways to innovate within the traditional bureaucracy, the use of cross-department or cross-government initiatives may increase in the years ahead. There is much to be learned from the Department of Agriculture about how to organize and foster such initiatives, without creating a new mini-bureaucracy to manage them.

The Race To The Top Program: The Department of Education

Undertaking innovation in government is a challenge. Government leaders must work with their existing toolkit, primarily grants and contracts, to bring about their desired results. It is rare that Congress gives government new authorities and a new portfolio of tools. (One exception is the creation of the Advanced Research Projects Agency-Energy in the Department of Energy). Thus, government must be creative in using the tools already on the books.

At the Department of Education, the Obama Administration used one of government's oldest tools—the 19th century grant-in-aid—to accomplish 21st century objectives. Under the leadership of Secretary Arne Duncan and former Deputy Secretary Anthony Miller, the Department focused on one of its primary goals: dramatically improving educational performance in all 50 states.

Given the budget of the Department (it accounts for only 10% of total national spending on education, with the remaining 90% coming from state and local governments) and its limited leverage over state and local education institutions, the Department had to be creative in developing new approaches that would encourage movement toward reforming schools and improving educational performance across the nation.

The new approach was to create a nationwide competition among the states to receive new funding authorized by the American Recovery and Reinvestment Act of 2009. In order to compete for the funds, each state had to develop a plan that set forth its educational reform goals and targets.

Former Deputy Secretary Miller recalls, "The program invited and challenged states to approach education reform systematically. In the first two rounds, 46 states applied, which demonstrated the widespread interest and appetite to do things differently, and dramatically improve education."

Each state was required to develop a reform plan which includes activities in the following areas:

- Adopting standards and assessments that prepare students to succeed in college and the workplace and to compete in the global economy
- Building data systems that measure student growth and success, and inform teachers and principals about how they can improve instruction
- Recruiting, developing, rewarding, and retaining effective teachers and principals, especially where they are needed most
- Turning around the lowest-achieving schools

As of 2012, there have been 19 winners (two in Phase One, 10 in Phase Two, and seven in Phase Three). One innovative feature about the Race to the Top approach is that both "winners" and "non-winners" developed state plans which set forth their reform agenda. That is, through the competitions, 46 states began working on the reform agenda of the Department of Education.

"Many of these states—not just the winners—are pursuing at least pieces of their reform plans," Miller reports. So the Department's objective of educational reform is being achieved in both the states that received funding and those states that did not receive federal funds.

Secretary Duncan emphasizes this aspect of the program: "Each of the states (that applied) now has in place—win or lose—a blueprint of how they would like to move forward, statewide, on education reform."

A second innovative feature of the Race to the Top program is its emphasis on outcomes.

"Race to the Top continues the movement toward performance-based measures," says Timothy J. Conlan, Professor of Government and Politics at George Mason University. "In the past, grant requirements have focused on procedures and outputs. Race to the Top focuses on outcomes, not outputs."

The Race to the Top competition model is now being replicated. In 2011, nine states (from the 35 states that prepared plans) received Race to the Top–Early Learning Challenge awards to build statewide systems of high-quality early learning and development programs for low-income children from birth to age five (the Challenge is jointly administered by the Department of Education and the Department of Health and Human Services).

In 2012, the next five highest ranked states from the 2011 competition were invited to reapply to receive funding for early learning programs. In describing the model, former Deputy Secretary Miller says, "Race to the Top is a good example of how our Department is working to transform from a bureaucratic agency to an engine of innovation, partnering with states to support their leaders in working together to produce real change that puts students first."

The 2013 Education budget contains plans to use the Race to the Top competition model to tackle the issue of college costs and quality by encouraging shared responsibility among states, families, and the federal government. Under the plan, the Education Department would invest $1 billion for a new Race to the Top focusing on college affordability and completion.

The goal of the new program is to drive reform, provide incentives to keep costs under control, and increase the number of work-study jobs. Plans are also underway to launch Race to the Top competitions at the school district level (in contrast to the previous state-level competitions). Other government Departments, including the Department of Transportation, are also considering using the Race to the Top approach for their programs.

In looking back on the success of the program, former Deputy Secretary Miller reflects, "Race to the Top—a competitive program whose funding is less than half a percent of total K–12 spending—has done more to advance systemic education reform than any other program in the Department's history."

In addition, Race to the Top exemplifies a new approach to the way government does business. Historically, many grants programs have been allocated by formula across all 50 states. In contrast, Race to the Top created a competition in which the states with the highest ranked plans (based on a very detailed scoring process) received funding. Most importantly, states were required to state explicitly their goals and targeted outcomes.

The Every Day Counts Program: The Department of Transportation

After being confirmed as Administrator of the Federal Highway Administration in July 2009, Victor Mendez quickly assessed the major challenges facing the agency.

"We decided on several priorities," recalls Mendez. "First was the Recovery Act, on which we had a major role. Second was the (transportation) reauthorization act. Third was innovation, because I felt that transportation projects were taking too long to complete. We need to cut delivery time. Finally, there were environmental issues. We wanted more green options for FHWA. We had to reduce our carbon footprint." The innovation initiative was named Every Day Counts (EDC).

"I talked to employees and stakeholders about this. We are trying to reduce project time for our construction projects by 50 percent, as well as to increase efficiency. We wanted ideas to improve operations. We didn't want to do a lot of studies, we wanted to implement new ideas ... I chose the name Every Day Counts to express the sense of urgency I feel about doing this. We really have no time to waste in building our 21st century transportation system and saving our planet."

The Every Day Counts program became a major vehicle for Mendez to work with the transportation industry. "I was concerned about the way the industry conducts business," comments Mendez. "Our construction projects take too long. It often takes 13 years to finish a project. I wanted to raise this as an issue and see if we could make progress in reducing the time it takes for major projects. I wanted to put more focus on innovation in the industry and demonstrate that shorter projects could be undertaken. People said that we could cut the time by 10 percent, but I said 'Why not cut it by 50 percent?' I wanted to find out whether we could use technology to be more innovative and could implement projects faster."

In his previous position as Director of the Arizona Department of Transportation, Mendez received praise for overseeing the building of the Regional Freeway System in the Phoenix area six years ahead of schedule.

EDC initiatives were developed to identify and deploy innovation aimed at shortening project delivery, enhancing the safety of highways, and protecting the environment. EDC is organized around three pillars:

- Reducing the carbon footprint of FHWA
- Accelerating technology and innovation deployment
- Shorter project delivery

Examples of Every Day Counts projects include a toolkit on specific strategies shortening project delivery time. One component of the shortening project delivery time pillar is the "Planning and Environment Linkages" module, focused on reducing duplication and making more informed project level-decisions.

Another EDC component focuses on using new technologies to accelerate project delivery, including prefabricated bridge elements and the use of geosynthetic reinforced soil for bridge systems. EDC projects result from a long vetting process which evaluates hundreds of ideas.

In addition to the above projects, EDC has an active website which includes a Communities of Practice landing page where those involved in transportation can join their peers, partners, and national subject matter experts to ask questions and participate in discussion on EDC initiatives. The site also includes an EDC Innovation box that allows the public to make suggestions to FHWA on how it can shorten project delivery and accelerate technology and innovation deployment. There is also an active EDC Forum and an Innovation Corner to which key FHWA staff members contribute.

In describing his experience launching and supporting the Every Day Counts initiative, Mendez says, "I think it has made a difference. It is bigger than I thought it would be. The entire industry is now talking about speeding up project delivery. We at FHWA saw this as a big issue and we raised people's attention to it and we now have industry working on this across the United States."

Chapter Three

The Deputy Secretaries

Understanding the Job of the Deputy Secretary

The job of the Deputy Secretary* is one of the most important in government. With the passage of the GPRA Modernization Act of 2010, the position now has additional responsibilities for the management of Cabinet Departments. The job is also one of the toughest in government for several reasons:

- **The job is big—involving managing complex federal Cabinet Departments, many of which are "holding companies" for a diverse set of agencies.** For example, the Department of Commerce consists of 12 agencies and 10 staff offices.

- **There is often much ambiguity surrounding the responsibilities of the Deputy Secretary.** There is no single, agreed-upon model for the position. One Deputy Secretary tells us that after nearly two years in office, "The job of the Deputy Secretary is still a little unclear to me."

- **The success of the job frequently depends on the working relationship and comfort level between the Cabinet Secretary and the Deputy Secretary.** As one Deputy Secretary puts it, "There is always tension in the role between the Deputy Secretary and the Secretary. You need to gain trust."

- **The challenge of being "number two" in any organization is often a difficult one at best.** We are told by one Deputy Secretary, "I had

The Deputy Secretaries

Rafael Borras, page 42

Under Secretary for Management, Department of Homeland Security

William V. Corr, page 44

Deputy Secretary, Department of Health and Human Services

W. Scott Gould, page 46

Deputy Secretary, Department of Veterans Affairs

Seth D. Harris, page 48

Deputy Secretary, Department of Labor

David J. Hayes, page 50

Deputy Secretary, Department of the Interior

Dennis F. Hightower, page 52

Deputy Secretary, Department of Commerce

---

* This chapter also includes an Under Secretary position, held by Rafael Borras at the Department of Homeland Security.

Maurice Jones, page 53

Deputy Secretary,
Department of Housing
and Urban Development

Kathleen A. Merrigan, page 54

Deputy Secretary,
Department of
Agriculture

Anthony W. Miller, page 56

Deputy Secretary,
Department of Education

Thomas R. Nides, page 58

Deputy Secretary for
Management and
Resources, Department
of State

Daniel B. Poneman, page 60

Deputy Secretary,
Department of Energy

never been a number two before, so this is a change for me. I didn't know how I would like being number two."

Key Components of the Job of the Deputy Secretary

While there will always be some ambiguity and tension in the role of the Deputy Secretary, several key roles emerge from our interviews. The Deputy Secretaries profiled fulfill the following roles:

• Alter ego for the Secretary
• Chief Operating Officer (COO) of the Department
• Convenor
• Policy advisor
• Leader of departmental initiatives
• Crisis manager
• Liaison to stakeholders

There is an ebb and flow between various roles over the course of a Deputy Secretary's tenure. One Deputy Secretary remarks, "We started out on management and we spent a lot of time on that during our first year. That was very important. Then the Secretary asked me to play a greater role in another area. There are also the unexpected events which nobody can predict. So you must learn to live with this ebb and flow and you have to be ready to respond to unanticipated events."

Serving as an Alter Ego for the Secretary

One Deputy Secretary describes this function: "My major role is backing up the Secretary. We want to make sure that we make the best use of his time. I'm the back stop. I'm available across the board on many issues. Your job [as Deputy Secretary] is to serve the Secretary in whatever capacity he or she desires. I support the Secretary and focus on what is important to him. That has been my view

Deputy Secretaries and the Senior Executive Service

In their role as Chief Operating Officer, many of the Deputy Secretaries we interviewed took a great interest in their Senior Executive Service corps. The SES corps consists of the most experienced career staff in the Department.

Scott Gould, former Deputy Secretary at VA, tells us, "We have over 400 SESers in the Department. I believe that working with the SES can make a real difference in the Department. We needed to work on the issue of performance ratings, as well as our allocation of SES members. This effort resulted in VA getting more SES slots. We are now working hard to get the right people into those jobs. We interview all SES candidates in the Office of the Secretary, which makes a significant impression on those interviewed. We have moved and removed some of our SES members."

At the Department of Labor, Deputy Secretary Seth Harris also focused on the SES. "Strengthening the SES corps was a critical management issue for the Department," says Harris. "I thought we had to start with our career managers and make changes there. We had to strengthen the organization. I had to move people around to improve management in the Department ... We need to improve the SES and develop an ever-stronger corps of SES members. We needed to define what it means to be an elite manager in the SES and what skills they needed. We needed to do more skill development."

During his time at the Department of Commerce, former Deputy Secretary Dennis Hightower also focused on the SES. Hightower recalls, "I think we clearly articulated a new approach for the Department among our SES members. We have made progress on performance measurement and we are moving on a balanced scorecard. We want to be sure that as a Department, we are working on the right things: things that move the needle in terms of outcomes—not just activities.

"We also detailed members of the SES to the Office of the Secretary to work on special initiatives. We wanted to increase the 'bandwidth' of our SES corps. We also wanted them to know how the fifth floor (the Office of the Secretary) works. We wanted to give people a firsthand look at the Department. We put high-powered teams together from across the Department—our best minds on our toughest problems. My direct involvement shows that we are serious about this. I've seen some extraordinarily talented people in the Department and I want to give them an opportunity to grow—some mini-succession planning in action. This has worked out well."

Like other Deputy Secretaries, Anthony Miller focused on the people side of the Department of Education. "We have a very talented organization, but we needed to get them aligned," says Miller. "We wanted to have the Senior Executive Service (SES) members in the Department assume more responsibility for organizational performance. So we based their performance plans on 80 percent individual performance and 20 percent organizational performance. We wanted the SES members to know that they are expected to contribute to the larger organization. Once we laid it all out, it became clearer to people. Making things clearer is actually unleashing the energy of our SES members. I think they are thriving."

from the first day I was here."

This role includes filling in for the Secretary when he or she is unavailable to attend key government meetings, and serving as "Acting Secretary" when necessary. As one Deputy Secretary tells us, "I have to be here when the Secretary is out."

Serving as the Chief Operating Officer (COO) of the Department

The role of a Department COO is clear. One Deputy Secretary reports that: "I work on the infrastructure of the Department. There are many actionable items and a bunch of moving parts. We need to work on many fronts." These fronts include working on the culture of the organization, as well as focusing on the people side of the Department. All of the Deputy Secretaries interviewed spend time working to strengthen their Senior Executive Service corps.

In addition to working with the departmental bureaucracy, Deputy Secretaries spend time on interagency committees, including the President's Management Council. In describing the COO role, one Deputy Secretary says, "My job is really a T-shape as I do a lot of collaboration across government with other agencies. It helps that I have a network of people I know across government. Then my job goes straight down the bureaucracy."

The concept of the Deputy Secretary serving as the COO of the Department is relatively new. The official designation of COO responsibilities dates back to an October 1993 Memorandum from President Bill Clinton establishing the

---

Setting Expectations for the Deputy Secretary

The Deputy Secretaries we interviewed emphasize that there is no one-size-fits-all job description for a Deputy Secretary. The job is highly dependent on the relationship between the Secretary and the Deputy Secretary. But it does appear that administrations can do a better job in setting expectations for the position. Based on observations of previous Deputy Secretaries in both Democratic and Republican Administrations, unmet expectations can decrease effectiveness in the job. A Deputy Secretary might accept the position expecting to work on policy and be surprised or disappointed to end up doing management.

To effectively accomplish an organization's mission, it is crucial that the Secretary and the Deputy Secretary (and perhaps the Office of Presidential Personnel) come to a fully understood agreement on expectations for the job of the Deputy Secretary—which of the roles described above will be fulfilled by the Deputy Secretary. Agreement on expectations by all parties is likely to result in a more fulfilling and satisfying set of experiences for future Deputy Secretaries, a more effective working relationship between the Secretary and Deputy Secretary, and accomplishment of the Department's agenda.

President's Management Council (PMC) and asking each Department to designate a Chief Operating Officer. With a few exceptions (most notably the Department of the Treasury and the Department of Defense), Departments designated the Deputy Secretary as COO. In July 2001, President George W. Bush issued a Memorandum reestablishing the PMC and continuing the COO role.

In December 2010, Congress passed the GPRA Modernization Act of 2010 which codified the Chief Operating Officer role into law. The bill, signed into law by President Obama in January 2011, states that the COO shall be responsible for improving the management and performance of the organization and "achieving the mission and goals of the agency through the use of performance planning, measurement, analysis, regular assessment of progress, and use of performance information ..." In June 2011, President Obama issued an Executive Order implementing the GPRA Modernization Act. The Memorandum calls for the COO to be designated as the Senior Accountable Official responsible for leading performance and management reform efforts and reducing wasteful or ineffective programs.

The 2010 law and 2011 Executive Order have the potential to change the role of Deputy Secretaries in government. One Deputy Secretary tells us, "I'll be interested in seeing the impact [of] the new GPRA law that says each Department must name a COO. The bill also establishes a new reporting relationship to the White House. It will be interesting to see how GPRA works and impacts the role of Deputy Secretaries."

Finally, the continued pressure to reduce spending has increased the time Deputy Secretaries spend on budget-related issues. Says one Deputy Secretary, "The budget is going to be a problem. Resources will become increasingly scarce in the future. I think we will continue to see reductions in the budget. We have been working long hours to come up with different budget scenarios. It's always more fun when you are budgeting for a good year, but management is tough and it is our job to make tough choices. We can manage our way through this. We will end up cutting some programs."

Serving as a Convener

Several of the Deputy Secretaries emphasize their role as "convener" of key decision-makers within their own Departments, and often key leaders from outside their Department. "The Office of the Secretary," says David Hayes, former Deputy Secretary of the Interior, "is the only place where everything comes together. Traditionally, the agencies have tended to work alone in the Department of the Interior. Integration can only happen when the Secretary, Deputy Secretary, and Assistant Secretaries get involved."

In describing his role at HHS, Bill Corr also emphasizes the importance of bringing people together to develop solutions and ensure continuous momentum. Corr says, "One key aspect of my job is to get the right people in the room, determine the decisions that need to be made and ensure that we not lose our focus on our goals."

Serving as a Policy Advisor

Because of their extensive careers inside and outside government, Deputy Secretaries bring a great deal of policy expertise and experience to their positions. This makes it natural for Deputy Secretaries to expect to play a policy role in the Department. Based on our interviews and observations of Deputy Secretaries in previous Administrations, the policy role varies dramatically from Department to Department.

In some cases, the Deputy Secretary may be asked by the Secretary to partici-pate in the policy making process on a specific issue because of his or her expertise in that area. In other cases, a Deputy Secretary may be thrust into a policy making role because of the need for a strong individual to lead the policy making process. One Deputy Secretary tells us, "I had to step into the policy development and policy agenda-setting process. I ended up driving the policy process. So I had to do two and a half jobs for a while. This isn't the regular job of the Deputy Secretary."

There are no clearly defined lines between policy and implementation, as they often blend together and Deputy Secretaries naturally get involved in both. As one Deputy tells us, "It is a combination of both a COO role and a decision-making role. Reality is that you have to do some of both. The Recovery Act forced me to get involved in both policy and implementation."

In the past, some Deputy Secretaries may have been attracted to Washington for the chance to work on policy issues. Since Washington has always been more of a policy town than a management town, the policy side of the Deputy Secretary position has often been appealing to many appointees. Over time, however, the Deputy Secretary position has begun to swing more toward the management role and away from the policy role.

Serving as a Leader of Departmental Initiatives

When there is a high-priority initiative, the Secretary often asks the Deputy Secretary to take the lead. An initiative can either start within the Department and move to the White House or it can start at the White House and move to a Department for implementation. For example, the American Recovery and Reinvestment Act, passed by Congress in February 2009, quickly became an Administration top priority. Deputy Secretaries in all Departments assumed some responsibility for oversight of the Act.

Serving as Crisis Manager

The Deputy Secretary often assumes the role of crisis manager. Bill Corr, Deputy Secretary of Health and Human Services, says, "A major difference between my tenure in the Obama Administration and my time at HHS in the Clinton Administration is that the Department now has a critical emergency preparedness role. We now have emergency response capabilities for natural and man-made disasters that we did not have the first time I was here." During Corr's tenure, HHS confronted a series of emergencies during the first term of the Obama Administration: the H1N1 swine flu crisis, the Haitian earthquake, the Japanese tsunami, and the oil spill in the Gulf of Mexico.

David Hayes also faced a crisis at the Department of the Interior. "I was the operations lead for the Department on the Gulf Oil spill," Hayes says. "I spent every day—as did much of our team—from April 2010 to September 2010 on the oil spill … We were also involved in the response, the cleanup phase. We negotiated with BP every step of the way. I am proud of what we did."

Serving as Liaison to Stakeholders

In the past, many Deputy Secretaries were selected because of their relationship to specific stakeholder groups of a Department. The Deputy Secretary would then serve as the key liaison between the Department and that community. This responsibility often entails giving speeches to stakeholder groups and spending time on the road. In other cases, the Secretary might decide that he or she wants to take the lead in outreach. One Deputy Secretary reports, "When I came in, I thought I would just be doing management. But the Secretary wanted me to do more public outreach. So I ended up with a mixed portfolio. Part of my time was on public policy. Part of it was interfacing with the public. The rest of my time was on management."

Deputy Secretaries in Action

Rafael Borras at the Department of Homeland Security

"I felt good coming into this position," recalls Rafael Borras, the fourth individual to hold the position of Under Secretary for Management at the Department of Homeland Security (DHS). While it is still a relatively new position, Borras says, "I did not feel constrained by the history of DHS. We are building on all the work that took place before I arrived. I talked to each person who previously held this position. There is now clarity in the Department about the position. I don't need to argue with anybody about turf."

"I joined the Department with a clear vision of what my priorities were," says Borras. "I felt we needed to focus on financial management, acquisition, and human capital. Those three items fit with my agenda, and it fits well with the Department's agenda, and it also fit my professional interests. These three priorities are also our major management responsibilities."

After he was confirmed, Borras says, "I found a great willingness to make improvements. Many of the staff here thought it was time to take on the major challenges. They wanted to show what they can do."

The Department of Homeland Security (DHS) was created by the Homeland Security Act of 2002 and came into existence in January 2003. The Department brought together 22 organizations from across government.

DHS is now the third-largest Department in the federal government. It has a budget of nearly $60 billion and more than 240,000 employees. Among its best-known agencies are the Federal Emergency Management Agency (FEMA), the Transportation Security Administration (TSA), the United States Citizenship and Immigration Services (CIS), and the U.S. Coast Guard (USCG).

The Directorate for Management at DHS is relatively unique in government. Borras is one of two Under Secretaries for Management in government. The other Under Secretary for Management is at the Department of State, where Under Secretary Patrick Kennedy reported to former Deputy Secretary for Management Thomas Nides (profiled on page 58). At DHS, the following members of the Department's C-Suite report to Borras:

- Chief Administrative Officer (CAO)
- Chief Financial Officer (CFO)
- Chief Human Capital Officer (CHCO)
- Chief Information Officer (CIO)
- Chief Procurement Officer (CPO)
- Chief Security Officer (CSO)

In his confirmation hearings, Mr. Borras described the three major challenges facing him in his new role as Under Secretary: acquisition enhancement, financial enhancement, and human capital management enhancement (Department of Homeland Security).

The challenges were thus very clear to Borras when he started his job. Borras says, "My position is unique. I am very mindful of this. It is a great position. I am doing things that other Departments can't do. In the legislation creating the Department, Congress provided the appropriate authorities to give this position more clout. I have the authority I need. It is useful to have all the management lines of business reporting to me. Today, we do not have a problem with lack of coordination and integration between and among the management business chiefs."

While Borras concluded that he had the authority and structure in place to improve and transform management at DHS, he realized that he had to work to change the culture of his directorate and DHS. "There is the cultural part of my job which is less about policies. Culture and priorities interact with each other. We have many agencies (in DHS) which have their own history. We needed to get them to interact with each other and interact differently with each other. We want to change people's DNA, not just to change their minds."

In undertaking cultural change, Borras borrowed from his local government experience. "This is a lot like my experience in local government. There is an expression that you turn around a neighborhood block by block. As a result, I have been constantly focused on our priorities and our ability to execute. I needed to spend a lot of time on acquisition. This was our greatest vulnerability from a risk management point of view. We buy goods and services. If we can't come together around the need to improve our acquisition processes, something is wrong."

As noted, one of the major challenges facing Borras was enhancing the Department's reputation and evaluations with its oversight organizations. Borras says, "Our efforts have helped enhance our conversations with the Government Accountability Office and other oversight groups. We have now come back with a plan when we have a problem we are trying to solve, and a way to measure our progress."

William V. Corr at the Department of Health and Human Services

Bill Corr held several positions at the Department of Health and Human Services (HHS) during the Clinton Administration, including Chief of Staff, so he knew his top priority when he started his work as Deputy Secretary in the Obama Administration. "I knew the career staff at HHS would be outstanding. They are highly trained, talented, and deeply dedicated to the Department's mission of protecting and promoting the health of the American people and providing essential health services to those in greatest need. And I knew that my first and most important responsibility would be to identify and recruit an outstanding team of senior leaders."

Corr drew upon his prior experience in HHS to know how to proceed in his job as Deputy Secretary. "The Secretary and I agreed that we wanted operating and staff division leaders who exemplified two key qualities—outstanding leadership and commitment to being a complete team player. We focused on these two qualities because we knew that to succeed in implementing President Obama's agenda for HHS, and to meet the ongoing responsibilities of our Department, we needed excellent coordination across our 10 operating agencies and we needed to work closely with other Departments on challenges we shared."

During the early days of the Administration, Corr worked closely with the White House Office of Presidential Personnel (OPP). In describing this experience, Corr says, "We worked closely with our colleagues at OPP to understand the experience and skills we needed in each senior level job. We valued the benefit of bringing in people from outside government to get private-sector experience, but we knew we needed leaders who could learn quickly how to operate within government because it is quite different in many respects."

In describing the beginning of his tenure as Deputy Secretary, Corr recalls, "You can be overwhelmed by all the issues and problems when you arrive, so you have to make time for hiring and personnel actions. It was the most important investment of time I made at the beginning."

The Department of Health and Human Services was created in 1953 as the Department of Health, Education, and Welfare. HHS was formed in 1979 when the separate Department of Education was created.

Today, the Department is one of the largest in government. It has a budget of over $900 billion and over 75,000 employees. The Department consists of 10 operating divisions, including such well-known agencies as the National Institutes of Health, the Food and Drug Administration, and the Centers for Medicare and Medicaid Services.

There were three major challenges facing Secretary Kathleen Sebelius and Deputy Secretary Corr at the beginning of the Obama Administration. The first challenge was a very ambitious agenda set forth by the Administration, including passage of health care reform. If the Administration succeeded in passing health care reform, it would become the responsibility of HHS to implement the new health care law.

Second, the Secretary and Deputy Secretary faced an enormous management challenge in running a Department as large as HHS with its diverse set of missions. The management challenge required coordination among the various components of HHS and a clear emphasis on implementation of the Department's strategic priorities.

Third, the Department also faced the challenge of unexpected events. Corr says, "A major difference between my tenure in the Obama Administration and my time at HHS in the Clinton Administration is that the Department now has a critical emergency preparedness role. We now have emergency response capabilities for natural and man-made disasters that we did not have the first time I was here." As it turns out, the Department did have to confront a series of emergencies during the first term of the Obama Administration: the H1N1 swine flu crisis, the Haitian earthquake, the Japanese tsunami, and the oil spill in the Gulf of Mexico.

In response to the challenges facing the Department, Secretary Sebelius and Deputy Secretary Corr formed a clear understanding of the role of the Deputy Secretary. "The Secretary is a strong leader with executive experience as Governor of Kansas," Corr recalls. "From day one, she expected that she, the Chief of Staff and I would operate as a team. We communicate daily, even when she is traveling, and we discuss a wide range of matters from the urgent to long-range planning.

"We had to hit the ground running as a team with the early, unexpected challenges we faced—particularly the worldwide H1N1 crisis and the Recovery Act implementation—as well as the early tasks of selecting personnel, policy priority-setting, the annual budget cycle, and other regular, annual challenges. My overriding job through all of this has been to ensure that we execute successfully."

A key component of the Department's success is to coordinate work across multiple agencies and with others outside HHS. In describing this role, Corr says, "The health and human service issues that HHS and other Departments face require us to engage in an unprecedented level of coordination across our agencies. When working with other Departments we try to identify the right people who are committed to the same issues and problems as our Department. For example, we work closely with the Department of Veterans Affairs and the Department of Housing and Urban Development on homeless issues and with the Department of Agriculture on nutrition issues. The passage of the Affordable Care Act," says Corr, "presented us with our greatest challenge in coordination. It impacted nearly every operating division of HHS and required us to work closely with the Departments of Treasury and Labor."

In describing his role as HHS Deputy Secretary, Corr emphasizes execution. "I have found that setting priorities and developing strategic plans are the easier set of tasks and that consistent implementation and execution are significantly more difficult. For example, designing a new approach or program to prevent HIV infection or reduce childhood obesity is easy compared to the challenges of implementing that approach or program over the several years needed to produce the desired improvements in health."

W. Scott Gould at the Department of Veterans Affairs

Scott Gould, like several other political executives profiled in this book, participated on President-Elect Obama's transition team. "I had been appointed to co-chair the transition team for the Department of Veterans Affairs (VA)," recalls Gould. "We assembled about 20 people and we conducted 100 interviews and reviewed over 100 documents. We wrote a two-page memo to the President-elect and a 20-page white paper. We also briefed Secretary-designate Eric Shinseki on the Department. We analyzed the major operating units and support functions in the Department and provided the Secretary-designate with a starting point for action."

The Veterans Affairs transition team developed a three-part plan which included reorganizing the Office of the Secretary, improving the Department's management systems, and developing a plan to get the Department ready for implementation of the Post-9/11 GI bill, which provided improved education benefits for veterans serving on active duty on or after September 11, 2011. After the inauguration of the President, Gould helped prepare the Secretary-designate for his confirmation. "By the time I took this position, I had a good baseline knowledge about VA," says Gould. "My time on the transition gave me a sense of the issues and problems facing the Department. We all agreed that we needed to undertake an intensive transformation initiative at VA which would involve career employees."

The Department of Veterans Affairs, elevated to Cabinet status in 1989, has a long history. Some date the nation's veterans programs back to 1636, when the Pilgrims of Plymouth Colony passed a law which stated that soldiers disabled during their war with the Pequot Indians would be supported by the colony. The Continental Congress of 1776 provided pensions for soldiers who were disabled in the Revolutionary War. In 1811, the federal government established the first medical facility for veterans. Congress established a system of veterans benefits when the United States entered World War I in 1917. During the 1920s, veterans benefits were administered by three different federal agencies. The Veterans Administration was created in 1930 to consolidate and coordinate government programs for veterans.

Today, VA is the second largest federal government Department, with over 300,000 employees. It operates over 1200 medical facilities (152 VA hospitals, 278 VA Vet Centers, and nearly 800 VA community-based outpatient clients), 131 VA cemeteries, and 58 regional offices delivering veterans' benefits. VA's budget for FY 2012 is over $130 billion, including nearly $70 billion in mandatory funding. VA saw over one million patients per week and issued 4.4 million benefit checks in each month in FY 2012.

Secretary Shinseki concluded that management improvement was a top priority for the Department. In reflecting on his previous experience working in government, Gould says, "Unlike previous Secretaries I had worked for who decided to focus on two to three priority issues, Secretary Shinseki decided to take on a broad array of issues simultaneously and exploit opportunities. We had a lot of things to do."

This management focus led to a clear division of responsibility between the Secretary, Deputy Secretary, and the Chief of Staff. "In many ways, I have the classic Chief Operating Officer job," says Gould. "I spend a lot of my time involved internally with our line and support units—health care, benefits, and cemetery, as well as information technology, procurement, financial management, human resources, and policy. I'm in charge of the operating plan to implement our vision, and working on budget issues. In general, I focus on working 'inside' issues, while the Secretary focuses on setting overall direction for the entire organization and managing 'outside' stakeholders."

Shinseki and Gould proceeded on their VA management transformation on two fronts: working on the processes and the infrastructure of the Department, and working on human resources.

Based on his assessment of the need for a stronger VA workforce, Gould moved out quickly on the people front. "We wanted to make the Department more people-centered," says Gould. One of the first major departmental HR initiatives was to rapidly increase the amount of training given to VA employees. "When we started our training initiative, people said it couldn't be done," says Gould. "We went all out to get it done. We worked with the private sector and the Office of Personnel Management to get as much done as we could. We wanted to train over 135,000 people per year in the Department—a goal we exceeded in FY 10 and are on track to accomplish in FY 11. We worked hard to get $200 million to invest in our people."

Seth D. Harris at the Department of Labor

There were several beginnings for Seth Harris. In January 2007, Harris began working with the Obama campaign team. Starting in August 2008, he worked three days a week for the Obama Presidential transition planning team while continuing to teach law at New York Law School. In November 2008, he was appointed to oversee the transition teams for the Departments of Labor, Education, and Transportation and 12 other agencies. "I worked closely with Secretaries-designate Solis, Duncan, and LaHood," says Harris. "After the transition, I worked with Secretary-designate Solis and handed off all the materials we had collected during the transition. I then arrived at the Department in February 2009 as a Senior Advisor to the Secretary after the announcement of my selection as Deputy Secretary-designate. So I had the opportunity to re-learn the Department prior to becoming confirmed as Deputy Secretary in May. I also worked closely with the Acting Deputy Secretary during the February–May time period."

Harris was very familiar with the Department of Labor because of his prior service in the Department during the Clinton Administration. Harris recalls, "I had worked six and a half years as a senior policy advisor at Labor. So I knew about the management structure of the Department and the role of the Deputy Secretary."

The Department of Labor dates back to 1884, when it was created as the Bureau of Labor in the Department of the Interior. In 1888, the Bureau became independent as a Department of Labor without executive rank. The Bureau of Labor returned to Bureau status when the Department of Commerce and Labor was created in 1903. In 1913, all labor programs were transferred from the Department of Commerce and Labor to a new Department of Labor.

Today, the Department of Labor has a more than $12 billion discretionary budget, over 17,000 employees, and administers and enforces more than 180 federal laws. The Department's programs cover more than 125 million workers and 10 million employers. The Department has over 25 organizational units, including the Mine Safety and Health Administration (MSHA), the Occupational Safety and Health Administration (OSHA), the Employment & Training Administration (ETA), the Bureau of Labor Statistics (BLS), and the Employee Benefits Security Administration (EBSA).

In describing the Department, Harris says, "I'm still amazed at the complexity of these organizations. I have 13 line agencies, with each having many different product lines. Our customers range from non-English speaking migrant farmworkers to corporate chief executive officers. We have many market niches and each of our agencies faces a different set of political issues."

Harris found a different Department of Labor than the one he had left nearly a decade earlier. "Since my last time here, I found that we had some new programs," recalls Harris. "We were also faced with implementing the new Recovery Act. Due to retirements and other departures by senior career staff, I thought the Senior Executive Service corps had lost talent that we needed to succeed. Strengthening the SES corps was a critical management issue for the Department. I thought we had to start with our career managers and make changes there. We had to strengthen the organization. I had to move people around to improve management in the Department. We also found a demoralized workforce."

Harris also faced the challenge of poor management processes and practices in some places. "We had to improve the business practices of the Department," asserts Harris. Harris concluded that the Department needed to launch a new strategic planning process. Harris also realized that, together with the strategic planning process, the Department needed new performance measures. "The Department was measuring the wrong things," says Harris. "The measures were typically internal and we were not measuring outcomes. The Department had focused on outputs and process measures previously. We realized that measuring outcomes is incredibly hard, but absolutely essential."

"How do you turn a giant ship?" asks Harris. This was the issue Harris had to answer for himself and the Department. He concluded that the Department had the right mission and a large staff which had much potential and a deep dedication to the Department's mission. "The raw material was there," comments Harris. "We needed to unleash the inner Labor.

"We concluded that we would use strategic planning as our tool for changing the Department," recalls Harris. "We articulated a vision for the Department— 'Good jobs for everyone.' That was a new goal we believed our staff would enthusiastically embrace. We wanted to articulate the vision clearly. We wanted to emphasize the lives of our customers. We asked our employees whether they were doing the Department's work to help people, and the answer was uniformly 'yes.' We wanted to get the organization to focus on [its] job of protecting workers. We wanted them to know that labor policy and labor still matter. We worked on a set of 13 outcomes which were a different set of measures than people had worked toward in the past. This turned out to be a very effective tool."

The Department of Labor's change management initiative thus consisted of four key components: a vision, a set of outcomes, performance goals and measures, and a strategic plan. "This has been a big change," says Harris, "both conceptually and intellectually for the Department. We also started agencies working on operating plans. I had been surprised by the lack of operating plans in almost half of our agencies. By using all these tools, we wanted to change the organization."

David J. Hayes at the Department of the Interior

"My current time at the Department is much different than my first experience at Interior during the Clinton Administration," recalls David J. Hayes. "This time I came in at the beginning of the Administration with Secretary Ken Salazar. We had to build a new team, and at the same time we were addressing a backlog of issues that needed attention. During my previous experience, I joined former Secretary Bruce Babbitt's excellent, well-established team, and I was able to focus on a more discrete agenda of key issues.

"I came back for a second tenure as Deputy Secretary because I love the Department's mission and I was inspired by the vision laid out by President Obama and Secretary Salazar," says Hayes. "I also wanted to expand the Deputy Secretary role beyond its traditional Chief Operating Officer role. I view my job as lining up the management of the Department with the policies of the Department. The Department of the Interior has a broad jurisdiction, and I enjoy the organizational challenge it represents.

"I knew Secretary Salazar very well. I had been President-elect Obama's transition head for the Departments of Energy, Agriculture, and Interior; and for the Environmental Protection Agency. So Ken and I worked together on the transition. I knew that Ken wanted a strong Deputy Secretary."

The Department of the Interior is one of the federal government's oldest Departments. Its origins date back to 1789 when portions of its activity were divided among the first three federal Departments (Foreign Affairs, Treasury, and War). Interior was formally created as a separate Department in 1849.

The Department has a budget of approximately $12 billion and over 70,000 employees. It contains nine major agencies, including such well-known organizations as the Bureau of Land Management, U.S. Geological Survey, the Fish and Wildlife Service, and the National Park Service. Lesser-known but equally important bureaus include the Bureau of Reclamation, the Bureau of Indian Affairs, the Bureau of Ocean Energy Management, the Bureau of Safety and Environmental Enforcement, and the Office of Surface Mining.

Among its responsibilities, the Department of the Interior manages over one-fifth of the land area of the United States, plus the development rights to the 1.7-billion acre outer continental shelf. Interior provides water to over 30 million Americans, manages relations with each of the 565 federally recognized

American Indian and Alaska Native tribes, and is home to the nation's premier earth sciences agency.

Hayes describes one of his various roles as that of convener. "I regularly broker meetings among our bureaus with stakeholders and with state and local governments. We have a major land, water, and wildlife management role throughout the United States, and our bureaus' missions and responsibilities can sometimes be in conflict."

Like the other Deputy Secretaries profiled in this chapter, Hayes has a major role in working closely with other federal Departments. "The President's Management Council is my link to the other Departments. For example, because the Department of the Interior manages energy development on one-third of the land mass of the United States and in our offshore waters, we are in the middle of the Administration's energy policy discussions. We routinely work closely with EPA and the Departments of Defense, Agriculture, and Energy on a broad range of energy-related issues," says Hayes. "Having strong lines of communication to my fellow Deputy Secretaries is an invaluable resource for me."

Another role played by Hayes as Deputy Secretary is crisis manager. "I was the operations lead for the Department on the Gulf Oil spill," Hayes says. "I spent every day—as did much of our team—from April 2010 to September 2010 on the oil spill." Joel Achenbach writes in *A Hole at the Bottom of the Sea* about the start of Hayes's involvement in the oil spill:

> David Hayes … arrived at his office that Wednesday morning, April 21, with no inkling that it would be anything other than a normal workday. He heard about the explosion within minutes of walking into Interior's massive building … by midmorning the scale of the disaster became more apparent, and Hayes's boss, Interior Secretary Ken Salazar, suggested that he jump on a plane and fly to New Orleans.
>
> Hayes would rather have stayed put; it was his daughter Molly's eighteenth birthday. He called his wife: "We may have a problem here."
>
> … Hayes and press secretary Kendra Barkoff raced to Reagan National Airport— no luggage, not even toothbrushes—and talked their way onto a US Airways jet that had already closed its door and was about to taxi toward the runway. (Achenbach)

In looking back on the Gulf Oil spill, Hayes is proud of his Department's work. He says, "Our Department worked closely with the national labs, and our scientists at the USGS and elsewhere contributed invaluable research." Says Hayes, "We were also involved in the response, the cleanup phase. We negotiated with BP every step of the way. I am proud of what we did."

The Interior Department took the oil spill as a chance for reform, Hayes says. "The oil spill was an opportunity for us to address a number of long-standing institutional issues at the Department. We had to revamp our processes in response to the oil spill, and we did a major bureau reorganization based on the lessons we learned." In the midst of the crisis, Hayes says his team gained invaluable experience. "We increased our skills. It was a huge lift. We all spent long days during that period, but we kept the trains running."

Dennis F. Hightower at the Department of Commerce

"I was sworn in at 9:00 a.m. and I was in my first budget meeting at 9:30 a.m.," recalls Dennis Hightower. "I quickly got the impression that running Commerce was like running a holding company—a collection of vastly different businesses, but with a common goal of helping U.S. businesses become more innovative and competitive. My first week there was *Commerce 101*. I did a lot  of listening and learning. I did, however, already know much about Commerce. As a business executive, I had used many of the services of the Department over the years."

Hightower spent time during his first months at Commerce on the road. "I spent time out in the field where the work gets done," recalls Hightower. "I wanted to meet the Commerce employees, and observe firsthand how they performed their work. I used different forums to talk with employees. I would ask a lot of questions. I used this time to think strategically about the Department."

Based on this outreach, Hightower says, "I began to select three to five very specific objectives on which we could focus. I also was interested in getting more cross-fertilization in the Department. After about 60 days, my office started developing brief position papers describing both short-term things we could do (the low-hanging fruit) as well as longer-term, sustainable projects; and mobilizing members of the Office of the Secretary to support these efforts."

Deputy Secretary Hightower got it right. The Department of Commerce is much like a holding company. The Department consists of 12 bureaus and 10 staff organizations. Its bureaus range from the Economics and Statistics Administration to the National Oceanic and Atmospheric Administration to the United States Patent and Trademark Office. The Department of Commerce was formed in 1903 when the Department of Commerce and Labor was split into two Cabinet Departments. The Department had a budget of over $17 billion and had nearly 55,000 employees.

During his time at Commerce, Hightower worked on many fronts. One major activity was oversight of several Administration priorities. "I worked on the 2010 Census, the broadband initiative of the Recovery Act, and the Export Control Reform Initiative," says Hightower. "In the broadband initiative, it was essential to accelerate the second and third phases to get the money out to the winning grantees to facilitate job creation. Successfully bringing NOAA's satellite program in-house was a major undertaking, involving close coordination with DoD,

NASA, and the prime contractor."

Another activity of Hightower's was reaching out to the business community and working with Commerce agencies that deal directly with large, medium, and small businesses. "I saw the many opportunities that the Department has to reach out and touch businesses on all levels," says Hightower. "A new Department initiative, 'CommerceConnect' brought all of the capabilities of Commerce to one location (piloted in Detroit) to help small and medium size companies in depressed communities redeploy their products, services, and skill sets to new growth areas. We are involved in speeding up granting patents at the United States Patent and Trademark Office, assisting manufacturers at the National Institutes of Standards and Technology and the International Trade Administration (ITA), and assisting exporters at both ITA and the Bureau of Industry and Security. I wanted to explore how the Department and its components—that touch every phase of the business life cycle—could help businesses become more innovative and competitive at home and abroad."

Another front was the people side of the Department. Along with several of his fellow Deputy Secretaries, Hightower took a special interest in meeting and talking with employees. "I always believed in management by walking around," says Hightower. "You have to reinforce your strategy. You have to tell people what you are doing and why, and how they fit. I like to go to Commerce offices when I'm on the road. These visits increase the visibility of the Office of the Secretary and facilitate a dialogue. Also, you never know where the next good ideas will come from."

In focusing on the people side of the Department, Hightower had been influenced by the time he spent working with Jack Welch at General Electric. "Welch taught me that business wasn't about just making your numbers," recalls Hightower. "I learned it was also about values and creating the right environment. Welch spent a lot of time on succession planning, too. He used to say that numbers don't get the job done. It is people who get the job done."

Maurice Jones at the Department of Housing and Urban Development

Like many of the Deputy Secretaries profiled in this chapter, Maurice Jones had a conversation with the Secretary about his role at the Department of Housing and Urban Development (HUD). Jones recalls, "I view myself as a partner to the Secretary. We had a discussion about my job. There was a job to be done. Among my other assignments, it was clear I was also going to focus on operational excellence. I had to identify the job to be done and then help lead us there. We needed more efficient processes in the Department."

There was clearly a need for an increased focus on management and operational excellence. "Our operational mission," says Jones, "was getting complaints. It was not just a question about us getting more money in our budget. We needed to make our processes more efficient. We needed budget data in a more timely manner. We believed that the Department would get more money to spend if we managed the money better. Historically, we have un-invested in our capacity for operational excellence."

The demand for operational excellence was coming from a variety of places. "Our stakeholders inside of government—the White House, the Office of Management and Budget, Congress—wanted operational excellence," says Jones. "Our external stakeholders also complained about how long it took us to get things done."

In assessing the Department's operations, Jones initially focused on the Department's human resource and financial functions. Jones recounts, "I started out wanting to know how well the Department was recruiting and developing our people. I also wanted to know about our Department's financial stewardship role. So I have been focusing on human capital and financial processes. You can have the greatest innovative policies in government, but without execution, those policies can't succeed."

In describing his role as Chief Operating Officer (COO), Jones says, "I spend a large part of my time making sure that we have the right people in the right jobs. We have made some changes since I arrived. We have a new Chief Human Capital Officer and a new Acting Chief Information Officer."

In placing an increased focus on operational excellence, Jones found much support from within the Department. Jones says, "Employers are welcoming this new direction and new focus. We receive many complaints from within the Department as to how long it takes to get things done. Nobody is against this. We believe we can do things differently. The opportunity is here. We just need to focus on operational excellence. As time evolved, I saw lots of opportunities to move operations to a much higher level. The passion I saw was compelling.

"I get up every day to work on these issues," says Jones. "I want to get our operations in top notch shape. I realize that you never get to perfection, but you have to keep it as a priority. It is tough. Government is not designed for speed. A problem is that people don't come to the federal government to do execution, which is what we need to do."

Kathleen A. Merrigan at the Department of Agriculture

Kathleen Merrigan recalls her first days as Deputy Secretary in the Department of Agriculture: "Knowing that everybody would want to come in and make a case for priorities for the new Administration, I accepted all

meeting requests for the first three months. This prevented a logjam of requests and allowed me to establish relationships with important constituent leaders."

The Department of Agriculture is one of the oldest Departments in government, created in 1862. It has a budget of approximately $145 billion and over 110,000 employees, 90,000 of whom are based in state field offices and in 99 countries across the globe. The Department consists of 18 agencies and 15 staff offices. Agencies in the Department include the Forest Service, the Food and Nutrition Service, the Agricultural Research Service, the Animal and Plant Health Inspection Service, and the Food Safety and Inspection Service. The Department is responsible for a wide variety of activities, ranging from food safety to rural development to delivering food and nutrition programs.

A challenge faced by Merrigan, along with the other Deputy Secretaries profiled in this chapter, was the size and scope of the Department, including the tendency for each internal agency to view itself as somewhat independent of the Office of the Secretary. "Historically, the power in the bureaucracy has been in the hands of agency administrators," says Merrigan, once an agency administrator herself. "Administrators run their own budget, Congressional outreach, and public affairs offices."

Deputy Secretary Merrigan introduced outcomes-based budgeting, demanding that all proposals demonstrate their relative contributions to four priorities established by the Secretary and his team. "This required agency administrators and Under Secretaries to work together to articulate and achieve cross-cutting objectives and outcomes. Four years goes by very quickly. Focus and speed are essential."

While one set of initial challenges focused on the internal management of the Department, another set was external. The average age of farmers and ranchers in this country is 59, and more than 30% of farmers are over age 65. "We need a recruitment strategy to repopulate Rural America. With less than 1% of Americans directly connected to farming, the challenge is to remind policy makers and the American public why USDA and agriculture matter."

In responding to the challenges she faced, Merrigan had to divide her time between the internal management of the Department and the need for external outreach to the broad and growing number of groups interested in agriculture. Internally, the budget consumed much of Merrigan's time as the ongoing budget process and debt negotiations required major management initiatives to narrow priorities and find efficiencies.

In describing her experience implementing a new outcomes-based budget process, Merrigan says, "It was uncomfortable at first as people tried out this new way of doing things. But eventually people recognized the value of going forward in this way, particularly as budgets are being downsized and with a public that is increasingly skeptical of government investments. We also identified high priority performance goals. We chose performance goals that required agencies to work together. When OMB asked for a goal leader, I responded that each goal had multiple leaders. While that may make accountability more difficult in the short term, the lasting value is the synergistic energy and cross-fertilization that comes from multiple agency engagement." Merrigan also led an effort to rewrite the Department's strategic plan, the first draft of which she and the Secretary concluded was not ambitious enough. "We wanted stretch goals," says Merrigan. "There is too much at stake to play it safe."

In addition to managing the Department's budget process, Merrigan launched an extensive outreach program. During her tenure as Deputy Secretary, Merrigan visited more than 40 states. "I've lectured at dozens of college campuses, held producer roundtables in nearly every state, and conducted oversight visits of Recovery Act-funded projects. One of my primary goals as Deputy is to increase interest in the work of USDA and in American agriculture. I want people who have had mixed experience with USDA in the past—women and minorities and those involved in alternative production techniques—to hear from me directly that this is a different, more inclusive USDA."

Given the vast array of field offices, Merrigan made visits with field staff a priority. "I try and visit our field offices whenever I travel. Many employees in our county offices had never had people from Washington visit, not just in this Administration, but some tell me not in the 35 years that they have worked for USDA. Employees come to these meetings expecting a big speech, but after five minutes of remarks, I turn to questions and assure them that they can be frank and that everything is on the table."

Anthony W. Miller at the Department of Education

When invited to join Secretary Arne Duncan's team at the U.S. Department of Education, Anthony Miller did not anticipate becoming Deputy Secretary of the Department—the number two position. "I came with five other individuals and we worked as Special Assistants to the Secretary," recalls Miller. "We were all new and none of us had been here before. My first impression of the Department was pretty overwhelming. I didn't know where to sit, who else was here, or where I should park.

"I started working on strategic planning from day one. We had initially thought about my serving in the Department as Chief Operating Officer," states Miller. "As our staffing needs became clearer, the President decided to nominate me as Deputy Secretary. I was formally nominated in May 2009 and confirmed by the U.S. Senate in July."

The Department of Education is the second "youngest" federal Cabinet Department (created in 1980) and is the smallest Department in terms of the number of federal employees (4,200). It has a budget of approximately $70 billion, making it the third largest source of discretionary funds in the federal government.

In higher education, the Department provides about 45 percent of scholarship aid and about 75 percent of total financial aid. The federal government's contribution to elementary and secondary education is about 10 percent of total national spending, with the remaining 90 percent coming from state and local government funding. While it is a relatively new Cabinet Department, the federal role in education dates back to the 1860s when the federal government started to collect information on schools and teaching to help states establish school systems.

During the first year of the Obama Administration, Deputy Secretary Miller faced two major challenges:

- **Implementing the Recovery Act in the Department.** Congress passed the American Recovery and Reinvestment Act on February 13, 2009 and it was signed into law by President Obama on February 17. The Department received $97 billion in Recovery Act funds, an amount of money larger than its annual budget. The funds were intended to avert layoffs of school personnel and also to advance critical reforms in education.
- **Strengthening the Department's internal processes.** With the addition of Recovery Act funds, it became essential that the Department's management processes operate effectively and efficiently.

The challenge in years two and three of the first term shifted for Deputy Secretary Miller. "I learned about the cycles of government," states Miller. "During your first year here, you are doing the planning for the first time and learning the planning process. You are still working from the old budget. In year two, you really start implementing your agenda as well as identifying opportunities to improve processes. In year three, you can more systematically drive your policy agenda. The reality is that this is a multi-year effort and you don't realize that at the beginning. In year three, we're now working to institutionalize changes to key planning and management processes and to implement a continuous improvement mindset as part of the Department's agenda."

The first order of business for Miller, in both his role as a Special Assistant and later Deputy Secretary, was getting the Recovery Act implemented. "We started working on the Recovery Act during our first days and that dominated our activities. Our first six months were devoted to getting the Recovery Act launched." In reflecting on this experience, Miller says, "If there was one thing we needed to do, it was the Recovery Act. We stood it up and got the money out. It's been a tremendous success in the education world, saving hundreds of thousands of educator jobs." Launching the program included developing guidance and providing technical assistance to recipients, including explaining the Act's unique requirements for how the funds could be used and the reports that needed to be submitted.

While the Department was successful in standing up the program and obligating the money to the states, it turned out that getting the money out was only part of the job. "After we got the money out, the states then had to work with local school districts to minimize the potential for waste, fraud, and abuse as funds were drawn down by districts to meet their most pressing needs," states Miller. "We encouraged them to spend the money early and wisely, but we didn't have any control over whether they kept part of the money to spend at a later date. We didn't want them to sit on the money. We wanted them to save jobs and advance reforms and do it as quickly as possible." Like many of the political executives in this book, Miller learned that there are many external factors outside the control of the Department that influence the ultimate impact of federal dollars.

The second order of business for Miller was strengthening the Department's administrative processes. During the early days of the Administration, it was essential to clarify the decision-making processes in the Department. "There are so many layers in government that you have to be clear about how and where decisions will be made," states Miller. "With the arrival of a new leadership team, you need to let people know how the decision-making process will operate."

Thomas R. Nides at the Department of State

"I spent 10 years in the private sector before returning to government service at the State Department," says Tom Nides. "My return to government has exceeded my expectations, in part because of the people I am surrounded by every day. The State Department attracts an incredible cadre of people. I would put them up against people I've worked with in the private sector any day."

The United States Department of State is the oldest federal agency, established in 1781 as the Department of Foreign Affairs. With over 270 missions in 190 countries, the Department of State is central to promoting America's economic prosperity and advancing national security interests around the world.

The Department has two Deputy Secretaries who serve as principal advisers to the Secretary of State, assist the Secretary in the formulation and conduct of U.S. foreign policy, and provide general supervision and direction to all elements of the Department. The Deputy Secretary of State for Management and Resources serves as the Chief Operating Officer of the Department, overseeing the allocation of the Department's budget of over $50 billion.

Mr. Nides is the second person to serve as Deputy Secretary of State for Management and Resources. In addition to the challenges inherent in the conduct of U.S. foreign policy in an ever-changing world, Nides faced the challenge of further defining a newly formed and not well-understood role. Nides arrived in January 2011, after his predecessor, Jack Lew, moved to the White House. "I learned a lot from Jack Lew and he helped smooth the transition. But because this is still a new position, the role continues to require definition," says Nides. A strong working relationship with Deputy Secretary Bill Burns helped Nides define the position's roles and responsibilities. "I work very closely with Bill Burns.

He understands the value and importance of this position for the Secretary and the Administration. He and I have a divide-and-conquer strategy in support of Secretary Clinton. We work closely together on managing the Department, as well as engaging other agencies and the White House. We work especially closely with the National Security Council and its director, Tom Donilon."

Secretary Clinton asked Nides to lead in five key areas:

- The Department's budget
- Economic statecraft
- The Quadrennial Diplomacy and Development Review
- The Iraq transition
- Afghanistan and Pakistan relations

Laying out clear goals within his areas of responsibility was important for Nides. He says, "I've learned you have to set goals. If you can't track it, no real progress can be made. My team keeps me informed as to what decisions I need to make and ensures that the President's and Secretary's priorities are reflected in the day-to-day work of the Department and our embassies and consulates abroad."

In describing his role, Nides says, "As Deputy Secretary of State, I could be focused on many issues and in many places. But few things are as important to me as fighting for the resources that our diplomats and development experts need to enhance our national security and economic security. Few things are more important than making the case for security, economic, and humanitarian assistance. And few things are more important than making sure that Washington appropriates funding in a rational way." (Department of State, 2011).

In managing the budget process for the Department, Nides says, "We work very closely with the Hill. We work closely with groups concerned about and interested in foreign assistance. We have to clearly communicate to the American public that the entire budget for the State Department and the U.S. Agency for International Development is a small fraction of the federal budget—less than one percent of the federal budget, not the 20 to 30 percent that most Americans believe is devoted to foreign assistance."

Another major component of Nides' job is to advise the Secretary of State on economic policy. During her tenure, former Secretary Clinton put "economic statecraft" at the forefront of foreign policy. Economic statecraft is "how we harness the forces and use the tools of global economics to strengthen our diplomacy and presence abroad; and how we put that diplomacy and presence to work to strengthen our economy at home." Nides championed this agenda during his two years on the job. Nides has said, "One reason I was so eager to work for Secretary Clinton is that I believe our foreign policy needs to be more engaged where business and diplomacy intersect."

Nides also had responsibility for leading the transition in Iraq from military-led to civilian-led operations. The transition was completed in December 2011. At the time, Nides said, "This is the largest military-to-civilian transition initiative since the Marshall Plan." Nides also led the Department's efforts to right-size its mission in Iraq, using a core set of principles to ensure that the United States has fulfilled its end of the Strategic Framework Agreement (the cornerstone of the U.S. and Iraq bilateral relationship), that both Iraqis and Americans expect effective programs that are mutually beneficial, and that the diplomatic presence should look like other U.S. missions across the globe. Nides said, "We'll continue to look … to make sure that our footprint is appropriate … we are going to look to ways to shift more of the cost structure locally … and continue evaluating (it) as this mission set is … being accomplished." (Department of State, 2012a)

Daniel B. Poneman at the Department of Energy

"In many ways, this was a homecoming for me," says Daniel Poneman. "I had been here in 1989 when I was a White House Fellow.

"My prior time in the Department helped me to understand how the Department operates. When you are young and working in the trenches, you can see what works well and what doesn't work well. My six years working at the National Security Council in the White House helped as well. You get a different view of the Cabinet from the White House. You can see the critical role the Cabinet agencies play in implementing the national agenda."

The origins of the Department of Energy can be traced to the Manhattan Project and the race to develop the atomic bomb during World War II. In the 1970s, the Atomic Energy Commission—the Department of Energy's predecessor—was split into two separate agencies: the Nuclear Regulatory Commission, to regulate the nuclear power industry; and the Energy Research and Development Administration (ERDA), to manage the country's nuclear weapons arsenal and energy development programs and to pursue technology research and development.

In 1977, Congress created the Department of Energy by combining agencies including ERDA, the Federal Energy Administration, and the Atomic Energy Commission. Today, the Department has a budget of over $25 billion, approximately 15,000 employees, and more than 100,000 contractors. In describing the Department, Poneman says, "The Department is organized around three major program areas—energy, science, and nuclear security. In addition, we have launched the Advanced Research Projects Agency-Energy, or ARPA-E. Other important Department elements include the Energy Information Administration and the Power Administrations."

A major activity during Poneman's first year was reaching out and engaging the Department's employees. "The Department is all about its people. It's a great organization that depends on a good esprit de corps. The people I work with are glad to be here. They have engaging work. Our employees are working on the major issues facing the nation—climate, energy, and national security. These are great challenges for the nation and reflect the President's and the Secretary's top priorities." Poneman concluded that the Department needed to develop a set of guiding management principles. "The purpose was to support our programmatic objectives," says Poneman. "They were all about how we will operate and manage the Department. You won't be surprised that as more people participated in developing these principles, the inclination was always to add more of them, more details and caveats. But the goal was to establish simple yet clear guidelines for how we do business at the Department that would apply equally to both our federal and our contractor employees. So we took and studied all the comments, but then boiled it all down to seven principles. The key is to incorporate them into our daily actions, so they don't become just empty rhetoric."

During his first year, Poneman also prioritized the Department's management efforts into the following areas: human capital, project management, transparency, and roles and responsibilities. Poneman says, "We wanted to emphasize management excellence, which we see as critical to achieving the Department's mission. It affects everything we do at DOE." Because of the major management challenges facing the Department, Poneman says, "I've spent more time on management issues than I thought I would. Everything is a balance, so sometimes that meant I had less time to devote to interagency meetings or policy issues. But getting management right is essential to succeeding as a Department."

Throughout his tenure as Deputy Secretary, Poneman continued to devote a significant amount of time to people issues facing the Department. "I've worked on ensuring that we have a process for getting good people into the Department and then retaining them once they are hired and are here," says Poneman. Poneman told *Government Executive* that he viewed hiring as only one part of the personnel challenge. Poneman says, "[Hiring] is just the front edge. Our mission is evolving, and we need to continue to provide career paths that are exciting so we not only attract but retain talent" (Peters).

Appendix to Chapter 3
Profiles of Deputy Secretaries Interviewed

Rafael Borras

Tenure
Mr. Borras was nominated by President Obama
to serve as Under Secretary for Management in
January 2011, and confirmed by the U.S. Senate
in April 2011. (Mr. Borras served as Under
Secretary in a recess appointment lasting from
March 2010 to his confirmation in April 2011.)

Private Sector Experience
Prior to being confirmed as Under Secretary,
Mr. Borras served as Vice President of the
Infrastructure and Environment Division, URS
Corporation, from 2000 to 2010.

Federal Government Experience
From 1997 to 2000, Mr. Borras served in the General Services Administration as
Regional Administrator, Mid-Atlantic region. From 1994 to 1997, he served as
Deputy Assistant Secretary for Administration in the U.S. Department of Commerce.

Local Government Experience
From 1993 to 1994, Mr. Borras served as Deputy City Manager and Commissioner,
Human Services in the City of New Rochelle, New York. He also served in the City
of Hartford, Connecticut from 1991 to 1993 and the County of Miami-Dade, Florida
from 1982 to 1985.

Non-Profit Experience
From 1985 to 1991, Mr. Borras served as Director of Communications for the
International City/County Management Association.

Education
Mr. Borras received his undergraduate degree from Florida International University.

Reflecting on DHS and Managing in Government
"It is the best job in government. I truly love this Department. We have a chance to
improve the Department and make long-lasting changes.

"I have observed some political appointees who haven't been in government before
get frustrated. I believe that you have to act like you are in charge. You set the agenda.
I have seen some political appointees be too passive … I tell them that it is not about
you or me. It is up to you to make [change] last with the career staff. My belief is that
it is shame on both of us if change goes away during a change of Administration."

William V. (Bill) Corr

Tenure
Mr. Corr was nominated by President Obama to serve as Deputy Secretary of the Department of Health and Human Services in January 2009, and confirmed by the U.S. Senate in May 2009.

Private Sector Experience
Prior to being confirmed as Deputy Secretary, Mr. Corr served as Executive Director of the Campaign for Tobacco-Free Kids from 2000 to 2009.

Federal Government Experience
Mr. Corr served as Chief Counsel and Policy Director for U.S. Senate Minority Leader Tom Daschle from 1998 to 2000. From 1993 to 1998, he served in a variety of positions at the Department of Health and Human Services, including service as Chief of Staff, Counselor, and Deputy Assistant Secretary for Health. From 1989 to 1993, he served as Chief Counsel and Staff Director for the Subcommittee on Antitrust, Monopolies and Business Rights, Senate Committee on the Judiciary. From 1977 to 1989, he served as Counsel to the Subcommittee on Health and the Environment, House Committee on Energy and Commerce.

Non-Profit Experience
From 1974 to 1977, he directed four non-profit, community-run primary health care centers in the Appalachian Mountain area of Tennessee and Kentucky.

Education
Mr. Corr received his B.A. in Economics from the University of Virginia and a J.D. from Vanderbilt University School of Law.

Reflecting on Serving in Government
"Public service is challenging and rewarding. I consider myself incredibly fortunate to be able to participate in our nation's efforts to address major national issues. Working at HHS in my position is the chance of a lifetime to make an important difference in the lives of all Americans."

W. Scott Gould

Tenure
Mr. Gould was nominated by President Obama to serve as Deputy Secretary of the Department of Veterans Affairs in March 2009, and confirmed by the U.S. Senate in April 2009. Mr. Gould resigned his position in May 2013.

Present Position
Mr. Gould is Executive Vice President, Medical Affairs, CareFirst BlueCross BlueShield, Baltimore, Maryland.

Private Sector Experience
Prior to being confirmed as Deputy Secretary, Mr. Gould was Vice President for Public Sector Strategy at IBM Global Business Services. He also served as Chief Executive Officer of O'Gara Company and Chief Operating Officer of Exolve. Earlier in his career, he was a consultant at Theodore Barry and Associates.

Federal Government Experience
Mr. Gould served as Chief Financial Officer and Assistant Secretary for Administration at the Department of Commerce, and as Deputy Assistant Secretary for Finance and Management at the Department of the Treasury. In 1993, he served as a White House Fellow at the Export-Import Bank of the United States and in the Office of the White House Chief of Staff. Mr. Gould is a veteran of the United States Navy. As a Naval Intelligence reservist, Mr. Gould was recalled to active duty in 2001 to support the war in Afghanistan.

Local Government Experience
In 1991, Gould was appointed by the Governor of Massachusetts to conduct a financial and operational work-out of the city of Chelsea, the first municipality in the state to be placed in receivership by the general court.

Education
Gould attained a B.A. degree in Philosophy from Cornell University and a M.B.A. and Ed.D. from the University of Rochester.

Reflecting on Serving in the Department of Veterans Affairs
"I consider myself lucky to be here. I like the mission and the people here; we are a team. I tell my colleagues that now is the time that we can make a difference. I've become especially interested in the problem of homeless veterans. Our goal is to reduce the number of homeless veterans to zero in five years. We are working on integrating our mental health programs, as well as reducing our claims backlog. It's all been very challenging and rewarding—every minute of the day."

Seth D. Harris

Tenure
Mr. Harris was nominated by President Obama to serve as Deputy Secretary of Labor in March 2009, and confirmed by the U.S. Senate in May 2009.

Academic Experience
Prior to being confirmed as Deputy Secretary, Mr. Harris served as a Professor of Law at New York Law School and as Director of its Labor and Employment Law programs.

Federal Government Experience
Mr. Harris served for nearly seven years at the Department of Labor during the Clinton Administration. During that time, Mr. Harris served as Counselor to the Secretary of Labor and as Acting Assistant Secretary of Labor for Policy, among other policy-advising positions. Mr. Harris served as a law clerk to Judge William Canby of the U.S. Court of Appeals for the Ninth Circuit and Chief Judge Gene Carter of the U.S. District Court for the District of Maine.

Education
Mr. Harris is a graduate of the New York University School of Law, where he was Editor-in-Chief of the Review of Law and Social Change. He received his B.S. degree from the School of Industrial and Labor Relations at Cornell University.

Reflecting on Serving in the Department of Labor
"I was involved in the campaign, so I knew what the President wanted us to do. But governing has been harder than I thought. I had a good understanding of the issues, but it still has been hard.

"I really do care about the Department's mission. I want it to be successful. I want it to be efficient and effective. I wanted to make sure that we had a performance measurement and performance management system in place so that the Department could work."

David J. Hayes

Tenure
Mr. Hayes was nominated by President Obama to serve as Deputy Secretary of the Interior in February 2009, and confirmed by the U.S. Senate in May 2009. Mr. Hayes resigned his position in April 2013.

Present Position
Mr. Hayes is a Senior Fellow at the William and Flora Hewlett Foundation and a Lecturer at the Stanford Law School.

Private Sector Experience
Prior to being confirmed as Deputy Secretary, Mr. Hayes was Global Co-Chair of the Environment, Land and Resources department of the law firm Latham & Watkins.

Federal Government Experience
From 1997 to 2000, Mr. Hayes served as counselor to Secretary of the Interior Bruce Babbitt and later as Deputy Secretary.

Academic/Non-Profit Experience
Mr. Hayes has served as a Consulting Professor at the Woods Institute of the Environment, Stanford University; as Chairman of the Board of Visitors for Stanford Law School; as a Senior Fellow at the World Wildlife Fund; and as Co-Chair of the Board of American Rivers.

Education
Mr. Hayes graduated *summa cum laude* from the University of Notre Dame and earned his J.D. from Stanford Law School, where he was an editor of the Stanford Law Review.

Reflecting on Serving in the Department of the Interior
"I have spent most of my career in the field of conservation. There is no place where you can do more to make a difference in conservation than at the Department of the Interior. We [have an] impact every day on a host of environmental issues. We have to be careful about managing our natural resources responsibly.

"I recommend public service. It is a wonderful opportunity to work on a host of important issues and explore personal growth. I tell people to jump in and try it. At the Department of the Interior, we came in at the start of the Administration with five major priorities, and we have worked as an entire Department to see them through. We have a shared mission, and that is working on behalf of the American people."

Dennis F. Hightower

Tenure
Mr. Hightower was nominated by President Obama to serve as Deputy Secretary in July 2009, and confirmed by the U.S. Senate in August 2009. Mr. Hightower resigned his position in August 2010.

Present Position
Mr. Hightower is Chairman of Hightower Associates, a strategic advisory firm.

Private Sector Experience
Prior to being confirmed as Deputy Secretary, Mr. Hightower served as Chief Executive Officer of Europe Online Networks S.A., a satellite-delivered, broadband Internet service provider based in Luxembourg. From 1987 to 1996, he was a senior executive of The Walt Disney Company, serving as President of Walt Disney Television and Telecommunications. During his career, he was a Managing Director at Russell Reynolds Associates, a Vice President at Mattel, Vice President and General Manager of General Electric's lighting business in Mexico, Senior Associate at McKinsey & Company, and a manager at Xerox Research and Engineering Group.

Federal Government Experience
Mr. Hightower was a regular Army officer for eight years, rising to the rank of Major. He is a decorated Vietnam veteran. He served as a member of the Department of Defense Business Board.

Academic Experience
Mr. Hightower served as a Professor of Management at Harvard Business School.

Education
Mr. Hightower holds an M.B.A. degree from Harvard Business School and a B.S. degree from Howard University.

Reflecting on Serving in the Department of Commerce
"This has been a very gratifying and exciting role for me at Commerce—facilitated in large measure by the Secretary's trust and confidence in my abilities to get things done as the chief operating officer. It uses everything I've done in the past, particularly my work on strategy, change management, and fixing organizations. I've always believed that there are core leadership skills in both business and government that are interchangeable—personal integrity, people skills, competence, and an infectious passion for what you do."

Maurice Jones

Tenure
Mr. Jones was nominated by President Obama to serve as Deputy Secretary of the Department of Housing and Urban Development (HUD) in September 2011, and confirmed by the U.S. Senate in March 2012.

Private Sector Experience
Prior to being confirmed as Deputy Secretary of HUD, Mr. Jones was President of Pilot Media. During his career at Pilot Media, he served as President and Publisher of *The Virginian-Pilot*, Vice President and General Manager of Pilot Media, and Vice President of the Landmark Publishing Group (now called Landmark Media

Enterprises). Mr. Jones also served as a partner in Venture Philanthropy Partners and worked for the law firm of Hunton & Williams.

State Government Experience
Mr. Jones served as Commissioner of the Department of Social Services for the Commonwealth of Virginia and Deputy Chief of Staff to Governor Mark Warner.

Federal Government Experience
Mr. Jones served as a Special Assistant to the General Counsel in the Department of the Treasury. He also served as Deputy Director for Policy and Programs in the Department of the Treasury and Director of the Community Development Financial Institutions Fund (CDFI)

Education
Mr. Jones graduated from Hampden-Sydney College and attended Oxford University as a Rhodes Scholar. He earned his law degree from the University of Virginia.

Reflecting on Serving in HUD
"When I arrived at HUD, I found a place with very committed individuals with a real passion for the mission. They have a real passion to help homeowners. I found people working hard and working late hours. I found people who knew the content of their jobs. The passion I saw was compelling."

Kathleen A. Merrigan

Tenure

Dr. Merrigan was nominated by President Obama to serve as Deputy Secretary of the U.S. Department of Agriculture in March 2009, and confirmed by the U.S. Senate in April 2009. Dr. Merrigan resigned her position in March 2013.

Present Position

Dr. Merrigan is an independent consultant.

Academic Experience

Prior to being confirmed as Deputy Secretary, Dr. Merrigan served eight years as Assistant Professor and Director of the Agriculture, Food and Environment graduate program at the Friedman School of Nutrition Science and Policy at Tufts University. She also served as an instructor at the Massachusetts Institute of Technology.

Federal Government Experience

Dr. Merrigan served as Administrator of the USDA Agricultural Marketing Service during the Clinton Administration. She served for six years as a senior science and technology advisor to the U.S. Senate Committee on Agriculture, Nutrition and Forestry.

State Government Experience

Dr. Merrigan served as a special assistant in the Texas Department of Agriculture where she worked on regulation and pesticide issues. She also served as Chief of Staff to a state senator in the Massachusetts State Senate.

Education

Dr. Merrigan holds a Ph.D. degree in Environmental Planning and Policy from the Massachusetts Institute of Technology, a Master of Public Affairs degree from the University of Texas, and a B.A. degree from Williams College.

Reflecting on Serving in the Department of Agriculture

"Even though I have worked in agriculture policy for the better part of my career, it still took me awhile to gain my footing. A bureaucracy this vast and complex is tough to manage. You have to know how to delegate, how to establish trust with your career managers, and then quickly decide where to leave your fingerprints. As a political appointee, time is not on my side and a critical skill is knowing when to say 'No.'"

Anthony (Tony) W. Miller

Tenure
Mr. Miller was nominated by President Obama
to serve as Deputy Secretary of the Department
of Education in May 2009, and confirmed by the
U.S. Senate in July 2009. Mr. Miller resigned
his position in May 2013.

Present Position
Mr. Miller is Partner, The Vistria Group,
Chicago, Illinois.

Private Sector Experience
Prior to joining the Department in 2009, Mr.
Miller was an operating partner with Silver
Lake, a private equity firm. From 2003 to

2006, he was with LRN Corporation, where he was Executive Vice President of
Operations. Prior to LRN, he worked for 10 years at McKinsey & Company, where
he was a partner specializing in growth strategies, operating performance improvement, and restructuring for companies. Mr. Miller began his professional career with
Delco Electronics, a subsidiary of GM Hughes Electronics, where he managed regional channel marketing.

Local Government Experience
Mr. Miller advised the Los Angeles Unified School District from 1997 to 2000, developing student achievement goals and strategies, aligning budgets and operating
plans, and designing metrics and processes for overseeing district-wide performance.
He undertook similar work with the Santa Monica-Malibu Unified School District
in 2001. He also served as an ex-officio member of the Los Angeles Unified School
District Board of Education Budget and Finance Committee in 2002–2003.

Education
Mr. Miller is a graduate of Purdue University and holds an M.B.A. from the Stanford
Graduate School of Business.

Reflecting on Serving in the Department of Education
"This is an important moment in time to be here. Congress gave the Department the
resources at the same time that there is a growing appreciation of the importance
of education in our nation. We have the President's attention on education issues.
We have a dynamic group of people working here, including an authentic leader in
Secretary Arne Duncan. Everything came together in the first year—we got important
legislation passed and we got resources. Secretary Duncan keeps reminding us that it
is all about the kids. It isn't about us."

Thomas R. Nides

Tenure
Mr. Nides was nominated by President Obama to serve as Deputy Secretary of State for Management and Resources in September 2010, and was confirmed by the U.S. Senate in December 2010. Mr. Nides resigned his position in February 2013.

Present Position
Mr. Nides is Vice Chairman of Morgan Stanley.

Private Sector Experience
Prior to being confirmed as Deputy Secretary, Mr. Nides was Chief Operating Officer of Morgan Stanley, where he also served on the

Management Committee and Operating Committee. He has served as Worldwide President and Chief Executive Officer of Burson-Marsteller and as Chief Administrative Officer for Credit Suisse First Boston.

Federal Government Experience
From 1986 to 1993, Mr. Nides served as an Assistant to the Majority Whip in the U.S. House of Representatives and Chief of Staff to the Speaker of the House. He also served as Chief of Staff to the United States Trade Representative.

Education
Mr. Nides received a Bachelor of Individual Studies from the University of Minnesota.

Reflecting on Serving in the Department of State
"You can intellectually understand the job, but until you get here you don't understand the complexity of everything," reflects Nides. "In the business world, you have unexpected events, like the 2007–2008 economic crisis. In this job—just as the saying goes about change—crisis is the only constant." In a briefing on the FY 2013 budget, Nides said, "Since I presented last year's budget, there hasn't been a day when we weren't managing multiple crises at once.

"You have to be patient in government. You have to bring people along. You can't 'roll' them into doing things. You need to keep pushing your agenda and be disciplined in decision-making. It is a real intellectual challenge."

Daniel B. Poneman

Tenure
Mr. Poneman was nominated by President Obama to be Deputy Secretary of Energy in April 2009, and confirmed by the U.S. Senate in May 2009.

Private Sector Experience
Prior to being confirmed as Deputy Secretary, Mr. Poneman served as a Principal of The Scowcroft Group, providing strategic advice to corporations on a wide variety of international projects and transactions. He practiced law for nine years in Washington, D.C., first as an Associate at Covington & Burling, later as a Partner at Hogan & Hartson.

Federal Government Experience
Mr. Poneman served as a White House Fellow in the Department of Energy in 1989. After serving as a White House Fellow, he joined the National Security Council staff as Director of Defense Policy and Arms Control. From 1993 to 1996, he worked as Special Assistant to the President and Senior Director for Nonproliferation and Export Controls at the National Security Council.

Education
Mr. Poneman received A.B. and J.D. degrees with honors from Harvard University and an M.Litt. in Politics from Oxford University.

Reflecting on Serving in the Department of Energy
"I am grateful to have the opportunity to wake up every day and come to work on crucial national issues. The Department has an important agenda and a chance to make a difference for tomorrow. We are trying to transform the way the nation produces and uses energy. It's an ambitious goal, but one that I'm confident we can achieve."

Chapter Four

The Producers

Understanding the Job of the Producer

This chapter is not about the recent Broadway show and movie *The Producers*. Instead it focuses on nine political executives who run production type organizations in the federal government. These executives are driven by numbers and producing the results expected of them.

    While the factory floor is not an image commonly associated with government organizations, there is an element of manufacturing in these organizations. Bill Taggart, former Chief Operating Officer, FSA, tells us, "We needed to think like a manufacturing plant. You have to get down on the floor, wander around, see folks, and engage them. During my first couple of weeks on the job, I visited FSA regional offices. I was the first COO that many of the regional office staff had ever seen. Headquarters had become isolated from the field."

    In his seminal work *Bureaucracy*, James Q. Wilson discusses "production" agencies—a concept similar to the Producers discussed in this chapter (Wilson). According to Wilson, the key distinguishing factor of production agencies is that the activities of their agencies are observable and they have *outputs* and *outcomes*. Wilson writes, "Where both outputs (or work) and outcomes are observable, managers have the opportunity to design (within the limits established by external constraints) a compliance system to produce an efficient outcome."

The Producers

Allison A. Hickey, page 81

Under Secretary for Benefits, Veterans Benefits Administration, Department of Veterans Affairs

David J. Kappos, page 83

Under Secretary of Commerce for Intellectual Property and Director, United States Patent and Trademark Office (USPTO), Department of Commerce

Alejandro Mayorkas, page 85

Director, U.S. Citizenship and Immigration Services (USCIS), Department of Homeland Security

John T. Morton, page 86

Director, United States Immigration and Customs Enforcement (ICE), Department of Homeland Security

Robert A. Petzel, page 88

Under Secretary for Health, Veterans Health Administration (VHA), Department of Veterans Affairs (VA)

Key Components of the Job of the Producer

Key to the success of producers are fulfilling the following three components of their job:
- Delivering the output
- Getting the metrics right
- Focusing on customers

Delivering the Output

While the image of the factory floor offered by Bill Taggart conjures up memories of Frederick Winslow Taylor and scientific management, the comparison is very apt for a select number of government organizations. Factory managers, like the producers in government, worry about inputs, accuracy and errors, cycle time, and outputs. Managers of factories aim to achieve routine and constant flow, and they pride themselves on reducing variation and increasing factory efficiency.

David Kappos, former Director, USPTO, tells us, "We understand our inputs and outputs at USPTO." A major initiative led by Director Kappos was to examine and reengineer the number of reviews of a patent submission. "We have good numerical data on this," says Kappos. "We want to reduce the number of reviews on a submission. We want to reduce the rewriting. We are at three reviews and we have gotten it down to between 2.3 to 2.4. The goal would be 2.0. That would be a major reduction." The PTO Patent Dashboard presented on page 77 provides information on three of the 14 indicators that PTO tracks on a monthly basis.

The nine individuals profiled in this chapter all had experience on the "factory floor." David Stevens spent the early part of his career as a loan officer. David Kappos spent his career working closely with USPTO and the intellectual property community to improve the patent application process. Bill Taggart and James Runcie's careers in the banking industry served them well in working with the student loan "ecosystem," which includes the lending industry in a key role. Retired Brig. General Hickey had spent 27 years in the military and had firsthand experience with the Department of Veteran Affairs as a retired military officer. John Pistole had firsthand experience in airline safety as Assistant Special Agent in Charge, Boston. While in that position, he helped lead the investigation and recovery efforts for the Egypt Air Flight 990 crash off the coast of Rhode Island. Robert Petzel spent 40 years in the Department of Veterans Affairs prior to being confirmed as Under Secretary for Health, including experience in running one of the VHA integrated service networks. So when it came to understanding the production tasks for their organization, all had firsthand experience on the front line and understood frontline production issues.

Getting the Metrics Right

A key component of the job of the producer is getting the metrics right. When the right metrics are selected and are used to determine if the desired outputs are being delivered, they become an effective management tool for agency leadership. In the case of the Veterans Health Administration and the United States Patent and Trademark Office, there was an obvious metric on which the agency was being assessed—their backlog. In the case of PTO, the backlog was patent applications pending. Former Director Kappos set forth the goal of getting the backlog under 700,000. Kappos felt strongly that citizens really cared about the backlog. Kappos told us, "We set the specific targets. Our goal is to get the backlog under 700,000. We haven't been under that figure for many years. We are aiming to reach the 325,000 goal by 2015. We couldn't just give people the goal of 325,000 by 2015. That goal was too far away. So we set 699,000 for FY 2011. Getting under 700,000 would be a major accomplishment." USPTO reached that goal in June 2011. In July 2013, the backlog of patents pending stood at 591,173. Kappos created a Dashboard to track key agency indictors, including the backlog, which is available to both the agency and the public. (Figure 4.1)

In the case of the Veterans Benefits Administration, the backlog became a major national issue. Several Congressional hearings were held on the backlog, and it attracted increased media interest. To decrease the backlog, VHA mandated overtime for VHA staff. As a result, the backlog has been decreasing. In June 2013, the backlog fell below 800,000 for the first time since April 2011. The backlog total in June 2013 hit 797,801. Of those claims, 524,711 (65%) were backlogged more than 125 days. In September 2012, the backlog was 895,248 with over 66% pending for more than 125 days. The departmental goal is to process all claims in less than 125 days with 98% accuracy by 2015. The reduction in backlog was also due to a new initiative to give priority to oldest claims.

In the case of U.S. Citizenship and Immigration Services (USCIS), the agency undertook a change in culture by moving from production-based metrics to a focus on quality. Alejandro Mayorkas, Director of USCIS, says, "We are a customer service agency, and by 'customers' I mean internal and external customers

Figure 4.1: USPTO Patent Dashboard* Selected Indicators

Unexamined Patent Application Backlog

August 2012

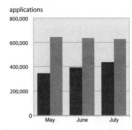

applications

Backlog vs. application filings

● Applications filings   ● Application backlog

The unexamined patent application backlog is the number of new utility, plant, and reissue (UPR) patent applications in the pipeline at any given time which are awaiting a First Office Action by the patent examiner. Continuation, continuation-in-part, and divisional applications are included in the total.

First Office Action Pendency (months)

August 2012

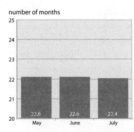

number of months

Last three months, FY 2012

First Office Action pendency is the average number of months from the patent application filing date to the date a First Office Action is mailed by the USPTO. Our goal is to reduce first action pendency to an average of 10 months by 2015. The term "pendency" refers to the fact that the application is pending or awaiting a decision.

Traditional Total Pendency (months)

August 2012

number of months

Last three months, FY 2012

This is the measure of total pendency, as traditionally measured. Historically, pendency has been measured as the average number of months from the patent application filing date to the date the application has reached final disposition (e.g., issued as a patent or abandoned) which is called a "disposal". Our goal is to reduce Traditional Total Pendency to an average of 20 months by 2015. This pendency includes the time periods awaiting action by the USPTO, as well as any time awaiting reply from an applicant.

*From USPTO website, http://www.uspto.gov/dashboards/patents/main.dashxml

Selecting Producers

When politicians talk about "running government like a business," they have a point when they are discussing the government agencies that are run by people whom we have labeled the producers. These agencies benefit greatly from having an individual with business experience. Nearly all of the producers profiled in this chapter brought significant backgrounds to their government positions. Most important, they served in leadership positions directing activities similar to those they would direct in government.

David Kappos spent his career in intellectual property at IBM. David Stevens, Commissioner, FHA, came from a real estate and banking background, including working at Freddie Mac. Bill Taggart came to FSA from the banking industry. Their prior private-sector careers had prepared them well for their government positions. In reflecting on his selection, David Stevens says, "I understood the business. I had lots of experience in the business. Some of the previous incumbents had not really understood the industry. I was one of the few Commissioners in this position who had practical industry experience."

Historically, many previous appointees selected to run production-type agencies came to their positions with strong policy backgrounds. Their experience in the private sector was often limited or nonexistent. While there were business leaders who were selected as Cabinet Secretaries over the years, the sub-cabinet has been largely dominated by "policy types." The shift from the hiring of "policy types" to "managerial types" began to pick up momentum in Washington during the 1990s with a growing recognition that managerial experience is often exactly the type of experience needed to run many government organizations.

The shift to managerial types was clearly seen in 1997, when the Clinton Administration actively sought to recruit a business person to run the Internal Revenue Service (IRS). Historically, the head of IRS had been a tax lawyer. While the tax lawyers knew the complexity of tax laws, many did not have any prior experience managing large organizations. In describing his recruitment to serve as Commissioner of IRS, Charles Rossotti writes:

> [I]n February 1997, I found a pink phone slip with a message from an executive search firm about its assignment to find a business executive to be IRS commissioner ... Putting a businessperson in charge of the IRS seemed to me like a sensible idea ...
>
> [The executive recruiter] convinced me that it would ... be helpful for the Treasury Department to hear my insights on how to recruit a businessperson for the job.
>
> [Deputy Secretary Summers] launched into an explanation of why the Administration needed a person with strong management experience to run the IRS. It was the largest civilian operation in the federal government and needed astute management, especially of its troubled computer program, he said ...
>
> The following Sunday night, I was surprised to get a call from Treasury Secretary Robert Rubin. He got right to the point—he would like to talk

to me seriously about taking the IRS job. The job was "the most important management job in the civilian government," he said, adding that my background in the information systems industry might make me the right person to fill it (Rossotti).

Rossotti ultimately agreed to accept the position and served a five-year term as IRS Commissioner from 1997 to 2002.

Since the appointment of Rossotti, the trend toward selecting individuals with management and private-sector experience as IRS Commissioner has continued. Mark Everson succeeded Rossotti in 2002 and brought extensive private-sector experience as a manager to the position, as well as his previous government experience. Everson's private-sector experience included his tenure as Group Vice President of Finance for SC International Services and his 10 years in senior financial positions with the Pechiney Group. The most recent Commissioner, Douglas Shulman, brought both public and private-sector experience to the position and continues the trend of non-tax lawyers selected to the position.

In August 2013, President Obama nominated John Koskinen to serve as the Commissioner of IRS. Mr. Koskinen's career has largely been in the private sector where he specialized in turning around companies. His federal government experience included serving as Deputy Director for Management at the Office of Management and Budget and as the Y2K "Czar." Koskinen also served as Deputy Mayor and City Administrator for the District of Columbia.

alike. We serve the public and, in our ongoing efforts to combat fraud and safeguard our nation's security, we also serve the intelligence community and other government agencies who share those aspects of our mission."

Focusing on Customers

In addition to delivering the output and getting the metrics right, another key component of the job of the producer is to focus on customers. All the agencies profiled in this chapter provide services to citizens who are eagerly awaiting a decision on a patent, a visa, a veteran's benefits, or a student loan.

This important role is highlighted by Alejandro Mayorkas, Director of U.S. Citizenship and Immigration Services (USCIS). Mayorkas says, "We are essentially a customer service agency." After arriving at USCIS, Mayorkas found that the agency had historically not focused on the customer service aspects of the job. This increased focus on customer service drove Mayorkas to modernize the operations of USCIS and move to greater transparency and consistency between USCIS offices. For USCIS, it is no longer a question of "production" or "quality." It is a focus on quality and all that term encompasses. Majorkas describes this emphasis: "Speed alone cannot be the central metric when one considers our mission and everything it involves. We have to make decisions that adhere to the facts and the law, that are sound and reflect a consistent application of the law and policy, that are comprehensive in reviewing and applying the factual record, and that are thorough in detecting issues of concern."

James Runcie had a similar experience at the Office of Federal Student Aid. Runcie recalls, "I thought the agency could improve how we assess, interact, and ultimately deliver to our broadening customer base." Runcie then moved toward establishing a greater customer focus. "We wanted to increase customer awareness and make our information more accessible to them. It took us a couple of years but we made significant progress. We ultimately rebranded the organization."

As a consequence of a focus on customers, several of the political executives profiled in this chapter devoted increased effort to segmenting their customers in order to improve service delivery. At the Veterans Health Administration, Allison Hickey pushed for "express lanes" for less complicated claims. Hickey recalls, "We are able to push these less complicated claims through at a faster pace. If we can do this, there will be less work on the front end … which will then allow us to spend more time on tougher, more complicated claims. We are trying to manage our throughputs."

At the Transportation Security Administration, a major initiative under John Pistole has been the TSA Pre✓™ program and other programs in which different segments of the traveling public are treated differently to speed their progress through security lines. Pistole recalls, "We had been using a one-size-fits-all approach. But I knew it didn't have to be this way… I knew we were already treating people differently. I knew that there many possibilities of doing things differently."

Working Style of Producers

We found that there is a unique profile for the selection of political executives to run production agencies. In addition to their managerial or business experience, there is also a working style which serves producers well in these types of agencies. This working style can be characterized as:
- Hard-charging and high energy
- Disciplined and focused on delivering the outputs of the organization
- Data-oriented
- Engagement-oriented, reflected in their outreach to employees as seen in the holding of town hall meetings, visiting regional offices, and regularly communicating with employees via blogs or newsletters.

Just as there is a desired professional background and working style for the ideal producer, there are also working styles which might *not* be conducive to leading production organizations. Such working styles might include:

- A tendency to like working on and looking at only big issues
- Low to moderate interest in the nitty-gritty details of the operations of the organization
- Low to moderate interest in reaching out to meet with or communicate with frontline workers in the organization
- Preference to work primarily in their offices with personal and headquarters staff

While the above are clearly generalizations, they are presented to serve as guidelines for appointing officials as they seek to place the right person in the right job. The concepts of a policy person and a managerial person are archetypes which can be used in sorting candidates for the right job. A policy person is clearly appropriate for the position of Assistant Secretary for Planning and Evaluation (ASPE) in the Department of Health and Human Services.

Based on observations over the years and research conducted for this book, a managerial person faces a high probability of being frustrated by the "lack of action" and "all that talking and debating" when placed in a policy job. Producers find greater satisfaction in agencies in which there are clear objectives and performance data. As Bill Taggart tells us, "There are two separate sets of skills—the implementers are not the policy folks and the policy makers are not implementers."

Producers in Action

Allison A. Hickey at the Veterans Benefits Administration, Department of Veterans Affairs

"I was obviously not a stranger [to] government," recalls Allison Hickey. "I knew the government, its culture, and rules. I had spent 27 years in the military and 17 years in the Pentagon. Part of my first day felt very normal, but there were differences. I came in without knowing anybody—not a single soul. This is different from the military where you know a lot of people.

"I had to learn a new set of languages and meet new people. I had a staff meeting quickly, so people could size me up. I was the brand-new person. I wanted them to know who I was. I wanted them to see me."

The Veterans Benefits Administration (VBA) is one of the three major components of the Department of Veterans Affairs: the Veterans Health Administration (page 88), the National Cemetery Administration, and VBA. VBA provided compensation and pension benefits to an estimated 4.3 million veterans and survivors in FY 2012, 10% of whom were 100-percent disabled. With a workforce of over 20,000 civil servants, VBA manages the following benefit programs: the Compensation and Pension Service, the Education Service, and the Insurance Service.

There was no shortage of challenges facing Hickey when she began her position as Under Secretary. "I starting asking questions," recalls Hickey, "and I identified the following major challenges:

- No integrated plan,
- No metrics for success,
- No common message, and
- Hardworking employees with their chins down."

Hickey started by looking at VBA's claims and benefit process. She was quick to conclude, "We needed to change our processes. I knew about process improvements." Hickey also knew about technology. "I was surprised," says Hickey, "by how far behind we were on using technology. We were still very paper-bound, touching over one billion pieces of paper manually in a year. That is equal to 200 Empire State Buildings stacked end to end. The Veterans Health Administration was ahead of us, having turned their paper medical records into a paperless environment a decade ago. We have all these paper files in VBA. I decided to take this on. We needed to reduce the paperwork."

Hickey found that in responding to one challenge, another became even more perplexing. "We are doing very well on increasing access," reports Hickey. "But it is a double-edged sword. We have done such a good job on access, we are now getting a historical demand for services never seen before. It was easy to open up access, now we have to work through this new demand."

Veterans today are filing more claims than their counterparts did in the past. Hickey reports, "This has resulted in an increase in complexity and workload. We are hitting a pressure point. Demand is growing through the roof. There is also an ongoing exodus of service members that will drive up demand and claims. Historically, veteran file rates have been 20 percent. We are now at 45 percent and we expect it to go up to as much as 90 percent as a result of the new mandatory Transition Assistance Program."

It was clear to Hickey that the agency needed to dramatically change the way it was doing business. Hickey found it very helpful to use the "People, Process, and Technology" framework in leading the VBA transformation initiative.

People. To improve its customer focus and to assist its employees in expediting claims, VBA created "express lanes" for certain claims. "We are able to push these less complicated claims through at a faster pace," describes Hickey. "If we can do this, there will be less work on the front end. We can get less complicated claims through which will then allow us to spend more time on tougher, more complicated claims. We are trying to manage our throughputs." These segmented lanes increase claims processing speed through handling of similar claims, placing a veteran's claim in one of three lanes: Express (30 percent), Core (60 percent), or Special Operations (10 percent) based on specific criteria. Another step was providing additional training to VBA employees through the Challenge Training Program, which both increased quality and reduced errors at an earlier point in the process.

Process. One key process improvement was releasing a simplified notification letter, which has enabled VBA to increase productivity by 15 percent and resulted in a 14-day reduction in average processing time. The simplified letters consolidated the previous two separate documents into one clear and concise letter containing the VBA decision and the reasons for the decision. Hickey notes that with one million claims annually, a 15 percent improvement is significant.

Additional process transformation initiatives include rater decision support tools, fully developed claims, and disability benefits questionnaires.

Technology. In the area of technology, the creation of the e-Benefits portal was a major step. Hickey says, "Right now, we are in the season of technology. All the parts are coming together now. We are happy with our e-Benefits website which has helped us increase access. We now have nearly two million users and there is increasing utilization by veterans. We are now preparing veterans to come into the system differently than they have in the past. In very short order, veterans will file their claims online through e-Benefits like they do their taxes at IRS."

David J. Kappos at the United States Patent and Trademark Office, Department of Commerce

The process of confirmation and transition into government is both exciting and challenging. David Kappos found that out. "The whole confirmation process places heavy demands on political appointees," recalls Kappos. "I was confirmed at 11:00 a.m. on a Friday and I was supposed to start work on the following Monday. I had to leave my family on short notice. There was no time to plan on where to stay. But I managed to get to D.C., find a hotel, and start on that Tuesday.

United States Patent and Trademark Office
An Agency of the Department of Commerce

"At 11 a.m. on Tuesday, I conducted my first staff meeting," says Kappos. "Everybody was a bit nervous about the new guy on board. I knew the issues facing the USPTO, so I wanted to get off to a fast start. I know you only have a certain period of time in these jobs so I didn't want to waste a single day. I wanted to get a running start and hit the ground running, but I didn't want to jump out of the chopper shooting."

Like several of the organizations described in this book, the responsibilities of the United States Patent and Trademark Office (USPTO) are set forth in the Constitution of the United States. Article I states that the federal government will "promote the progress of science and useful arts, by securing for limited times to authors and inventors the exclusive rights to their respective writing and discoveries." The USPTO organization was created by an act of Congress in 1952 and placed in the Department of Commerce. The Patent Office within the USPTO (headed by the Commissioner for Patents) reviews newly filed applications, publishes pending applications, and issues patents to successful applicants. The Trademark Office (headed by the Commissioner for Trademarks) examines and approves applications for trademark registration.

A major activity of the USPTO is to review newly filed patents and move the application patent from receipt to final disposition—either issuing a patent or declining the patent. A key indicator of USPTO is the number of patent applications awaiting the "First Office Action." As Director of USPTO, Kappos has led the effort to reduce the backlog and speed up the review process. The task is made even more challenging by the continued increase in number of patent applications, now over 500,000 annually.

"The USPTO has a critical role to play in our economic recovery," says Kappos. "And that's why people really care about the backlog, which hinders innovation and economic growth. In response, we set specific targets. Our goal is to get the backlog under 700,000. We haven't been under that figure for many years. The goal is to get it down to a backlog of 325,000. That would be about 70 dockets per examiner, which is about right. We have a production inventory system. We are aiming to reach the 325,000 goal by 2015. We couldn't just give people the goal of 325,000 for 2015. That goal was too far away. So we set 699,000 for FY 2011. Getting under 700,000 would be a major accomplishment."

In response to these myriad challenges, Kappos launched an aggressive campaign on many fronts. As described by Kappos, "The job of leadership is to work on all the challenges. You need to do it all. There is no one single thing that you have to do; you have to do a hundred things. Change is the sum of a lot of little things. I don't believe there is a magic bullet or a single fix. I believe it is about making day-by-day changes and continuously working toward improvement. I believe philosophically that you are never done. Change goes on forever."

In addition to the usual challenges of budget uncertainty and budget reductions that faced all the political executives profiled in this book, Kappos and the USPTO faced a unique set of budget challenges. With the 1990 legislative changes, USPTO became a 100-percent fee-funded operation. Under the existing funding system, however, USPTO only has access to the portion of its collections provided in the annual appropriations bills. Thus, when actual fee collections exceed the level of spending authorized by Congress, the additional funds collected by USPTO remain unavailable for spending. Legislative changes were sought to replace the current funding system. Changes in the funding system, according to Kappos, would reduce the patent backlog and enable the completion of a high-quality patent examination in a shorter amount of time.

Patent reform legislation, the Leahy-Smith America Invents Act (AIA), was passed by Congress in September 2011 and represented the first major reform to the patent system since 1952. The new legislation, however, did not include the creation of a public enterprise revolving fund that would have ensured that all fees collected by USPTO supported processing efforts of the agency without fiscal year limitations. That change had been included in the Senate-passed legislation.

The backlog continued to rise in April 2011 to over 706,000, but then went down in May 2011 to just over 703,000. In June 2011, the number of patents pending fell below 700,000 for the first time—to 695,086. In the following 14 months (through August 2012), the number continued below 700,000. In August 2012, the number fell to its all time low—623,168. Throughout the remainder of 2012 and 2013, the number of patents pending have continued to fall. In January 2013, the backlog fell below 600,000. In July 2013, the number was 591,173.

Alejandro Mayorkas at the U.S. Citizenship and Immigration Services

"When I arrived at USCIS," Mayorkas recalls, "I found extraordinary workers with antiquated systems. I had a talented workforce and complex laws to administer with old systems in place. The agency lacked access to the best and most updated support  that industry has to offer. The agency receives seven million applications annually and we have to process those applications with antiquated systems. There is a great divide at USCIS between people and technology."

In many ways, U.S. Citizenship and Immigration Services (USCIS) is a prototypical production agency—a large number of inputs (applications) and outputs (approved citizenship applications and work applications). In addition to citizenship and work applications, USCIS is responsible for immigration of family members of permanent U.S. citizens, verification of eligibility to work (the E-Verify program), administrating humanitarian programs and adoptions, and promoting civic integration. USCIS has a budget of over $3 billion and 13,000 employees in 240 domestic and foreign offices.

"We are essentially a customer service agency," says Mayorkas. But Mayorkas found that the agency had historically not focused on the customer service aspects of the job. Mayorkas also wanted to modernize the operations of USCIS, as well as achieve more transparency and consistency between USCIS offices.

Like many producers, Mayorkas faced the challenge of how to manage his production line

---

Production at USCIS

In FY 2012, USCIS:
- Naturalized 763,690 citizens
- Processed 21 million queries through the E-Verify program
- Interviewed more than 76,750 refugee applicants
- Completed 36,000 asylum applications
- Produced nearly 3.8 million secure identity documents, including 2 million permanent resident cards, 1.3 million employment authorization documents, and 90,000 refugee travel documents and reentry permits

and decide what trade-offs the agency should make. Mayorkas describes the dilemmas facing a production agency: "One key challenge I face is metrics. What are the appropriate metrics for admitting people into the United States? I think a lot about managing the workforce we have. We also have to search for fraud, so achieving the goals of speed and fraud detection is a balancing act. How fast should we go versus how careful should we be? We are doing national security work."

During his first year at the agency, Mayorkas held local town hall meetings with employees. In recalling those meetings, Mayorkas says, "I found that our culture was one of production by the clock. We could do 10 cases in 10 hours. People will do what they are asked to do. But I think it is important to understand our mission. I believe that people will do more if they understand the mission. We are trying to shift away from just speed as a goal and metric. We needed to change the dialogue to quality. We want to shift to a culture of quality. We have processing time and service level agreements. Timeliness is one measure, quality is another."

Because the agency is funded by fees from applications, USCIS is adequately staffed and can adjust staffing based on demand and revenue. Mayorkas says, "We have worked through our backlog. Our backlog is a matter of the law. Timeliness is important. We do have processing time goals. Citizens need to know when they might expect a response. I have spent time thinking about how do you achieve the goal of timeliness. What is the culture of the agency and how do you motivate people?"

Another challenge facing production agencies is consistency in decision-making between offices within the organization. Mayorkas describes this phenomenon: "There has been criticism of USCIS because of the lack of consistency between offices. We have different policies in different offices. I found that different decisions were being made in different offices. We had to work hard on achieving transparency, consistency, and integrity."

John T. Morton at the United States Immigration and Customs Enforcement, Department of Homeland Security

"It was a great honor to be selected as Director of ICE," recalls Morton. "I was a career person. I had been a criminal prosecutor in the Department of Justice. So I had been a long-term observer of the agency. I knew the mission quite well and I knew the people in the agency."

In 2009, Morton took over an agency that was then six years old. The agency had been created in 2003 as a component of the new Department of Homeland Security. The new agency included the investigative and enforcement elements of two prior agencies: the U.S. Customs Service and the Immigration and Naturalization Service. The new agency, ICE, was given the mission to "promote homeland security and public safety through the criminal and civil enforcement of federal laws governing border control, customs, trade, and immigration." The agency has a budget of over $5.7 billion and 20,000 employees located in all 50 states and in 47 foreign countries.

"My job," says Morton, "was to move the agency beyond the merger. I wanted to chart and fulfill our destiny as an agency. The agency needed a champion. We were doing fantastic work but the agency felt underappreciated. I felt that the men and women of the agency should get the recognition they deserved. It was the most misunderstood agency in government. I wanted to reshape the perception of the agency. I wanted us to be known as major players in law enforcement."

Reshaping ICE was a major challenge for Morton. Morton recounts, "The problem is that nobody gets past our first name. Our name has a real impact on how the agency is perceived. Immigration is an unsettled part of our national policy. Immigration dominates how our agency is perceived, but it is only half of what we do."

Thus Morton focused his energies on the twin challenges of immigration and criminal investigation. On the criminal investigation side, Morton says, "I wanted to promote and champion our investigative work. I wanted it to be recognized that we have a strong investigative arm that I wanted to tell people about. We are the fifth largest criminal investigative staff and have over 7,000 special agents. We have broad jurisdictions and are involved in arms trafficking, narcotics, and stolen art investigations. We are going from not being a force to becoming a major player in law enforcement. We renamed the investigative arm of the agency from the Office of Enforcement to the Homeland Security Investigation. Our investigations arm tracks the illicit movement of people and goods."

The immigration side of the agency was more problematic. Morton recalls, "I wanted to give us space to look at our organization. I told people that we cannot do everything. I wanted the agency to focus more on certain groups of immigrants. This was not a simple question. We had to look at what Congress asks us to do. There are 11 million immigrants in the United States. Asking us to remove all those people is not right. We are not funded to do that. So there was a conflict between policy and our capability. We had to occupy the contentious middle ground."

When the mission of an agency is politically contentious, the job of the producer is indeed challenging. Morton says, "Immigration enforcement brings out passion in people. It is an unsettled mission. We go about this in a very public way. We want to remove the right 400,000 people annually. There is more work than we can do. We focus on criminals. Congress has supported our approach on focusing on criminals. Some people think we are not enforcing the law. We are doing what we can. We are trying to reshape our world and develop solutions. I think it is better to take control of our destiny."

Robert A. Petzel at the Veterans Health Administration, Department of Veterans Affairs

Robert Petzel knew the Veterans Health Administration very well when he assumed its leadership in February 2010. "I had worked for 40 years in the organization," says Petzel. "So I knew the people and the processes in the agency."

Before arriving at headquarters in May 2009 to serve as VA's Acting Principal Deputy Under Secretary for Health, Petzel had been the Network Director of the VA Midwest Health Care Network in Minneapolis, Minnesota. One of Petzel's key agenda items after arriving in Washington was to develop a vision for the organization. "When I got here," Petzel recalls, "we were unclear about where we wanted to go. The vision was articulated when I was the Acting Principal Deputy. When we looked at the entire system, quality was assumed. We had excellent quality, but the key was the nature of the experience that was being delivered. We wanted to be the place where people wanted to go. The patient experience is now second in importance only to access for veterans. We wanted to move toward patient driven care."

The Veterans Health Administration operates the nation's largest integrated health care system, consisting of 152 medical centers and nearly 1,400 community-based outpatient facilities. The medical centers and outpatient facilities are operated by 21 Veterans Integrated Service Networks (VISNs) which provide regional systems of care to better meet local health care needs and provide greater access to care. These facilities have over 53,000 health care practitioners who provide comprehensive care to 6.2 million veterans annually. VHA has a budget of $54 billion and employs over 270,000 staff.

Like Alejandro Mayorkas at the U.S. Citizenship and Immigration Services (and other producers), Petzel faced the problem of consistency and standardization. Petzel describes the challenge: "All of the VISNs were functioning differently. There was little standardization. We wanted services to be standard. There are a lot of different aspects to standardization. There is now evidence-based medicine, so we wanted standardization of care and treatment. Treatment of patients varied from VISN to VISN. We also wanted standardization of medical equipment. Many of the VISNs were wedded to their existing vendors. We wanted a higher level of standardization. Standardization of equipment does save money, saves on maintenance, and makes it easier when the equipment moves around. We had to overcome obstacles to standardization and standardize how the VISNs worked."

Another challenge facing Petzel is the effective use of all the data that VHA collects. One characteristic of production agencies is that they do collect data and have the potential to use it to gain increased knowledge of how to improve their programs. Petzel says, "We have a lot of data. We want to push using that data for continuous improvement. The key is adding value. We also want to move to an increased prevention focus, while also becoming more patient driven."

Petzel emphasizes the long-run nature of continuous changes. "We are making progress," says Petzel, "but we are not done. Improvement is a continuous ongoing event. You can't have an impact in one or two years. We are making progress on e-connected health and telemedicine, but still have much to do."

John S. Pistole at the Transportation Security Administration, Department of Homeland Security

"I was impressed with the quality of the people here," recalls John Pistole, "especially the senior staff. We had a top-notch Deputy who had been Acting Administrator for 18 months. The agency was only eight years old at that point. The staff had a combination of different experiences and disciplines which impressed me.

"My second observation was the enormity of the task. Our job is to get people from point to point safely, with a 100-percent customer satisfaction as well. We literally have hands-on contact with the American public."

The Transportation Security Administration (TSA) was created by legislation in November 2001 in the aftermath of the 9/11 attacks. The agency began operations in 2002. In 2003, TSA was moved from the Department of Transportation to the Department of Homeland Security (DHS) after the creation of DHS. TSA is responsible for:

- Security screening of passengers and baggage at over 450 airports
- Vetting more than 14 million passenger reservations and over 13 million transportation workers against the terrorist watch list each week
- Conducting security regulation compliance inspections and enforcement activities at airports and for cargo screening operations

TSA has over 51,000 employees and a budget of over $8 billion.

Like the other producers in this chapter, Pistole quickly came to the conclusion that his agency needed to change the way it was operating. "We had been using a one-size-fits-all approach," says Pistole. "But I knew it didn't have to be this way. As an FBI agent, I would get on a plane with special treatment. So I knew we were already treating people differently. I knew that there were many possibilities of doing things differently."

As TSA approached its 10th anniversary as an organization, Pistole engaged in a reexamination of the agency. Pistole says that the agency had an enormous mission in its early years and had not yet had time to step back and review everything it does. "I believe we are not about avoidance," states Pistole, "but instead about risk management ... We need to focus on the unknown. We have to be sure that we spend our resources on the right things. We want to expand the TSA Pre✓™, which we are now testing at 15 airports." By the end of 2012, TSA Pre✓™ will be in 35 airports.

In describing TSA Pre✓™, Pistole says that it is dedicated lanes for individuals who have already been vetted. Pistole recalls, "We needed to change our mindset. In Fall 2010, we added World War II veterans who were coming to Washington, D.C. on charter flights. I had seen some gracious pat-downs but I thought we could go further. I had to find out whether I had the authority to change protocols. I did not see our current protocols as sustainable long-term. We want to keep traveling safe, but we can redefine mission. It will take common sense. We need to look at things from a risk-based approach."

In October 2011, TSA began the TSA Pre✓™ program with Delta Air Lines and American Airlines in which selected individuals could receive expedited screening. The TSA Pre✓™ program is part of TSA's movement toward a strategy for enhanced use of intelligence and other information to implement a risk-based security (RBS) approach in all facets of transportation, including passenger screening, air cargo, and surface transportation. In testimony before the House Committee on Homeland Security, Pistole said, "Our objective is to mitigate risk in a way that effectively balances security measures with privacy, civil rights, and civil liberties concerns while both promoting the safe movement of people and commerce and guarding against a deliberate attack on our transportation systems. RBS in the passenger-screening context allows our dedicated TSOs to focus more attention on those travelers we believe are more likely to pose a risk to our transportation network while providing expedited screening to those we consider pose less risk." (Pistole)

Pistole says, "TSA Pre✓™ is important to us. We are expanding the populations eligible to participate. We want to expand so that different populations can participate." Since the start of the program, TSA has expanded TSA Pre✓™ benefits to military active-duty members traveling through Reagan Washington National Airport and Seattle-Tacoma International Airport. TSA has also implemented other risk-based security measures, including modified screening procedures for passengers 12 and younger and 75 and older. Flight attendants and pilots are now receiving the expedited screening.

The RBS approach is driving major changes at TSA and new ways of doing business with the public. To successfully implement these changes, Pistole needed the support of the organization. He recalls, "I asked our senior staff in D.C. how they felt about making these changes. It turned out that there was widespread support at headquarters, not total support but significant support. I then had a two-day conference with our 120 security directors and regional staff to get their feedback. Everybody seemed supportive. I needed people fully on board and needed my top managers to lead their people. I wanted the entire organization to have buy-in. If senior staff did not feel comfortable with all this, that was okay with me and I told them that we can make other arrangements for them. Several people ended up moving."

David H. Stevens at the Federal Housing Administration, Department of Housing and Urban Development

The process of being nominated and confirmed to a federal position is slow. With the exception of the Cabinet and selected other positions which usually are confirmed between the end of January and mid-February at the start of a new Administration, the remaining appointees arrive throughout the year. Many of the individuals profiled in this book, with several exceptions, arrived in the summer of 2009—five to six months after the inauguration of the new President. David Stevens arrived in July 2009 after being nominated in April. "I started talking to Secretary Donovan about this position in February," recalls Stevens. "The appointments process was slow. It's never quick. You have the White House review, the FBI review, and the financial review. It's a long process."

The Federal Housing Administration (FHA) was created in 1934 as a key component of New Deal legislation. In 1965, it was incorporated into the newly created Department of Housing and Urban Development. The FHA provides mortgage insurance on loans made by FHA-approved lenders throughout the United States. The FHA does not directly issue loans itself. Since its creation, the FHA has insured over 39 million home mortgages and over 52,000 multi-family project mortgages. It has a portfolio of $1 trillion in insured mortgages. FHA has 3,000 employees.

"I spent my first days at FHA assessing the organization," recalls Stevens. "I would go out into the field and talk with our staff. We held large staff meetings and an off-site planning retreat. I wanted to better understand the major issues facing the Department. I focused on what I thought I could accomplish and would make a real difference."

During his initial assessment, Stevens says, "It became obvious to me that we needed to better manage risk. We needed a risk office and a Chief Risk Officer. I felt FHA needed to go outside of the organization to recruit some top-notch Deputy Assistant Secretaries. We needed to recruit people with experience in credit risk, credit policy, and lending."

Unlike several of the executives profiled in this book, Stevens concluded during his assessment of the organization that a full-scale reorganization was not needed. "I decided," recalls Stevens, "that I didn't want to reorganize. So I put my efforts into assessing the talent already in the organization. At Freddie Mac, I had spent too much time on reorganization rather than on dealing with other crucial issues. My time at Freddie Mac was very valuable to me. I worked on multiple issues there which turned out to be excellent training for this position."

While Stevens did not launch a major reorganization, the creation of a new Office of Risk Management and the new position of a Deputy Assistant Secretary for Risk Management (the Chief Risk Officer) demonstrated the need to fill in gaps in the organization's capability. Stevens sought Congressional approval to formally establish the position and create a permanent risk management office. "This will be a permanent change," says Stevens, "and last beyond any single Administration." Stevens told Congress that the creation of this office would expand FHA's capacity to assess financial and operational risk, perform more sophisticated data analysis, and respond to market developments.

While the creation of new capability was an important step in increasing the effectiveness of FHA, Stevens concluded that there remained major skill gaps in the agency. "The staff here hasn't received much management training over the years. We set a requirement that everybody receives at least 20 hours of training. This was never done before." On related fronts, Stevens worked to improve the hiring process and to bring on additional staff to FHA to respond to the increased workload. "One of our big initiatives was improving the hiring process. We got it down to 76 days from 180 days. This is now a model across the government. It was simply taking too long. We did a flow chart to lay out the process, which the Office of Personnel Management has used. We now think that we can shave off even more days from the process. In addition, we hired about 100 new people."

The major challenge to which Stevens had to respond was strengthening the financial stability of the organization. "We had to sort out the reserve fund and get it above the two percent requirement," says Stevens. "It was below the required two percent when I arrived. This was a major concern at the White House and the National Economic Policy Council. We needed to get a bunch of new policies so the agency won't face financial problems in the future. We also had to change the entire system. We worked with lenders on many issues." Stevens also worked closely with the Administration in raising insurance premium rates, which put FHA on a much sounder financial footing for the years ahead.

Because of the crisis situation confronting Stevens when he arrived at FHA, he adopted a management strategy to focus on just a few major issues. "I've learned to just focus on two or three issues and give those my full attention," says Stevens. "That meant I gave other issues much less attention. On the other issues, I just needed to know enough to give people my go-ahead to keep them going. You really have a short time here and you have so much to get done, you have to focus on just a few things. I had to focus on a couple of things and dig in to get them done."

William J. Taggart and James W. Runcie at the Office of Federal Student Aid, Department of Education

We had the unique opportunity to interview the two individuals who have headed the Office of Federal Student Aid (FSA) in the Department of Education since 2009. FSA is a good example of a

production agency. Like the other production agencies profiled in this book, the agency has inputs (applications) and outputs (approved loans). By interviewing both Bill Taggart and his successor James Runcie, we were able to observe the evolution of a production agency over a five-year period of substantial transformation.

William Taggart (2009 to 2011)

Bill Taggart performed extensive due diligence prior to accepting the position of Chief Operating Officer (COO) at Federal Student Aid. "As a former management consultant," says Taggart, "I knew how to assess organizations. Therefore, I had a good idea of the situation I was walking into. I began discussions with the Department in February 2009 ... I read about the pending legislation that would substantially change the way FSA operated. All of these sources of information helped me to obtain a clear view on the current state of affairs at FSA. After careful consideration, I determined that I was well suited for this type of leadership challenge. As a former recipient of federal financial aid, I felt honored to be appointed the COO of FSA."

The Office of Federal Student Aid was the first performance-based organization (PBO) in government. It was created by the 1998 Reauthorization of the Higher Education Act. The legislation creating FSA designated that the office would be led by a Chief Operating Officer with a strong background in technology and management who would have a performance-based contract and report directly to the Secretary of Education. The agency also received flexibilities in procurement and personnel management. FSA provides over $130 billion in financial aid to nearly 14 million college students annually. FSA administers both the Department's education grant programs (about $30 billion) and loan programs (about $100 billion). In March 2010, Congress passed the Health Care and Education Reconciliation Act of 2010 that assigned additional responsibilities to FSA to ensure that student aid was operating efficiently and effectively. The Act ended the provision of subsidies to private banks to give out federally insured loans. Instead, loans are now administered directly by the Department of Education.

After arriving at FSA in June 2009, Taggart spent his initial days assessing the state of FSA. "The organization had a very experienced staff with a great passion for students. However, employee morale was down," recalls Taggart. "The previous several years had been difficult ones for the organization and it had a big impact on employees. I found there were many unhappy employees. I also found that the working relationship between FSA and the rest of the Department of Education needed improvement. I assessed that the organization was very good at crisis management and could respond to unplanned events quite well. In addition, FSA was a leader in working with private-sector firms through its public-private partnership framework. That said, the organization did not have a current strategic plan and was not fully prepared for the passage of new legislation if and when it was enacted."

One top priority for Taggart was employee engagement at FSA. "Human capital challenges were significant," recalls Taggart. "Many of the staff worked at

FSA an average of 18 years but did not feel valued by senior management. Nearly 20 percent of them will be eligible to retire in the next five years. We had only 975 people, with headcount falling, while our workloads were up 200 percent in some cases. It was clear that we needed to hire more staff to perform tasks that were deemed as 'inherently governmental.' We needed to hire the right people, with the right competencies, who knew how to work in a team-based environment. I held several town hall meetings to get the employees' unfiltered feedback. They had a lot on their minds and were very vocal. That meant to me that they cared about the organization. It would have been much worse if I had been met with silence. It was essential for me to help the employees to feel better about the organization. I decided to get them involved in developing a new vision, mission, and core values for the organization. Over 200 employees participated in the process and helped to develop a new working relationship between the FSA employees and the COO."

Like many large operational organizations, FSA has a clear sense of purpose that Taggart capitalized on. "The good news was that I found that FSA employees have great passion for students," he recalls. "Many told me about how they had received student loans when they were in college. I realized that I could use the natural energy for postsecondary students to rally the employee base and move the organization forward. They all believe in federal financial aid for postsecondary students and are proud that FSA provides assistance to students."

In addition to the commitment of his organization to its mission, Taggart had a transformational event to bring about significant change in the organization. "On March 30, 2010, new legislation was passed making FSA the sole originator of federal student loans," he says. "The team started planning for this change well before I arrived in June 2009. We needed a plan in place just in case the legislation passed. We wanted to show the American people that we could accomplish this task. I kept telling the organization that we were moving into a more visible role in government similar to a new play opening on Broadway. There were a lot of people looking at us. The new law gave us something to rally around. The entire organization could participate in moving FSA into the future. Everybody felt part of the process. Our organization jelled at this moment. We were all in the same boat together."

In addition to increasing the morale of the organization and implementing the new legislation, Taggart also set about to reevaluate and reengineer, where necessary, the entire ecosystem that goes along with FSA. "The FSA organization is the core of student financial aid," he says. "After understanding FSA, you then have to learn about the entire ecosystem that goes with it. The ecosystem includes our 10,000 contractors, over 2,500 lenders, 34 GAs and the 6,200 colleges and universities we serve. The COO at FSA is not just running FSA, he or she provides oversight to the entire ecosystem. Your job is to influence how the entire system works. You have to know how to give the right amount of guidance. You can't just focus on the interworkings of FSA."

James W. Runcie (2011 to Present)

James Runcie joined FSA as an advisor in 2009 and was named Deputy Chief Operating Officer in 2010. He served as Acting Chief Operating Officer after the departure of Bill Taggart in June 2011 and was named COO in September 2011.

Runcie faced the challenge of following up on the transformation initiatives started by Taggart. Runcie recalls, "I worked closely with Bill and my goal was not to whiplash the agency by moving in another direction. We needed a level of continuity. The original five-year strategic plan remained relevant and it made sense to stay the course. There was relief throughout the organization when I indicated that there were no immediate plans for major strategy or operational shifts."

There were, however, additional improvements that needed to be made in the agency. Runcie recalls his impressions of the agency. "Federal Student Aid was a very mature organization in some ways, with a very good performance culture. While I thought it was high-performing, the organization relied heavily on key people and maybe to a lesser extent on organizational processes. This created risks around institutional capacity as changes to the student aid programs and the general marketplace continued to accelerate. We needed to build process or governance models in areas such as policy implementation, change management, project development and delivery, investment management, and risk management."

In areas of strategic importance, Runcie concluded that the agency needed improvement in customer engagement. While FSA had a strong track record in the execution of programs that benefited students and borrowers, he believed that the agency could do better. "I thought the agency could improve how we assess, interact, and ultimately deliver to our broadening customer base. The changing profile of a prospective post-secondary student and the Administration's goal of increasing the number of college graduates required a dynamic understanding of customer behavior. Also issues around how students and borrowers deal with debt management were becoming more critical as the amount of student aid-related debt increased." Runcie adds, "We had the opportunity to leverage a lot of the customer and market segmentation analytics that leading private sector organizations were using.

"We built some immediate momentum by leveraging our existing experience with the web and social media," says Runcie. "It took us a couple of years but we made significant progress. We rebranded the organization. Multiple websites were integrated into one that was designed to better suit the needs of the broadening definition of our customer. On the social media side, we substantially increased our presence and now run analytics around followers, subscribers, tweets, and other forms of interaction. The agency has expanded its outreach to smartphones and tablets, in addition to the more standard venues. I might add that we have won several awards based on this body of work."

Another area of improvement is risk management. Runcie recalls, "We had limited ability to strategically assess risk. We spent most of our energy dealing with tight operational deadlines and expanding scope. Some of what we do is unplanned, driven by the policy process or as a result of unforeseen changes in the marketplace. I did not want to be in a position where we damaged our reputation and provided poor service because we couldn't adequately manage the risk around additional initiatives. Taggart was also very focused on risk management and began the process of building a good risk management practice. My focus is to make sure that we create a risk management culture. Not one central oversight body or a set of processes, but an environment where all of our staff consider the risk around any activity."

In looking forward, Runcie says, "We have operational constraints and increasing complexity. We are focused on building a sustainable and higher capacity platform. We need to update some of our aging systems infrastructure, manage the acquisition of new systems and services, and make sure we invest in our human capital through development and hiring."

Appendix to Chapter 4
Profiles of Producers Interviewed

Allison A. Hickey

Tenure
Retired Brig. General Hickey was nominated by President Obama to serve as Under Secretary for Benefits of the Department of Veterans Affairs in January 2011, and confirmed by the U.S. Senate in May 2011.

Private Sector Experience
Prior to being confirmed as Under Secretary, Brig. General Hickey served as a leader of Human Capital Management at Accenture.

Federal Government Experience
Brig. General Hickey served for 27 years in the U.S. Air Force, having served on active duty in the Active Air Force, Air National Guard, and Air Force Reserve. Her positions in the Air Force included serving as Director of the Air Force's Future Total Force Integration office at the Pentagon where she handled strategic planning, mission development, and resource implementation for more than 140 new Air Force units. Prior to holding that position, she served as Assistant Deputy Director of Strategic Planning for the Air Force and Chief of the Air Force Future Concepts and Transformation Division. As a pilot and aircraft commander, she accumulated more than 1,500 hours of flight time in KC-10A, KC-135A, T-38, and T-37 aircraft.

Education
Brig. General Hickey graduated from the U.S. Air Force Academy in 1980.

Reflecting on the Relationship between the Department of Veterans Affairs and the Department of Defense
"We still have to work on the DoD-VA handoff. There is a cultural transformation starting at DoD and there is great interest there in improving the handoff. Historically, DoD has viewed the new veteran as somebody else's problem. DoD lets go and then VA takes on. I didn't realize how quick the drop was after folks leave the military. There are still too many cases where VA doesn't own the case yet. All the key information we need to do our job comes from DoD. But we are getting there and Secretary Shinseki and Secretary Panetta are committed to improving the handoff."

David J. Kappos

Tenure
Mr. Kappos was nominated by President Obama to serve as Under Secretary of Commerce for Intellectual Property and Director of the United States Patent and Trademark Office in June 2009, and confirmed by the U.S. Senate in August 2009. Mr. Kappos resigned his position in December 2012.

Present Position
Mr. Kappos is a partner at Cravath, Swaine & Moore.

Private Sector Experience
Prior to being confirmed, Mr. Kappos was Vice President and Assistant General Counsel for

Intellectual Property Law at IBM. During his career at IBM, he served in a variety of positions as an intellectual property law attorney and as Assistant General Counsel for IBM Asia Pacific. In addition to his position at IBM, he served on the Board of Directors of the American Intellectual Property Law Association, the Intellectual Property Owners Association, and the International Intellectual Property Society.

Education
Mr. Kappos received his B.S. degree in Electrical and Computer Engineering from the University of California, Davis in 1983, and his law degree from the University of California, Berkeley in 1990.

Reflecting on Running PTO
"It's been an enjoyable experience. But the final results are not yet in. We have made progress and are still working on many items on our agenda. If I leave and haven't achieved our goals, then I would have failed. Fulfillment in this job is all about accomplishing our mission and improving our organization."

Alejandro Mayorkas

Tenure
Mr. Mayorkas was nominated by President Obama to be the Director of U.S. Citizenship and Immigration Services (USCIS) in April 2009, and was confirmed by the U.S. Senate in August 2009.

Private Sector Experience
Prior to being confirmed as Director of USCIS, Mr. Mayorkas was a partner in the law firm of O'Melveny & Myers LLP from 2001 to 2009.

Federal Government Experience
Mr. Mayorkas served as the U.S. Attorney for the Central District of California from 1998 to 2001. From 1989 to 1998, Mr. Mayorkas served as an Assistant U.S. Attorney for the Central District of California.

Photo: Doug Sanders

Education
Mr. Mayorkas received a B.A. in History from the University of California, Berkeley in 1981 and a J.D. from Loyola Law School in 1985.

Reflecting on the Mission of USCIS
"I, myself, am a refugee from Cuba. My parents, my sister, and I fled Communist Cuba in 1960. The issue of immigration has been very close to me. I'm very drawn to the mission of USCIS."

John Morton

Tenure
Mr. Morton was nominated by President Obama to serve as Director of Immigration and Customs Enforcement (ICE) in March 2009, and confirmed by the U.S. Senate in May 2009. Mr. Morton resigned his position in July 2013.

Present Position
Mr. Morton is a Senior Vice President at Capital One.

Federal Government Experience
Prior to being confirmed as Director of ICE, Mr. Morton spent 15 years at the Department of Justice. At the Department, Mr. Morton served in several positions including Assistant

Photo: Doug Sanders

United States Attorney (Criminal Division, Virginia–Eastern District), Counsel to the Deputy Attorney General, and Acting Deputy Assistant Attorney General of the Criminal Division.

He served as a trial lawyer in the Office of General Counsel for the Immigration and Naturalization Service. Mr. Morton also served in the Peace Corps.

Education
Mr. Morton received his B.A. from the University of Virginia and his law degree from the University of Virginia School of Law.

Reflecting on Serving at ICE
"The job has challenges. ICE is a hard job. The artillery keeps coming. There are wonderful people here who are doing good work. There is enormous capability here. We are doing sophisticated work. I am impressed with the scale and breadth of our ability to tackle issues. It has been a welcome surprise. The agency has come a long way in the last couple of years. When the dust settles, we have smart people here."

Robert A. Petzel, M.D.

Tenure

Dr. Petzel was nominated by President Obama to serve as the Under Secretary for Health, Veterans Health Administration (VHA), Department of Veterans Affairs in November 2009, and confirmed by the U.S. Senate in February 2010.

Federal Government Experience

Prior to being confirmed as Under Secretary, Dr. Petzel served as VA's Principal Deputy Under Secretary for Health. From 2002 to 2009, Dr. Petzel had been the Network Director of the VA Midwest Health Care Network (VISN 23) in Minneapolis, Minnesota. From 1995 to 2002, he served as the Director of Network 13. Prior to that, he served as Chief of Staff at the Minneapolis VA Medical Center. He has over 40 years of service in the Department of Veterans Affairs.

Academic Experience

Dr. Petzel served on the faculty of the University of Minnesota Medical School.

Education

Dr. Petzel graduated from St. Olaf College and from Northwestern University Medical School.

Reflecting on Serving in VHA

"It's a real gift to have this job. I believe you don't make change by yourself. I elicit people's support. I believe that people need to share the vision.

"If you are going to make change, everybody needs to understand his or her role in moving toward that vision. You need to have a vision of where the organization is going and you have to communicate that vision to the whole organization."

John S. Pistole

Tenure
Mr. Pistole was nominated by President Obama as Administrator of the Transportation Security Administration in May 2010, and confirmed by the U.S. Senate in June 2010.

Federal Government Experience
Prior to being confirmed as Administrator, Mr. Pistole served for 26 years with the FBI. Mr. Pistole served as Deputy Director of the FBI from 2004 to 2010, and was heavily involved in the formation of terrorism policies. He also served as Deputy Director of the FBI and Executive Assistant Director for Counterterrorism and Counterintelligence. He

Photo: Brigitte Dittberner

is the second-longest serving Deputy Director of the FBI. Pistole began his career as a Special Agent in 1983, serving in the Minneapolis and New York divisions before serving as Supervisor in the Organized Crime Section at FBI headquarters in Washington, D.C. During his career, he led or was involved in several high-profile investigations, including the Christmas Day 2009 attempted attack on Northwest Flight 253 and the 2010 Times Square bombing attempt.

Education
Mr. Pistole received his undergraduate degree from Anderson University in Indiana and his law degree from the Indiana University School of Law–Indianapolis.

Reflecting on his Tenure at TSA
"I knew there would be criticism in this job, but I saw challenges and opportunities in nearly every situation.

"I have found that change is not easy. Risk-based security is a paradigm shift. We have to manage expectations. Since 2002, we have screened seven billion people. We need them all to arrive safely while we provide the most effective security in the most efficient way."

James W. Runcie

Tenure

Mr. Runcie was appointed in September 2011 by U.S. Secretary of Education Arne Duncan as the fourth Chief Operating Officer (COO) for the Office of Federal Student Aid (FSA).

Federal Government Experience

Prior to his appointment as COO, Mr. Runcie was Acting Chief Operating Officer after the departure of William Taggart in June 2011. Mr. Runcie joined FSA as an advisor in 2009 and was named Deputy Chief Operating Officer in 2010.

Private Sector Experience

From 2002 to 2009, Mr. Runcie served as Co-Head of Equity Corporate Finance of UBS Investment Bank. Prior to that position, Mr. Runcie served in executive positions with Banc of America Securities Corporation, Donaldson, Lufkin & Jenrette Securities Corporation, and the Xerox Corporation.

Education

Mr. Runcie received his undergraduate degree from the College of Holy Cross and received his Master of Business Administration degree from Harvard University's Graduate School of Business.

Reflecting on Serving in FSA

"This is a very transaction-heavy environment. The key is our ability to manage the process. Decision-making is very collaborative, with many individuals involved in the process. You need to work to get closure on decisions. You need to communicate with key players and give them lead time on decisions."

David H. Stevens

Tenure
Mr. Stevens was nominated by President Obama to serve as Assistant Secretary for Housing at the United States Department of Housing and Urban Development (HUD) and Commissioner of the Federal Housing Administration (FHA) in April 2009, and confirmed by the U.S. Senate in July 2009. Mr. Stevens resigned his position in April 2010.

Present Position
David H. Stevens is President and Chief Executive Officer of the Mortgage Bankers Association (MBA), the national association representing the real estate finance industry.

Private Sector Experience
Prior to being confirmed as Assistant Secretary, Mr. Stevens served as President and Chief Operating Officer of Long & Foster Companies, which includes Long & Foster Real Estate and its affiliated businesses, including mortgage, title insurance, and home service connections.

Mr. Stevens served as Senior Vice President of Single Family Business at Freddie Mac and Executive Vice President, National Wholesale Manager at Wells Fargo. He also worked 16 years in a variety of positions at the World Savings Bank, including Senior Vice President running its national lending practice.

Education
Mr. Stevens earned a B.A. from the University of Colorado at Boulder in 1983.

Reflecting on Running FHA
"The job ended up being bigger than I thought. I came here in the middle of the storm. We were really fighting a housing crisis. In the past, the job had really not had much visibility. The agency is important again and nobody would think of appointing somebody not fully qualified for this job. We were able to accomplish much of what we have done because of the crisis. FHA is now a major player in Washington. We have become the voice of housing in government. The White House, the National Economic Policy Council, and the Department of Treasury all now call upon us when there is a housing issue facing the Administration."

William J. (Bill) Taggart

Tenure
Mr. Taggart was appointed in June 2009 by U.S. Secretary of Education Arne Duncan as the third Chief Operating Officer for the Office of Federal Student Aid. Mr. Taggart resigned his position in June 2011.

Present Position
William J. Taggart is the President and CEO of Atlanta Life Financial Group (ALFG).

Private Sector Experience
Before joining the Department of Education, Mr. Taggart was President and Chief Executive Officer of Veritas One Consulting, LLC. Prior to Veritas One, he served in a number of leadership positions at Wachovia Corporation, including Chief Operating Officer of Corporate and Investment Banking, Head of Client Services, President of Info-One, and Chief Administrative Officer for Wachovia Insurance. Mr. Taggart also worked for First Union Corporation as Managing Director of Strategic Support Services for the automation and operations division, and for IBM in technology, consulting, and marketing roles.

Education
Mr. Taggart received a Master's degree from Harvard University's Graduate School of Business Administration and a Bachelor's degree in Business Administration from Howard University.

Reflecting on Running FSA
"You can look at projects like this (e.g., 100% Direct Lending) from a risk/ reward perspective," Taggart tells *Inside Higher Education.* "If someone looked at this project purely on risk, they probably would have run the other way … But how many times in your career do you get an opportunity to lead an effort of this size and magnitude for the benefit of American students and their families and the taxpayers?" (Lederman).

Chapter Five

The Regulators

Understanding the Job of the Regulator

Government regulators are modern tightrope walkers who perform a constant balancing act between what some might call too much regulation and others might call not enough regulation. The stakes are high for government's regulators. Their decisions impact the well-being of the nation's citizens (in some cases, their life and death) and the nation's economic well-being. When asked what is most fulfilling about his job, Joe Main, Assistant Secretary of Labor for Mine Safety and Health, says, "It is the daily update on mining incidents. It is a good day when we don't have any incidents. The number of incidents has been declining. I am satisfied when miners go to work in the morning and then go home safely each night."

The regulators profiled in this chapter are constantly balancing the cost implications of their regulations with the agency's desired result (such as reductions in deaths on the nation's highways, in the nation's mines, or due to faulty consumer products). David Strickland, Administrator of NHTSA, describes his balancing act:

The Regulators

Michael R. Bromwich, page 114

Director, Bureau of Ocean Energy Management, Regulation and Enforcement (BOEMRE), Department of the Interior

Margaret Hamburg, page 115

Commissioner, Food and Drug Administration (FDA), Department of Health and Human Services

Allison M. Macfarlane, page 117

Chairman, Nuclear Regulatory Commission (NRC)

Joseph A. Main, page 118

Assistant Secretary of Labor for Mine Safety and Health (MSHA), Department of Labor

"We understand the relationship between safety and costs and we want to work with manufacturers on safety. We want cars to be very safe but we are aware that we don't want them to be too costly for people to buy them."

Inez Tenenbaum had to be a tightrope walker at the Consumer Product Safety Commission (CPSC). In a *New York Times* article describing her tenure at CPSC, it was emphasized that before Chairman Tenenbaum could make headway on child safety issues, she "had to persuade consumer advocates that she would work for them while reassuring manufacturers that the agency would not be unfair in carrying out its new powers. It was a difficult juggling act that some industry officials say Ms. Tenenbaum has managed to pull off. 'What I was most glad about is that she treated industry as a resource, rather than the enemy,' said Carter

David L. Strickland, page 119

Administrator, National Highway Traffic Safety Administration (NHTSA), Department of Transportation

Inez Moore Tenenbaum, page 121

Chairman, Consumer Product Safety Commission (CPSC)

Jon Wellinghoff, page 123

Chairman, Federal Energy Regulatory Commission (FERC)

Keithly, president of the Toy Industry Association. 'We didn't agree on everything, but she was always fair." (Nixon)

There is no agreement on the number of regulatory agencies in government. Figures range between 25 and 50, depending on which agencies are counted. Some of the financial regulatory agencies are well-known—the Securities and Exchange Commission, the Commodity Futures Trading Commission, and the Federal Deposit Insurance Corporation. Another group of regulatory agencies are well-known for their oversight responsibilities in the area of food and drug safety—the Food and Drug Administration in the Department of Health and Human Services, and the Food Safety and Inspection Service in the Department of Agriculture. In addition, many government agencies have some regulatory responsibilities in their portfolio of activities.

There are two governance models for regulatory agencies. The first, common in the financial regulatory agencies, is the Commission model, in which there is one Chair and four Commission Members. In the case of a five-person Commission, the laws creating regulatory agencies usually stipulate that no more than three of the Commissioners should be affiliated with the same political party. The party that holds the White House names the person to serve as Chair. The second model is to have a single Administrator for the organization. In the profiles presented in this chapter, four of the agencies profiled have single Administrators (FDA, NHTSA, MSHA, and BOEMRE) and three have a Chair and four Commissioners (CPSC, FERC, and NRC).

Key Components of the Job of the Regulator

Serving as a government regulator involves many challenges. In our interviews with the seven political executives profiled in this chapter, each describes facing one or more of the challenges discussed below. The four key job components are:
* Operating in a politically contentious environment

- Getting the rules out *and* running an organization
- Responding to unexpected events while keeping the organization running
- Constantly engaging with and responding to stakeholder concerns

Operating in a Politically Contentious Environment

While all the positions described in this book are to some degree politically contentious, the job of the regulator is highly contentious. Public and Congressional attitudes toward regulation are highly volatile and subject to wide swings in support depending on the current political environment. Inez Tenenbaum, Chair of the CPSC, tells us, "It has been a roller coaster. We have so many contentious issues. Many of our rulemaking initiatives were mandated by Congress ... I was expecting a more positive environment. I wasn't expecting so much conflict."

Coupled with a politically contentious environment is the high visibility that comes with being a regulator. Tenenbaum says, "I've been surprised at the high visibility and high profile of the agency. Many of our issues—cribs, baby bumpers, window coverings—have received much attention." Michael Bromwich, former Director of BOEMRE, was surprised "at the great press attention and political intensity that surrounded our issuing of permits. Things are somewhat quieter right now in summer 2011, but not much."

One of the compelling findings from our research is the difference between federal agencies, including the regulatory agencies. At the Federal Energy Regulatory Commission, Chairman Wellinghoff describes a non-contentious five-member Commission which, he says, "does not think in partisan terms. We look at rates and make judgments." At the Nuclear Regulatory Commission, Chairman Macfarlane observes that differences of opinion between Commissioners is not partisan, but more a matter of professional judgment. Macfarlane says, "Our 'ideology'—if we can call it that—is over nuclear issues. Commissioners bring different regulatory and technical perspectives to their work. Our internal procedures drive us to work through these differences."

Getting the Rules Out *and* Running an Organization

Due to the unique nature of the job, the regulators have both policy and management responsibilities. In a five-member Commission, the Chairman becomes the individual responsible for managing the organization in addition to his or her responsibilities as a voting member of the Commission. At the CPSC, Tenenbaum's responsibilities include running the organization, managing the rulemaking process, and voting on the rules that the Commission will issue. At NHTSA, David Strickland is charged with getting the rules out and serving as the leader of the

Selecting Regulators

For the Office of Presidential Personnel, the selection of the regulators and their successful confirmation by the U.S. Congress are a continuing challenge. To gain confirmation, nominees to regulatory positions cannot be viewed as too close either to industry or to consumer interest groups. Recent Administrations have run into difficulty getting their nominees confirmed for positions at the Consumer Product Safety Commission, the National Highway Traffic Safety Administration, and the Mine Safety and Health Administration. In October 2013, President Obama's nominee to serve as Chair of the Federal Energy Regulatory Commission, Ron Binz, withdrew his nomination due to controversy over his positions.

The regulatory executives profiled in this chapter are exceptions to the recent trend of highly controversial and contentious nominees. In the case of Tenenbaum, her state government experience had prepared her for dealing with stakeholders, but she had not had any direct experience in the consumer product safety field. In the case of Strickland, he had spent his career as a Congressional staff member dealing with automobile safety issues but had not worked for industry or a consumer group. Joe Main came to the position with a career-long background in working on mine safety issues, both as a miner himself and a staff member of the United Mine Workers.

The experience of Michael Bromwich is somewhat atypical. He was chosen because of his management and turnaround experience, not his expertise on energy-related issues. Because of intense interest in the events surrounding the Deepwater Horizon incident and its aftermath, future nominees to the successor agencies of BOEMRE are likely to receive close scrutiny both in the selection and confirmation process.

In selecting future nominees for regulatory positions, the following factors should be considered:

- **Prior experience in the field is highly useful, as is knowledge of industry stakeholders.** While experience and knowledge of the stakeholder community are important, the appointee must not be viewed as too closely aligned with either side of the regulatory spectrum (whose attitudes range from support of heavy regulation to support of lighter regulation). In the case of Joe Main, his prior experience in mining helped him to know exactly how to respond to the Upper Big Branch mine explosion. Main says, "I've lived through these experiences before, so I knew what to expect." As with all the positions described in this book, there is often no shortcut for relevant experience. There is also no shortcut for knowing many of the stakeholders in the arena before arriving. Strickland recalls, "I knew (the stakeholders) from my days on the Hill—the automobile manufacturers, the safety advocates …"
- **Appointees to regulatory positions must be able to deal with conflict, handle controversy, and operate in a highly contentious environment.** Regulatory positions are not for those who like to avoid conflict. While often difficult to find, individuals who are well-respected on both sides of the regulated industry are needed to mediate the vast difference of opinion in any regulated arena.

organization.

A major initial activity of both Tenenbaum's and Strickland's was to speed up their agency's process for getting its new rules out. Chairman Tenenbaum describes one of her initial actions at the agency: "I told our staff and the Office of General Counsel to pick up the pace. Everything was simply taking too long. The delays were burdensome on industry. Industry needed to know what we were going to do, so they could be ready to respond." David Strickland expresses a similar frustration, "It was taking six months to elicit comments on some of our rules. We didn't have that long. We had to speed it up." The job of managing the rulemaking process falls to the agency Administrator or the Chair. In the Chair model, individual Commission members have little or no responsibility for oversight of the speed and management of the rulemaking process.

Another aspect of running the agency is making sure that the organization is prepared for the future. Since her arrival in 2009, FDA Commissioner Hamburg has spent a significant amount of her time on strengthening the institution and implementing several new pieces of legislation that were the first major changes in food and drug laws in 70 years. Hamburg recalls, "I found that I had to focus on positioning FDA for the future. I wanted it to be as effective as it could be. This required a whole new level of engagement with the agency. I wanted to strengthen the quality of the work done here. The agency needed an advocate for itself. There was no beginning and end to the initiative of improving the agency. I felt that if we didn't address this issue, we would be losing critical ground."

Responding to Unexpected Events While Keeping the Organization Running

Two of the political executives profiled in this chapter—Joe Main at MSHA and Michael Bromwich at BOEMRE—faced a major national crisis during their tenures. Joe Main confronted the challenge of investigating and responding to the Upper Big Branch mine explosion which occurred in April 2010, six months after his confirmation in October 2009. Michael Bromwich arrived at BOEMRE in June 2010, two months after the Deepwater Horizon explosion and subsequent environmental crisis, with a charge to serve both as a crisis manager and a turnaround manager for the organization.

David Strickland and Inez Tenenbaum also faced crises, albeit somewhat less dramatic ones. Strickland arrived at NHTSA in January 2010 in the middle of the Toyota recall crisis. When Tenenbaum arrived at CPSC in 2009, the organization was still responding to the aftermath of the 2007 recall of Chinese-made toys contaminated with lead paint.

While all seven political executives were prepared to deal with the crisis at hand (or in the case of Tenenbaum, the aftermath of a previous crisis), they also had to continue to run their organizations while dealing with the crisis. In effect, their workload doubled and they acted in the roles of both crisis manager and Chief Executive Officer concurrently. Joe Main recounts, "I'm very proud that I was able to keep the agency running in spite of Upper Big Branch. We had a successful strategy in place and we kept it going. We kept doing our work ..." In reflecting on his experience at BOEMRE, Bromwich recalls that he not only had to deal with the immediate aftermath of the Deepwater Horizon crisis, but also faced the challenge of reorganizing the agency, getting the permits issuance process running again, and getting the organization's employees back on track.

Constantly Engaging with and Responding to Stakeholder Concerns

Each regulatory agency has its own distinct set of stakeholders, all of whom make their views well-known. It is possible to map each regulatory organization's stakeholders, which range from citizens/consumers to corporations to foreign governments. While most regulatory agencies interact with regulated industries, there is a group of regulatory agencies that deals directly with citizens. These agencies include NHTSA and the CPSC. In the case of NHTSA, David Strickland recounts meeting with families of individuals who have died in car crashes. "They come to meet with me," says Strickland. "It gives me a sense of the importance of my job."

In the case of NHTSA, the passage of the Cameron Gulbransen Kids Transportation Safety Act mandated that the agency prepare new safety regulations to avoid accidents such as the one in which a minivan backed over Cameron because he was not visible from within the automobile. Cameron's father worked with Congress to pass the law mandating new regulations. In the case of CPSC, a major activity of Inez Tenenbaum's was to implement the requirements of the Virginia Graeme Baker Pool & Spa Safety Act which was enacted by Congress in 2007. Virginia Graeme Baker, granddaughter of former Secretary of State James Baker, drowned when the powerful suction from a hot tub drain trapped her underwater. In 2010, CPSC launched *Pool Safety: Simple Steps Save Lives,* a national public education campaign to raise public awareness about drowning and entrapment prevention. Tenenbaum went on the road to several cities to launch the campaign.

Tenenbaum also works directly with corporations. "I have been reaching out to stakeholders, instead of waiting for them to come to me," Tenenbaum recounts. "I want to work with companies on voluntary standards. Voluntary standards are the first step. We let industries regulate themselves, unless their regulations are ineffective. Sometimes voluntary standards are too little and too late. We want the stakeholders to come talk to me and the other Commissioners. I have really reached out to industry. I must talk to an industry representative three or four times a day."

There is also great sensitivity to many of these discussions. Margaret Hamburg describes her experience at FDA: "We expect companies to give us information. Companies do not want that information discussed publicly. We need to be aware of what is for public consumption and what is not. However, we still want more transparency. We want to increase trust in the agency. We are getting stakeholders involved and sharing information."

Regulators in Action

Michael R. Bromwich at the Bureau of Ocean Energy Management, Regulation and Enforcement, Department of the Interior

"I was first contacted by the White House about taking this job just 11 days before I started," recalls Michael Bromwich. "I was on the job exactly one week after I said 'Yes.' In that week, I had to wind up a 10-year law practice. I arrived almost exactly two months after the Deepwater Horizon oil spill: the spill occurred on April 20, 2010 and I got here on June 21st. The Department was then focused on capping the well and stopping the flow of the oil."

Michael Bromwich took over an agency in crisis. The Bureau of Ocean Energy Management, Regulation, and Enforcement (BOEMRE) was created in May 2010. Bromwich was chosen to lead BOEMRE in June 2010, one month after its creation. Its predecessor agency, the Minerals Management Service (MMS), had been created in 1982. Since its creation, MMS has had conflicting missions. One part of the agency was responsible for resource assessments and evaluation, environmental reviews, and leasing and permitting activities. The other part of the agency was responsible for collecting, accounting for, and distributing revenues associated with minerals produced on federal and American Indian-leased lands.

The life of BOEMRE was a short one. In response to the Deepwater Horizon explosion and the resulting oil spill in the Gulf of Mexico, the Obama Administration reformed the management of the federal government's activities related to offshore oil and gas regulations by splitting the agency into three separate organizations:

- **Office of Natural Resources Revenue (ONRR)** was moved to the Office of the Assistant Secretary for Policy, Management, and Budget. The office is responsible for revenue collection activities.
- **Bureau of Ocean Energy Management (BOEM)** is responsible for managing the development of the nation's offshore resources in an environmentally

and economically responsible way.

- **Bureau of Safety and Environmental Enforcement (BSEE)** enforces safety and environmental regulations.

"A significant part of my early time here was spent on the oil spill and its aftermath," recalls Bromwich. "We also faced some very substantial legal issues when the original moratorium on deepwater drilling was overturned by a federal judge the first week I was here. I then got swept up into that issue."

One key lesson learned by Bromwich was the importance of understanding the situation into which you have been placed. "You have to gauge what the crisis really is," recounts Bromwich. "We were the most heavily criticized agency in government when I started in June 2010, which did create a crisis mentality in the agency and in Interior generally. We were being criticized in the media every day—every media outlet felt obliged to publish numerous critical pieces about the agency. Morale was as low as I've ever seen it in any organization. There was a lot of tension in the agency, and a stream of negative commentary about it, including from inside the government. There was no end in sight to the negative publicity. I was very careful not to reinforce all this negative feedback by jumping on the bandwagon of criticism, but on the other hand I could not defend past acts of misconduct or lack of competence. I had two major tasks. The first was to manage the crisis and the second was to manage the reorganization. Those are the reasons I was brought in."

One challenging part of coming into a crisis situation is that you are never sure how long the crisis will last. Bromwich reports, "The crisis didn't end as quickly as I had anticipated. The external attention from the media and Congress continued. I expected it to diminish more quickly, in about 60 to 90 days after I arrived, but it continued for much longer. Then the issue of issuing new drilling permits in deepwater became a highly charged political issue, especially with the sharp rise in gasoline prices.

"I thought the crisis atmosphere would diminish, which would then give people more time for reflection and planning the best way forward," recalls Bromwich. "But it didn't happen. The legal controversies continued."

In looking back on his first year at BOEMRE, Bromwich says, "We did a lot. We got the oil well plugged. We reorganized the agency. We started issuing permits again. We are putting the organization back on its feet and getting our employees back on track. But we aren't done yet. The battle for more resources is proving harder than I thought it would be."

Margaret Hamburg at the Food and Drug Administration

After being nominated to serve as Commissioner of the Food and Drug Administration (FDA), Dr. Margaret Hamburg was advised by several former Commissioners to just pick out a couple of issues and focus on those items.

"Instead," Hamburg recalls, "I found that I had to focus on positioning FDA for the future. I wanted it to be as effective as it could be. This required a whole new level of engagement with the agency. I wanted to strengthen the quality of the work done here. The agency needed an advocate for itself. There was no beginning and end to the initiative of improving the agency. I felt that if we didn't address this issue, we would be losing critical ground. We needed to forge stronger working relationships with many groups. We have gone up in public approval of the agency."

In assuming the Commissioner position at FDA, Hamburg found an agency that has responsibility for protecting the nation's public health by ensuring the safety, efficacy, and security of human and veterinary drugs, biological products, and medical devices; and the safety of the nation's food supply, dietary supplements, cosmetics, and products that emit radiation. Most recently, FDA has authorities to regulate tobacco. FDA has a budget of $4.7 billion and over 15,000 employees. "I had worked with FDA previously," says Hamburg, "but I did not know all of its broad scope and responsibilities. It's a huge set of activities ... I faced a steep learning curve. It was quite demanding. Our decisions impact people's lives. Every decision by FDA is scrutinized."

Hamburg arrived at FDA when the globalization of food and drugs was dramatically increasing. "I was surprised by the impact of globalization," says Hamburg. "Over 40 percent of our drugs are manufactured outside the United States and over 15% of our food is from outside the U.S. Over 80% of our seafood is from outside of the country. So we now need to be globally engaged. One of our challenges is that the original set of FDA laws was written when most everything was made in the U.S. and there was no globalization." In July 2013, FDA issued proposed rules that would place responsibility on companies to police the food they import. The new rules would subject imported foods to the same safety standards as food produced domestically.

The proposed new rules were part of the Food Safety Modernization Act of 2010. The Act was the first significant update of FDA's food safety authority in 70 years. "Over the last four years," says Hamburg, "we have gotten several important pieces of legislation updating the agency. All of this is a challenge for us. The laws needed to be updated. We still need some additional tools."

While we have categorized FDA as a regulatory agency, the agency has many characteristics of a science agency. "We have made great strides forward on the science side of the house," says Hamburg. "We are creating new collaborations with the academic community. We are now working together to develop the new field of regulatory science. FDA must invest in science. There is a complex pathway to real-world products. Getting real-world products requires a different kind of science."

Allison M. Macfarlane at the Nuclear Regulatory Commission

In July 2012, Allison Macfarlane also took over an agency in crisis. It was a different kind of crisis, however, than those faced by Michael Bromwich at BOEMRE or Joe Main at MSHA. Macfarlane had been selected in May 2012 to serve the remaining year of her predecessor who had resigned after controversy over his management style, perhaps triggered in part by an unusual letter from the former Chairman's four colleagues to President Obama expressing "grave concern" about his actions at NRC.

"When I arrived," recalls Macfarlane, "the agency was in trouble. It had just been through a very turbulent time. The staff was suspicious of the Commission and the Commissioners were suspicious of the Chairman's office. I met quickly with the Executive Director and other senior managers. I talked to people. I took the time to learn the organization. I worked aggressively to build relationships."

The mission of the NRC is to license and regulate the nation's civilian use of nuclear materials to ensure protection of public health and safety. It now has a $1 billion budget, with a staff of over 3,700 employees. NRC performs continuous oversight activities of 100 currently licensed operating nuclear power reactors and 31 research test reactors to ensure that they operate safely and securely in accordance with NRC rules and regulations. NRC also has an active role in the handling of nuclear materials and waste safety.

Getting the agency back on track was a major focus of Chairman Macfarlane during her first year at NRC. In June 2013, she was reconfirmed to serve a full five-year term as Chairman that expires in June 2018. Macfarlane recounts, "I brought in my values. I thought it was important to get things resolved. I met with all the staff and each of the Commissioners. These early meetings were very helpful … This required me to do a lot of communication. We formulated a communications plan.

"I had to be a good listener," says Macfarlane. "I wanted to show that staff that I was concerned and that I understood the issues. I had an open door policy. I walked around a lot. I found a lot of opportunities to communicate. I also met with each of the Commissioners on a weekly basis. I was able to establish collegial working relationships with my fellow Commissioners."

NRC is different from some regulatory agencies that can be politically contentious on partisan grounds. Macfarlane describes the differences as grounded more in professional judgment: "The Atomic Energy Act envisioned five Commissioners engaged in robust—albeit collegial—debate. A lot of our discussions are technically based. Our 'ideology'—if we can call it that—is over nuclear issues. Commissioners bring different regulatory and technical perspectives to their work. Our internal procedures drive us to work through these differences." In addition to working with the Commissioners on nuclear issues, Macfarlane spends considerable time with representatives from industry, state and local government, tribal communities, citizens, and the academic community. "A wide variety of folks come by to see me," states Macfarlane. "I think it is important to listen to all views." She also believes these visits should be transparently available to those interested and maintains her calendar of these meetings, as well as her travel, on her website.

Joseph A. Main at the Mine Safety and Health Administration, Department of Labor

"I had been working with the agency since the 1970s, so I knew the place," states Joe Main. "I have worked with people in the agency for many years. On my first day in office, I was struck by the weight of my new responsibilities and the realization that I was going to have to run this place. I had used the time before my confirmation to get up to speed. I focused on the key issues and key challenges facing the agency. I asked the agency to send me over lots of information and reports which I could read before taking over."

The Mine Safety and Health Administration (MSHA) is responsible for the safety and health of the nation's mines. The agency develops and promulgates safety and health standards, ensures compliance, assesses civil penalties, and investigates accidents. The federal government's role in mine safety dates back to 1891 when Congress passed the nation's first law regulating mining activities.

Joe Main faced two sets of challenges at the Mine Safety and Health Administration. Upon arriving in October 2009, Main faced his first set of challenges. The first set of challenges is common to all regulatory agencies: fulfilling an ambitious mandate with limited resources, working with Congress to update and fine-tune existing legislation, and working with the regulated industry to develop initiatives.

The second set of challenges was a consequence of Massey Energy's Upper Big Branch Mine explosion on April 2010 in Raleigh County, West Virginia, in which 29 miners were killed. This challenge involved both responding to intense Congressional and media interest in the explosion and conducting an agency investigation into the tragedy. Main says, "You have to ask yourself and the agency, 'What did we miss?' 'How did this happen?' 'What have we learned?' and finally, 'What changes do we need to make?'"

By April 2010, Main was making significant progress on his original agenda. Main recalls, "When I came in, a major issue facing us was reforming the Black Lung Disease Program. There had been two prior attempts to reform the program but they had not worked. Our initial agenda was also to reduce coal mining fatalities. We have too many mining deaths. So we again implemented a multifaceted program: an education program and a new compliance plan with enhanced enforcement. But I didn't want this to be just a gotcha program. I wanted to try to fix the problem."

On April 5, 2010, the mine explosion at Upper Big Branch occurred. Main recalls, "I've lived through these experiences before, so I knew what to expect. It is important to manage all the different groups involved with mine explosion. My experiences earlier in my career were crucial. I had been involved in the 2001 Jim Walter mine explosion and the 1984 Wilberg Mine explosion. You have to be careful not to let everyone run into the fire. I knew I had to leave some people here in headquarters in order to keep the place running.

"I was there from Tuesday to Saturday on the front line. I got there as fast as I could. I first found out about it at 5:30 p.m. on Monday. We set up a command center. I left for the mine at about 4 a.m. and got there about 9 a.m. on Tuesday morning. That day was hectic. We had meetings to decide what to get done that day. What were the pieces that needed to get done? We had Congress, the press, and the President all interested in what we were doing. We had to put together quality information for the President. You can't imagine the intensity of the situation. You can always do more in these situations than you think you can.

"After the incident, we had to figure out what went wrong and we had to make corrections. We did find that there was a computer error in the pattern of violations software. Upper Big Branch had a pattern of violations that we had not caught up with. They had many violations and were at the top of the list nationwide.

"All the violations did not show up because some of the violations were being appealed under the old process. We clearly had to improve our pattern of violations procedures, which date back to 1977."

David Strickland at the National Highway Traffic Safety Administration, Department of Transportation

"I arrived on January 4, 2010," recalls David Strickland. "I got briefings all day long. I moved into my office, which I thought was big compared to my space in Congress. I had been doing oversight over NHTSA for nine years. I knew the agency, the structure, and the issues facing the agency. But I needed grounding on how NHTSA worked day to day. I knew a lot of the NHTSA senior staff. I knew Ron Medford, who is the Deputy Administrator. He had been Acting Administrator the year before I arrived. I needed to find out what I didn't know. I had many questions."

The National Highway Traffic Safety Administration (NHTSA) was established by the Highway Safety Act of 1970 with the mission to reduce the number of deaths, injuries, and economic losses resulting from motor vehicle crashes. NHTSA is the successor agency to the National Highway Safety Bureau, which was created in 1966. NHTSA has a budget of over $850 million and over 600 employees.

When David Strickland arrived in January 2010, the Department of Transportation was in the midst of intense Congressional and media scrutiny over the recall of Toyota vehicles due to unintended acceleration problems. Strickland and former Secretary Ray LaHood were testifying frequently before Congress on NHTSA's oversight of this safety issue. In addition to the crisis atmosphere surrounding the Toyota recall, NHTSA was facing an ambitious agenda: issuing new Corporate Average Fuel Economy (CAFE) standards, issuing a rear-view visibility rule, working with Congress on updating vehicle safety legislation, and undertaking the ongoing activities of the agency.

"When I got here in January, there had already been a significant amount of work in progress on Toyota," recounts Strickland. "There was much work underway, including a study by the National Academy of Sciences and a research initiative with the National Aeronautics and Space Administration. My first task was to determine whether NHTSA was broken. Some people were saying that we had a broken culture here. I decided that they were wrong and that NHTSA was not broken. That decision was a risk I had to take, but I believed it. It turns out that I was right. The final analysis showed that NHTSA had done a fantastic job on the Toyota recall."

In reflecting back on the Toyota perfect storm, Strickland recalls, "I thought the Department did exactly the right thing in going to Japan and telling them that we were going to enforce the recall regulations. We were doing our job. It was the right call to stop selling the cars. It got people's attention." After the Toyota crisis passed, Strickland says, "I could finally turn my attention elsewhere." One pressing item on Strickland's agenda was the issuing of CAFE standards. It is the responsibility of NHTSA to set the standards for fuel economy of cars and light trucks.

Like many of the regulators profiled in this chapter, Strickland spends much of his time working closely with his stakeholders, which include automobile manufacturers, equipment manufacturers, Congress, citizens and advocacy groups, and the states. Strickland says, "I knew a lot of them from my days on the Hill—the automobile manufacturers, the safety advocates. We all want a safer fleet of cars. It's our job to put out consumer alerts and narrow the safety gap. We understand the relationship between safety and costs and we want to work with manufacturers on safety. We want cars to be very safe but we are aware that we don't want them to be too costly for people to buy them. We don't want to price out the public. We want them to have choices."

State governments are also key stakeholders who play a crucial, lesser-known role in automobile safety. "People don't realize," says Strickland, "that states have a big role to play in regulation. It is the states that govern many safety laws. We target our efforts with the states. There is a framework we use that has been successful in the past. First, we work with the states to get new laws passed. Second, the laws are enforced by state and local policy. Third, NHTSA supports this effort with an active media campaign. We followed this framework with seat belts and are now following it with the distracted driving initiative led by Secretary LaHood." As of October 2012, 39 states, the District of Columbia, and Guam had passed laws banning text messaging while driving.

Inez Moore Tenenbaum at the Consumer Product Safety Commission

Some political appointees might expect to have the red carpet rolled out for their arrival. Inez Tenenbaum's experience was different. "The physical office space was a real mess," recalls Chairman Tenenbaum. "The walls had not been painted. I found old furniture in my office that needed replacing. The building itself was run down. It was a pretty dreary place. We had very few supplies, and we also had no business cards or stationery. At the start, I just had one staff member whom I brought with me from South Carolina. We have since improved the physical look of the building and created standard operating procedures."

The Consumer Product Safety Commission (CPSC), created by Congress in 1972, is the independent federal regulatory agency charged with protecting the public against unreasonable risks of injury or death from consumer products. The Commission consists of five Commissioners who are appointed by the President with the advice and consent of the Senate for staggered seven-year terms. The President appoints one of the Commissioners as Chairman, with confirmation by the Senate. As with most regulatory commissions, the 1972 law stipulated that no more than three of the Commissioners should be affiliated with the same political party.

The Commission's organizational structure has proven to be more difficult than Chairman Tenenbaum expected. "It's been harder than I thought working with the five Commissioners. I didn't come here to talk about the role of government. I'm here to enforce the statute. The agency should not be about ideology. Once something becomes a statutory mandate, you have to develop the rules."

While 87 percent of the Commission's votes are unanimous, the Commission is more partisan than Chairman Tenenbaum anticipated. "I was expecting a more positive environment. I wasn't expecting so much conflict. I initially viewed the Commissioners being more like administrative law judges than partisan Commissioners. I thought that once a decision was made, we would all put the decision behind us and move on. It hasn't turned out like that."

As is common with many incoming regulatory executives, Chairman Tenenbaum did not start off with a clean slate when she arrived in 2009. CPSC was still operating in the aftermath of the 2007 recall of millions of Chinese-made toys that were found to be contaminated with lead paint. The issue of dangerous cribs then surfaced in 2008. The publicity surrounding these incidents led Congress to pass the Consumer Product Safety Improvement Act (CPSIA) in August 2008. The new legislation updated the 1972 law and expanded the agency's regulatory mandate. The CPSIA mandated new federal safety standards in numerous areas. The new law also increased the agency's budget and staffing levels. One provision of the law mandated the creation of a publicly searchable web-based database of reports of injury, illness, or death, or risks of injury, illness, or death associated with consumer products.

Chairman Tenenbaum's initial response to this set of challenges was to devote much of her time during her first year to the internal management of the organization. "I found that the agency had no standard operating procedures. So everything we did was brand new. I had to issue directives on internal operations, like our directive on travel. We set up a six-month matrix schedule. I had to start setting deadlines. I wanted to know where people were on all the things we had to do."

Like many of the political executives profiled in this book, Tenenbaum wanted to speed up the agency. Given the number of rules mandated by the CPSIA and pending regulations, there was much to be done. Tenenbaum recalls, "I told our staff and the Office of General Counsel to pick up the pace. Everything was simply taking too long. The delays were burdensome on industry. Industry needed to know what we were going to do, so they could be ready to respond." In reflecting on her experience at the agency, Tenenbaum says, "I think organizations respond to the speed of the leader. Agency personnel can see that my staff and I are working very hard. I try hard to let everybody know what is expected."

Speeding up the agency also required Chairman Tenenbaum to try to change the culture of the agency. "You have to work on the processes of the organization," reflects Tenenbaum. "We are trying to create a new culture here and get people to change the way they are doing business. We want to create a culture of excellence. We want to bring in new talent and get new people." Like many federal organizations, CPSC is facing a dramatic increase in staff retirements as over one-third of the agency has worked at CPSC for over 35 years. Replacing that experienced staff will be a major challenge to Tenenbaum over the next several years.

Tenenbaum also concluded that the agency suffered from a lack of strategic direction. In response to this problem, the agency hired a consulting firm to assist in developing a five-year strategic plan. The outside consultant interviewed 76 stakeholders to get their views on the agency and how the agency might more effectively interact with industry. The resulting strategic plan included the development of measurable goals against which the agency could be evaluated. The strategic plan initiative also addressed the issue of a potential agency reorganization.

Jon Wellinghoff at the Federal Energy Regulatory Commission

Unlike some other regulatory Commissioners, Jon Wellinghoff describes a non-contentious five-member Commission during his seven years at the Federal Energy Regulatory Commission (FERC). "When I arrived at FERC," recalls Wellinghoff, "I wanted to get a feel for the place and find out what everybody did. I talked to my fellow Commissioners. We work very collaboratively and we understood the two laws that FERC administers (the Federal Power Act and the Natural Gas Act). We don't think in partisan terms. We look at rates and make judgments. When we have differences, they are substantive and not political. It is not a partisan agency. I enjoy being here."

The mission of FERC is to assist consumers in obtaining reliable, efficient, and sustainable energy services at a reasonable cost through regulatory and market means. The agency regulates the interstate transmission of electricity, natural gas terminals, and interstate natural gas pipelines. It also licenses hydropower projects. It has a budget of $304 million and a staff of 1,480.

Wellinghoff concluded that he needed to create two new offices within FERC to better align the agency for the future. Wellinghoff recalls, "I thought we needed to analyze new ideas. There were specific issues on which I wanted to work. I thought we needed a new policy office. We now have 11 offices, including a new Office of Energy Policy Innovation and an Office of Energy Infrastructure Security. In creating the Office of Energy Infrastructure Security, we needed to have more expertise on the Interstate grid to mitigate threats, including cyber threats and physical threats. This has been an extremely successful office. It has helped us become better prepared to work on cybersecurity and other infrastructure issues."

During Wellinghoff's tenure in leading FERC, the agency developed a strategic plan. "The key," says Wellinghoff, "is having a vision and a plan. We incorporated other Commissioners' views and priorities into our strategic plan. A second key is that you need a competent staff. You should then be aware of opportunities for positive actions."

Another key component of the job of a regulator is reaching out to stakeholders. "I spend a lot of time with stakeholders," says Wellinghoff. "I spend as much time as I can with them. I talk to consumer groups, power groups, pipelines and transmission operators." As part of its outreach to increase stakeholder involvement, FERC organizes technical conferences and workshops designed to explain and explore issues related to the development and implementation of its policies. The Commission also holds regional conferences to identify infrastructure conditions, needs and investments, as well as environmental and landowner concerns.

Appendix to Chapter 5
Profiles of Regulators Interviewed

Michael R. Bromwich

Tenure
Mr. Bromwich was selected to serve as Director of the Bureau of Ocean Energy Management, Regulation and Enforcement (BOEMRE) in June 2010. After the reorganization of BOEMRE, Mr. Bromwich served as the first Director of the Bureau of Safety and Environmental Enforcement. He resigned from that position in November 2011.

Present Position
Michael R. Bromwich is a litigation partner in Goodwin Procter's Washington, D.C. and New York offices, and a member of the firm's Securities Litigation & White Collar Defense Group.

Private Sector Experience
Prior to his selection as Director of BOEMRE, Mr. Bromwich was a Litigation Partner at Fried Frank Harris Shriver & Jacobson. He has also been a Partner in the Washington, D.C. office of Mayer, Brown & Platt and an associate in the Washington, D.C. office of Foley & Lardner.

Federal Government Experience
From 1994 to 1999, Mr. Bromwich served as Inspector General for the Department of Justice. From 1987 to 1989, Mr. Bromwich served as Associate Counsel in the Office of Independent Counsel for Iran-Contra. From 1983 to 1987, Mr. Bromwich served as an Assistant U.S. Attorney in the U.S. Attorney's Office for the Southern District of New York. He served as Deputy Chief and Chief of the Office's Narcotics Unit.

Education
Mr. Bromwich received his undergraduate degree, *summa cum laude,* from Harvard College in 1976. He received his law degree from the Harvard Law School in 1980 and a master's degree in Public Policy from Harvard's John F. Kennedy School of Government the same year.

Reflecting on Serving in BOEMRE
"This has been on the whole an extremely satisfying and enjoyable experience. In a career where I have spent 14 years in four very different public-sector jobs, I would say this has been the most satisfying single year of public service. I helped an agency that was in a very deep hole and helped to bring it back when many people—in and out of government—had given up on it. There is a lot of satisfaction in doing this."

Margaret A. Hamburg

Tenure
Dr. Hamburg was nominated by President Obama to serve as Commissioner of the Food and Drug Administration (FDA), Department of Health and Human Services, in March 2009, and confirmed by the U.S. Senate in May 2009.

Non-Profit Experience
Before being confirmed as Commissioner of FDA, Dr. Hamburg was the senior scientist at the Nuclear Threat Initiative. She also served as the foundation's Vice President for Biological Programs at the Initiative.

Photo: Stephen Voss

Local Government Experience
From 1991 to 1997, Dr. Hamburg served as Commissioner of the New York City Department of Health and Hygiene.

Federal Government Experience
From 1997 to 2001, Dr. Hamburg served as Assistant Secretary for Planning and Evaluation in the Department of Health and Human Services. From 1989 to 1990, she served as Assistant Director of the National Institute of Allergy and Infectious Diseases, National Institutes of Health. From 1986 to 1988, she served as Special Assistant to the Director of the Office of Disease Prevention and Health Promotion, Department of Health and Human Services.

Education
Dr. Hamburg graduated from Harvard Medical School. She received a B.A. degree from Harvard University.

Reflecting on Public Service
"I would encourage people to come into public service. You cannot always accomplish everything you want, but you can have a huge impact. You can gain different perspectives and have an extraordinary experience."

Allison M. Macfarlane

Tenure

Dr. Macfarlane was nominated by President Obama to serve as Chairman of the Nuclear Regulatory Commission (NRC) in May 2012, and confirmed by the United States Senate in June 2012. In March 2013, Dr. Macfarlane was renominated by President Obama to serve for a full five-year term, and reconfirmed in June 2013.

Academic Experience

Prior to being confirmed as Chairman of the NRC, Dr. Macfarlane was an Associate Professor of Environmental Science and Policy at George Mason University. During her aca-  demic career, she held fellowships at Radcliffe College, MIT, and Stanford and Harvard Universities. From 1998 to 2000 she was a Social Science Research Fellow-MacArthur Foundation Fellow in International Peace and Security. During her academic tenures, she served on National Academy of Sciences panels on nuclear energy and nuclear weapons issues. From 2003 to 2004, she was on the faculty at Georgia Tech in Earth Science and International Affairs. Her academic research focused on environmental policy and international security issues associated with nuclear energy, especially spent nuclear fuel and the back-end of the nuclear fuel cycle.

Federal Government Experience

Dr. Macfarlane served as a member of the Blue Ribbon Commission on America's Nuclear Future.

Education

Dr. Macfarlane received a doctorate in geology from the Massachusetts Institute of Technology and a Bachelor of Science degree in geology from the University of Rochester.

Reflecting on Leading in Government

In August 2013, Dr. Macfarlane told the *Washington Post*, "I've developed a very inclusive, collegial style of leadership. I'm not hierarchical and I expect the folks who are supposedly below me to be more of my equals. I expect to have a back and forth with them, where I respect what they say and they respect what I say. I think that creating that kind of respect and openness makes employees feel better and then work better. Giving your colleagues the respect that's due to them also means that you meet with them frequently and you understand their views, but that you ultimately make your own decisions." (Fox)

Joseph A. (Joe) Main

Tenure
Mr. Main was nominated by President Obama as Assistant Secretary of Labor for Mine Safety and Health (MSHA) in July 2009, and confirmed by the U.S. Senate in October 2009.

Private Sector Experience
Prior to being confirmed as Assistant Secretary, Mr. Main was an independent mine safety consultant. Mr. Main began working in coal mines in 1967. In 1974, Mr. Main joined the United Mine Workers of America (UMWA) to be an Assistant to the International President. In 1976, he joined the Safety Division of the UMWA, serving as Safety Inspector, Administrative Assistant, and Deputy Director. In 1982, Mr. Main was appointed Administrator of the UMWA Occupational Health and Safety Department.

Education
Mr. Main attended the National Mine Health and Safety Academy.

Reflecting on Serving at MSHA
"My goal has always been to make life better for miners. Miners are our first priority, as are their families.

"I'm proud that I was able to keep the agency running in spite of Upper Big Branch. We had a successful strategy in place and we kept it going. We kept doing our work, while also responding to requests from Congress. We had to respond to all the issues raised by Upper Big Branch. The key thing is to stay focused.

"The job is tougher than I thought. It's been crisis after crisis. You constantly ask yourself 'How did this happen?' You have to find the confidence in yourself. It was quite an experience to go to the White House. I hadn't slept much in two weeks and I was at the White House to give the President news about the event. You have to be able to manage stress in these situations."

David L. Strickland

Tenure

Mr. Strickland was nominated by President Obama to serve as Administrator of the National Highway Traffic Safety Administration on December 4, 2009, and confirmed by the U.S. Senate on December 24, 2009.

Federal Government Experience

Prior to being confirmed as Administrator, Mr. Strickland served from 2001 to 2009 as Senior Democratic Counsel to the Subcommittee on Consumer Protection, Product Safety, and Insurance of the U.S. Senate Committee on Commerce, Science, and Transportation.

Education

Mr. Strickland received his J.D. degree from Harvard Law School in 1993, and his B.S. degree in Communication Studies and Political Science at Northwestern University in 1990.

Reflecting on the Next Set of Challenges at NHTSA

"We are going to have to devote more attention to pedestrian safety issues. We have more bike riders and walkers now. We are developing regulations in this area. We are also doing some pedestrian pilot projects and are making progress in this area. I see this as a long-term issue and we have to increase safety awareness on this.

"Our next big horizon is crash avoidance. We are working on evaluating the new technologies in this area. Electric cars will also be making a big difference. We will work with manufacturers on safer and greener products. A remaining question is how we go about updating the CAFE fuel economy standards."

Inez Moore Tenenbaum

Tenure
Ms. Tenenbaum was nominated by President Obama on June 9, 2009 to serve as the ninth Chairman of the U.S. Consumer Product Safety Commission, and confirmed by the U.S. Senate on June 19, 2009. Ms. Tenenbaum announced her departure from CPSCP in October 2013 after completion of her four-year term.

Present Position
Ms. Tenenbaum is an attorney with Nelson Mullins Riley & Scarborough LLP.

Private Sector Experience
Prior to being confirmed as Chairman, Ms. Tenenbaum served as Special Counsel to the McNair Law Firm in the area of public school finance. Ms. Tenenbaum practiced health, environmental, and public interest law with the firm Sinkler & Boyd, P.A.

State Government Experience
Ms. Tenenbaum was elected South Carolina's State Superintendent of Education in 1998 and completed her second term in 2007. Ms. Tenenbaum also served as the Director of Research for the Medical, Military, Public and Municipal Affairs Committee of the South Carolina House of Representatives. She carried out the Committee's responsibilities for all legislation relating to public health, the environment, child welfare, social services, adult and juvenile corrections, state military affairs, and local government.

Non-Profit Experience
Ms. Tenenbaum served as an attorney at the South Carolina Center for Family Policy.

Education
Ms. Tenenbaum received her B.S. degree in 1972 and Master of Education degree in 1974 from the University of Georgia and her law degree in 1986 from the University of South Carolina.

Reflecting on the Next Set of Challenges at CPSC
"I'd like to cut back on our rulemaking activities. I want to spend more time now on developing partnerships and working with manufacturing groups. I want to expand our outreach. I want us to do more education and outreach. We want to do more prevention. We want to work closely with manufacturers because voluntary standards are the first step for the agency."

Jon Wellinghoff

Tenure
Mr. Wellinghoff was named Chairman of
the Federal Energy Regulatory Commission
(FERC) by President Obama in March 2009. He
was nominated to complete the remainder of a
two-year term as Commissioner in March 2006,
and confirmed by the U.S. Senate in July 2006.
He was nominated to a full five-year term on
December 11, 2007, and confirmed by the U.S.
Senate on December 19, 2007.

Private Sector Experience
Prior to being confirmed as a Commissioner of
the FERC, Mr. Wellinghoff was in private law
practice, focusing on renewable energy, energy
efficiency, and distributed generation. He also served as Managing Principal and
Regulatory Attorney, Efficient Energy Systems, Inc.

Federal Government Experience
Mr. Wellinghoff served as Assistant Staff Counsel to the Consumer Subcommittee
of the Committee on Commerce, Science, and Transportation, United States Senate.
He also served as a Staff Attorney in the Energy and Product Information Division,
Federal Trade Commission.

State Government Experience
Mr. Wellinghoff served two terms as the State of Nevada's first Consumer Advocate
for Customers of Public Utilities. He also served as a Staff Counsel to the Nevada's
Public Utilities Commission, as well as Assistant to the Commissioner.

Local Government Experience
Mr. Wellinghoff served as a Deputy District Attorney, Consumer Fraud Division,
Office of the District Attorney for the County of Washoe, Nevada.

Education
Mr. Wellinghoff received his Bachelor of Science degree from the University of
Nevada, Reno. He received an M.A.T. degree from Howard University and his law
degree from the Antioch School of Law.

Reflecting on Serving in FERC
"We have a very dedicated staff. They know our mission is to ensure fair and just
rates. I am very happy with the staff. I have never seen a better group and never had
a better experience with a government agency. The agency works very well."

Chapter Six

The Infrastructors

Understanding the Job of the Infrastructor

During our interviews for this project, we invited a group of political executives to participate who appeared at first to be only loosely connected: Jonathan Adelstein at RUS, Arun Majumdar at ARPA-E, Victor Mendez at FHWA, and Joseph Szabo at FRA. By the time the project was completed, we realized that they had much in common. All facilitate the development and enhancement of the nation's economic infrastructure. All are seeking cheaper and better ways to provide energy, highways, broadband, and railroads. Their efforts directly enable our nation's economic growth. We discovered that in different ways, each is focused on developing a crucial aspect of the nation's infrastructure.

During the period in which we interviewed them, all four were involved in the implementation of the American Recovery and Reinvestment Act. In two agencies, RUS and FRA, Recovery Act activities substantially transformed the organizations into faster, more flexible agencies. In the case of ARPA-E, a

The Infrastructors
Jonathan S. Adelstein, page 135
Administrator, Rural Utilities Service (RUS), Department of Agriculture
Arun Majumdar, page 137
Director, Advanced Research Projects Agency-Energy (ARPA-E), Department of Energy
Victor M. Mendez, page 140
Administrator, Federal Highway Administration (FHWA), Department of Transportation
Joseph C. Szabo, page 142
Administrator, Federal Railroad Administration (FRA), Department of Transportation

new agency was built from the ground up to support and develop transformative energy approaches and technologies. For FHWA, the Recovery Act provided increased funding for highway infrastructure projects. All faced the challenge of publishing notices of funding, receiving and reviewing applications, and making awards—all in a very short timespan under increased scrutiny and transparency. In the case of three of the agencies—FRA, RUS, and FHWA—the Recovery Act dramatically increased their workload. "Getting the broadband money out was really a major accomplishment for us," recalls Adelstein. "You have to understand that our workload increased 20 times over our previous workload."

Key Components of the Job of the Infrastructor

The infrastructors uniquely blend several key job roles:
* Instructor
* Producer
* Engineer

Serving as an Instructor

All four political executives profiled in this chapter had substantial outreach and instructor responsibilities in their positions. They all had to collaborate with their stakeholder groups, as well as educate them on the government's funding availability for infrastructure. All viewed information sharing with stakeholders as part of their jobs. Because of their educational role and their role in infrastructure development, we labeled this group as the infrastructors.

While we were familiar with the traditional government grant-making process, we found that all four individuals profiled in this chapter played a teaching/instructor role to state governments, their respective industries, applicants for funding, and the recipients of their funding. Building the nation's infrastructure is not a "hands-off" activity. At RUS, staff was active in reaching out to organizations that had not applied in the first round of applications. Adelstein recalls, "We got people to apply in the second round who had not applied in the first round. We developed an interactive process in which we communicated more effectively with potential grantees. This process led to the outcomes we desired. We got some good applications. We wanted to encourage the right people to apply." In addi-

---

Selecting an Infrastructor

In Chapter One, we discuss how important it is for the Office of Presidential Personnel (OPP) to identify the right set of experiences for political executives. This is especially crucial in the selection of infrastructors. OPP must determine the right mix of experience for these positions. Should they emphasize the technical/engineering aspects of these jobs, or the collaborative nature of the positions? There will also be times in an agency's history when an individual with a strong production background will be needed.

Regardless of the mix of experience selected, we believe that the ability (and experience) to effectively collaborate should become a requirement for infrastructor positions. In building the nation's infrastructure, the federal government has become a funder to other organizations (state and local governments, the private sector, nonprofit organizations) that actually build or create the infrastructure required. Thus, ability to work with and to share information with the "builders" has now become crucial.

tion to reaching out to new applicants, RUS sent selected first-round submissions (which had not been accepted) back to applicants to be revised and resubmitted in the second round. These efforts, believes Adelstein, resulted in improved applications in the second round.

A significant stakeholder for both Victor Mendez and Joseph Szabo is state government. Because of his background as Director of the Arizona Department of Transportation, Mendez brought the perspective of a state transportation official to DOT headquarters in Washington. A major priority for Mendez was to find new ways for FHWA to engage with the states. One new vehicle for FHWA was the Every Day Counts (EDC) program. As part of that program, FHWA partnered with the Association of State Highway Transportation Officials (ASHTO) to host 10 Regional Innovation Summits. The summits are a vehicle for FHWA to disseminate EDC strategies and technologies. The EDC program also enabled Mendez to engage the transportation industry to find innovative ways to reduce the time it takes to complete highway construction projects (see *The Every Day Counts Program: The Department of Transportation* on page 33 for a further discussion of this initiative).

In the case of Joseph Szabo and FRA, the agency had to take an aggressive role in reaching out to the states to assist them in completing the Stakeholder Agreements with rail owners or rail operators who would operate the proposed projects—a key requirement to receiving Recovery Act funding. Szabo recalls, "We thought the states and the private sector would be able to negotiate the agreements, but that wasn't happening. We had to help them on their service agreements. We helped get them to where they needed to be." This involvement followed an aggressive outreach at the start of the program. FRA held listening sessions with key stakeholders at which they explained the high-speed rail initiative, and received feedback on the program.

Outreach was also high on the agenda of ARPA-E Director Majumdar during his first year. A major part of an infrastructor's job is reaching out to the community in two-way conversations—both to learn what the community is doing and to inform the community of federal government funding opportunities. Majumdar recalls, "I reached out to universities. I set up informal meetings to just chat with experts to find out their issues and thoughts. I wanted to know what people were already doing."

The teaching role is also seen in working with Congress. Majumdar says, "I tell them (Congress) what we do. I like to explain our agency in laymen's terms. I try to make it easy for them to understand and talk to them in terms of impacts and savings, which gives them the big picture."

Serving as a Producer

All four political executives had to aggressively manage their organizations to produce the results expected of them. In all four cases, the expectation was to get the money out quickly in response to the Recovery Act. At FRA, Szabo had to borrow staff from other parts of the Department of Transportation to handle the increased workload. Szabo, like Adelstein, had to work with his agency to speed it up and make it more flexible. Just like the producers discussed in Chapter Four, the four individuals profiled in this chapter had to closely manage their organizations' inputs and outputs and make sure all the organizational tasks associated with the Recovery Act were completed in a timely, efficient, and transparent manner.

Serving as an Engineer

All four jobs require substantial expertise. In the case of Mendez and Majumdar, they had the engineering backgrounds necessary in their respective positions. In launching ARPA-E, Majumdar confronted many of the same challenges faced by the scientists profiled in Chapter Seven: serving as the interface between his organization and political leaders in Congress and in government, contributing to the national debate about new approaches to energy, and strengthening (or in this case, building) the institution. Majumdar devoted a substantial amount of his time and energy to recruiting talent to join the newly created ARPA-E. In reflecting on his tenure at ARPA-E, Majumdar says that one of his proudest accomplishments is recruiting a first-rate technical team at ARPA-E.

In the case of Adelstein, his service as a Congressional staff member and Commissioner at the Federal Trade Commission gave him expert knowledge of the issues associated with broadband. Joseph Szabo's firsthand experience working in the rail industry assisted him in understanding the technical aspects of rail.

Infrastructors in Action

Jonathan S. Adelstein at the Rural Utilities Service, Department of Agriculture

"When I got here," recalls Jonathan Adelstein, "I quickly found that we had a crisis in management regarding the information technology system we were using to accept applications for broadband projects. The process was in meltdown due to the unprecedented number of applications for loans and grants. RUS was working with another agency on application intake and it just wasn't working.

"It was a pretty stressful situation in the beginning. On top of the technology problems with incoming applications, there were issues arising with the way the rules had been set up. We had to quickly dig out of a hole on the broadband program. The rules for the first funding round had been put together before I arrived and the program was not working in the way that those who put it together had anticipated. The agency also had not had a boss for awhile prior to my arrival. So there was also a lot of unfinished business to complete."

The Rural Utilities Service traces its roots back to the Rural Electrification Administration (REA), a New Deal agency created in 1936 with the primary goal of promoting rural electrification. In 1994, REA was reorganized into the Rural Utilities Services (RUS). "RUS has a different history from other parts of the Department of Agriculture," says Adelstein. "We were put together with other rural development agencies."

Today, RUS is one of three agencies that make up the Department of Agriculture's Rural Development mission area, which is headed by the USDA Under Secretary for Rural Development. The other agencies reporting to the Under Secretary include the Rural Housing Service and the Rural Business and Cooperative Service. RUS has a budget of over $9 billion and over 700 staff working to deliver the electric, telecommunications, water, and environmental programs of the agency.

The challenge was clear. The American Recovery and Reinvestment Act provided $7.2 billion to the Department of Commerce's National Telecommunications and Information Administration (NTIA) and the Department of Agriculture's Rural Utilities Service to expand access to broadband services in the United States. The funding was administered through the Broadband Technology Opportunities Program (BTOP) at NTIA and the Broadband Initiatives Program (BIP) administered by RUS. BIP provided over $3.5 billion in funding for loans, grants, and loan/grant combinations to assist in rapidly expanding the access and quality of broadband services across rural America. The challenge was both to get the money out and to do so without any waste or abuse. The goal of the program was to provide access to over seven million residents and 350,000 businesses in rural America.

In addition to implementing the Recovery Act's rural broadband initiative, Adelstein also had to continue to manage the other programs within RUS, which included the electric program, the water and waste program, and the loan programs. "I had always thought of the Rural Utilities Service as a scrappy little agency in a big behemoth of a Department, with an independent streak," recalls Adelstein. Mr. Adelstein had the opportunity to test RUS to see how scrappy it really was.

A key step for Adelstein was to set his agenda and decide on its implementation. "I had to focus on the execution of the broadband program," states Adelstein.

"I had to defend its progress on the Hill, and that meant moving the ball forward so I had a better case to make. This became my key role. So there was a fairly set agenda when I arrived which I couldn't change until we launched the second round of funding. The policy decisions of the first round had already been made. As we entered into the second phase of the broadband initiative, we were able to draw on the lessons of the first round." In the second round of applications, Adelstein made significant changes. "First," recalls Adelstein, "we had another agency managing the intake contract and we worked hard to better manage that process. It worked much more smoothly thereafter.

"Second, the Vice President encouraged us to become more flexible in implementing the program. His support of flexibility was very important, as I used it as a mantra during the policy development process. We got more flexibility and a better balance between grants and loans, creating a new 75 percent grant/25 percent loan combination which contained incentives for higher loan components. Obtaining this flexibility was essential in reaching the most underserved areas. We worked closely with the White House on it. In round two, we were driving the process, which made it easier for us to determine what changes needed to be made."

In defining his job, Adelstein says, "My job was to let the staff see the goal and keep the political pressures off them. We didn't let politics interfere with our awards process. I was aware of the politics of it all but I didn't let it interfere with the agency. We made our decisions on merit. That took some time. I couldn't micromanage it, but I tried to stay focused on our job and we exceeded expectations. It was a collaborative process. I think this will have a long-term impact on how the agency operates. We knew the goals we wanted to accomplish.

"You have to understand that our workload increased 20 times over our previous workload," emphasizes Adelstein. "This was a massive increase in funding which had to be distributed in a small amount of time. Our staff really did step up to get this done. We proved the naysayers wrong. We showed that we are more flexible than people thought we were. We pushed the organization to become more flexible and to move faster. Everybody worked together. The agency became less balkanized. We changed how the agency was operating. The agency had been around for 75 years and they had never done anything like this. We worked as a team. We pulled it off."

Arun Majumdar at the Advanced Research Projects Agency-Energy, Department of Energy

"I had a very good and fulfilling academic career in California," recounts Arun Majumdar. "I would have been happy to stay in academia, but the ARPA-E opportunity came up. I thought the time was

ripe to look at energy and the environment. It was an opportunity to shape a new program in an important area.

"My first day was October 26, 2009, when I met with Secretary Chu, who was in California on that day to announce the first set of ARPA-E awards. I then took the red-eye flight to Washington that night, so I could arrive and start the job the next morning. I found a team that was already here and very hard at work to get the program up and running."

The Advanced Research Projects Agency-Energy (ARPA-E) was created by the America COMPETES Act, which was signed into law in August 2007. The creation of ARPA-E had been recommended by the National Academies in a 2006 report. While ARPA-E was authorized in 2007, it did not have an initial budget until April 2009 when the American Recovery and Reinvestment Act provided $400 million in funding. The first Funding Opportunity Announcement was made in May 2009, with the first awards being made in October. In response to this Announcement, ARPA-E received 3,700 concept papers. From the 3,700 concept papers ARPA-E requested 334 full proposals and selected 37 projects for funding.

The challenge was clear: to launch a new organization, develop program areas, make awards, provide technical oversight to awardees, and demonstrate results in the creation of transformational energy technologies. The unique mandate to ARPA-E is to support energy technologies that would fundamentally transform how the nation uses energy. The agency was created to make revolutionary improvements in energy, not evolutionary improvements.

Majumdar faced three distinct tasks during his first two years at ARPA-E. The first task was to focus externally to form new relationships crucial to the success of ARPA-E. The second task was to focus internally on creating a new government organization. The third task was to launch the right projects and start demonstrating results.

In undertaking his external outreach activities, Majumdar recalls, "During my first days, I reached out to key people in the Department of Energy. It was a new agency and I needed to reach out. I put together an advisory committee of notable individuals in the field to get their feedback. I wanted to know if we were doing the right things. I also spent time reaching out to the Office of Management and Budget during my first months on the job. I found that understanding Congress was really crucial. I was learning on the job."

The outreach activities were crucial in launching the organization. "I reached out to other relevant government agencies to see if there is synergy with what we do. I reached out to universities. I set up informal meetings to just chat with experts to find out their issues and thoughts. I wanted to know what people were already doing. We decided to have a big meeting in Washington, D.C., in which we would bring together all of our stakeholders. We held the meeting just two months after we decided to undertake it. It was quite an impressive event. People were engaged. We want to be a catalyst for change." Based on his outreach activities, Majumdar concludes, "There is no substitute for retailing. You have to go see people one on one and get to meet them. You also have to meet the right people."

Majumdar was very aware of the opportunities inherent in creating a totally new organization. "We came in with a clean slate," says Majumdar. "There was no 30-year history to overcome. I think it is difficult to change existing organizations. The pace of change in older organizations is much slower. The pace here is really fast. We have a 'let's get it done' attitude. We have a sense of urgency. We are, in fact, building the plane while we are flying it."

According to Majumdar, the next step after hiring the right people is to create the right culture in which they can flourish. "I want innovation to be the DNA of ARPA-E. It is part of our core strategy. Once you get people here, you have to give them the freedom to solve problems. We want people who like being challenged. You have to create an atmosphere to allow them to have a real impact. You need to create a culture of openness and discussion. You don't want a top-down environment. What I have done is to create a culture which empowers people at ARPA-E, while also holding them accountable. I want people to succeed and want to create an environment for success. So the key elements to creating a culture are getting talent, creating an open dialogue, and allowing people to realize their potential."

The final internal task facing Majumdar was to create the operating style of ARPA-E in developing program areas and selecting projects. "Our model," says Majumdar, "is to give people 'white space' and let them pitch an idea. We have good exchanges when we bring people together. We discuss ideas and exchange opinions. We are looking for big changes, not incremental changes. This process might take six to eight months until a program manager has put together a project. It all begins with a program idea. We then hold a technical deep dive or a workshop. Our program managers are key. There is the concept paper review and full proposal review prior to project selection. After project selection, they become part of the team of people we support. The program managers provide technical advice and visit the projects twice a year and sit down with awardees to provide technical guidance. We want to make sure the idea succeeds."

In undertaking the third key task of picking the right set of projects, Majumdar says, "I think we are looking at the right kinds of technology. We are imagining new ways to approach energy. I think we have done very well. We are doing some neat stuff. We have the private sector fully engaged. We are telling people about our early successes." One set of projects that ARPA-E is watching closely are renewable power projects that focus on innovative technologies in several sustainable energy areas such as extremely efficient photovoltaic solar collectors, wind turbines, and geothermal energy. Another promising area is the development of batteries for transportation, which would make electric cars cheaper and with longer range than those based on gasoline technology.

Victor M. Mendez at the Federal Highway Administration, Department of Transportation

"I was anxious to get started," recalls Victor Mendez. "The confirmation process had taken longer than I had anticipated. I was nominated in April 2009 and confirmed in July.

"I had experience with the Federal Highway Administration (FHWA) during my time as Director of the Arizona Department of Transportation. I had a good sense of the career leadership at FHWA. I thought they were very solid. And I thought that FHWA was well positioned to make a difference."

The Federal Highway Administration has a long history. A predecessor agency, the Office of Road Inquiry, was founded in 1893. In 1905, the name of that organization was changed to the Office of Public Roads and it was placed in the Department of Agriculture. The name was changed in 1915 (to the Bureau of Public Roads) and in 1939 (to the Public Roads Administration). The Public Roads Administration was abolished in 1949 and was then reestablished as the Bureau of Public Roads and placed in the Department of Commerce. The Federal Highway Administration was created as part of the Department of Transportation legislation in 1966 and began operations in DOT in 1967.

FHWA has a budget of $42 billion and a staff of nearly 3,000 civil servants. The FY 12 budget requested a major increase in FHWA's funding ($70 billion) to rebuild the nation's infrastructure of highways and bridges.

The challenge became quickly apparent to Mendez upon his arrival. "We decided on several priorities," recalls Mendez. "First was the Recovery Act, on which we had a major role. Second was the Reauthorization Act. Third was innovation, because I felt that transportation projects were taking too long to complete. We need to cut delivery time. Finally, there were environmental issues. We wanted more green options for FHWA. We had to reduce our carbon footprint.

"I spent time on the Recovery Act from day one," says Mendez. "My top priority was to focus on what we should be doing to implement the Act. We had to ensure that funds to the states got allocated and that they received their funding in time. We didn't want any state to lose funding by not getting their funding requests to us on time. We wanted to put people to work. Nearly all the states did a good job in getting their funding requests to us. Secretary LaHood and the Vice President did, however, have to make some phone calls to the states. I think we had to call 10 or 12 states to speed up their request for funding.

"We got all of the funds out by February 27, 2010," says Mendez. "Our deadline had been March 1. Meeting the deadline took a tremendous effort by our staff and I'm very proud of them. Then on Monday, March 2, we had to start to furlough our staff due to the Congressional standoff on unemployment benefits. People often talk about how government should be run like a business. In this case, I don't think business would treat its people this way. Furloughing people is not treating them very well. This is not a way to run any type of business. We want high energy and high performance from our employees and then something like this happens. We did the best we could in this situation and tried to limit the impact of the furlough."

Essential to the successful implementation of the Recovery Act was enlisting the support of FHWA workers and stakeholders. Mendez comments, "I learned a lot from working with Janet Napolitano when she was Governor of Arizona. She knew about the importance of working with stakeholders and employees. I've learned you have to work with different groups of people and it is best to be open with them."

In addition to communicating with his employees, Mendez also wanted to improve communication and the relationship between Washington and state transportation officials. "There is a real gap," reflects Mendez, "between people in Washington, D.C., and people out in the states who are actually delivering. I've been on the receiving end at the state level, so I understand the types of engagement you can have with the federal government. I found that people in D.C. often don't have a lot of 'on-the-ground' experience. I've tried to create new ways for FHWA to engage with the states. My only disappointment is that I would have liked to have spent more time with states. I came here to work with the states and then my attention quickly shifted to the Recovery Act."

One initiative to improve engagement with all stakeholders, including states and FHWA employees, was the Every Day Counts program launched by Mendez. "I talked to employees and stakeholders about this. We are trying to reduce project time for our construction projects by 50 percent, as well as to increase efficiency. We wanted ideas to improve operations. We didn't want to do a lot of studies, we wanted to implement new ideas."

The Every Day Counts program became a major vehicle for Mendez to work with the transportation industry. "I was concerned about the way the industry conducts business," comments Mendez. "Our construction projects take too long. It often takes 13 years to finish a project. I wanted to raise this as an issue and see if we could make progress in reducing the time it takes for major projects. I wanted to put more focus on innovation in the industry and demonstrate that shorter projects could be undertaken. People said that we could cut the time by 10 percent, but I said 'Why not cut it by 50 percent?' I wanted to find out whether we could use technology to be more innovative and could implement projects faster." In his previous position as Director of the Arizona Department of Transportation, Mendez received much praise for overseeing the building of the Regional Freeway System in the Phoenix area six years ahead of schedule.

Joseph C. Szabo at the Federal Railroad Administration, Department of Transportation

"With a strong background in railroad safety and operations, I was thrilled for the opportunity to join the Federal Railroad Administration (FRA)," recalls Joseph Szabo. "Through the Recovery Act, we were providing a boost to local economies across America by investing in rail infrastructure. As a result, the high-speed rail program was being built from the ground up and we had to ensure it was done in an expedited and efficient manner. Since my first day at FRA, we were squarely focused on launching the high-speed rail program. It was a time of change and growth for the agency and the FRA team was up for the challenge."

The Federal Railroad Administration was created as part of the Department of Transportation Act in 1966. It inherited the railroad safety functions previously performed by the Interstate Commerce Commission (which was abolished by Congress in 1995). The Federal Railroad Safety Act of 1970 and subsequent legislation granted FRA plenary authority in regulating railroad safety in areas such as the inspection, testing, and maintenance of track, signals, and mechanical equipment, as well as railroad operating practices, hazardous materials, and other areas.

The signing of the American Recovery and Reinvestment Act of 2009 on February 17, 2009, expanded the mission and reach of FRA. The Recovery Act gave FRA responsibility to assist states, localities, other federal agencies, and industry and transportation sector stakeholders to ensure the appropriate coordination among all parties in managing Recovery Act rail investments. FRA was tasked to administer $8 billion in high-speed rail grants, something unimaginable in the past.

The enormity of the challenge was clear to Szabo when he arrived. While his interest had long been in railroad safety and operations, Szabo found that implementation of the Obama Administration's high-speed rail program would take much of his time and energy. He faced the challenge of leading FRA during a significant transformation as it evolved from being primarily a railroad safety regulatory agency to one also responsible for grant management of a sizeable new program that happened to be a top DOT priority. In addition to administering a high volume of grant dollars, Szabo had the responsibility to ensure that quality projects were selected through a merit-driven process, and that the funds were spent in a prudent and transparent manner.

The challenge of overseeing a Presidential and departmental priority initiative should not be underestimated. Szabo reflects, "We clearly had the attention of the Secretary and Deputy Secretary. We were coordinating numerous activities simultaneously and providing daily progress reports. We were operating under immense scrutiny while facilitating change, and we had to get the job done right.

If not, our missteps would have been magnified. However, it is extremely reward-ing to work on a Presidential spotlight initiative and know we're transforming the way Americans will travel now and in the future."

Instead of focusing solely on railroad safety (as other administrators have done in the past), Szabo faced a challenge similar to that faced by Jonathan Adelstein at the Rural Utilities Service (RUS): transforming an old-line agency to undertake an entirely new set of activities under a very tight time schedule. That is, FRA had to establish a major grant program from the ground up, distributing $8 billion to states through the Recovery Act. In reflecting on his experience at FRA, Szabo says, "We really did transform the agency. Almost overnight, it went from being a relatively small safety agency to one that was also a grant-making organi-zation supporting both Amtrak and other passenger rail investment programs. We were required to strategically ramp up our efforts due to the wildly enthusiastic response of applicants seeking grant funds under a program that didn't yet exist."

Another change is that the agency, again much like RUS, had to become more agile. "A major accomplishment," says Szabo, "is that we became more proactive in getting out our rules and regulations on high-speed rail to ensure a fair and eq-uitable application evaluation and review process. We took great pains to look at things from our stakeholders' point of view and anticipate their needs."

In describing his relationship with the states, Szabo says, "The relationship between FRA and the states has evolved considerably. We had to adopt an aggressive approach to support our state partners if they were to successfully negotiate stakeholder agreements where needed. These so-called service outcome agreements (SOA) required states to secure the cooperation of freight railroads and/or entities that would ultimately operate the new and expanded intercity pas-senger rail services."

Working closely with the states required FRA to change the way it had cus-tomarily done business. Szabo recalls, "It meant we needed to fully understand the legitimate concerns and fears of stakeholders as they developed mutually ben-eficial agreements. It was a critical point in the process, and it proved that by bargaining in good faith, win-win outcomes could be reached."

In implementing its piece of the Recovery Act, FRA assumed a new role that it had not played before: that of technical advisor to the states. "It was a major undertaking to harness and leverage the necessary resources to provide such assis-tance," states Szabo. "For some states, we had to walk them through the complex, competitive application process and how to initiate and complete the stakeholder agreements. Many state departments of transportation had no dedicated railroad staff or divisions. Some had only one or two folks working on rail issues. Only a handful had a dozen or more working on rail issues. Assessing and addressing our own needs would prove to be critical in helping states define their own. It was an invaluable learning experience for our agency as we determined the most effec-tive tools and resources needed to provide that assistance."

Appendix to Chapter 6
Profiles of Infrastructors Interviewed

Jonathan S. Adelstein

Tenure
Mr. Adelstein was nominated by President Obama to serve as the Administrator of the Department of Agriculture's Rural Utilities Service in April 2009, and confirmed by the U.S. Senate in July 2009. Mr. Adelstein resigned his position in September 2012.

Present Position
Mr. Adelstein is President and Chief Executive Officer of PCIA–The Wireless Infrastructure Association.

Federal Government Experience
Prior to being confirmed as Administrator, Mr. Adelstein served as Commissioner of the Federal Communications Commission from 2002 to 2009. Previously, Mr. Adelstein worked for 15 years as a staff member in the United States Senate. During that time, he served as a senior legislative aide to Senate Majority Leader Tom Daschle, as a professional staff member on the Senate Special Committee on Aging, and as a legislative assistant to Senator Donald W. Riegle, Jr.

Academic Experience
Mr. Adelstein was a Teaching Fellow in the Department of History, Harvard University. Mr. Adelstein was also a Teaching Assistant in the Department of History, Stanford University.

Education
Mr. Adelstein received a B.A. in Political Science and an M.A. in History from Stanford University

Reflecting on the Future of RUS
"I've had a long interest in rural broadband development. I've been working on this for a long time. Rural broadband is a good investment and very cost-efficient. Its benefits spill over into health care, education, the environment, energy uses, and many other applications. It is an indispensable part of rural development. Rural areas need these projects or they may turn into ghost towns. It is like the impact in the past of rail lines or highways. Rural Americans need broadband for job development and to stimulate businesses in these areas. I'm convinced that it will save money if we do it right and not on the cheap. Rural areas have special needs. We want to get it done right."

Arun Majumdar

Tenure
Dr. Majumdar was nominated by President Obama to serve as the first Director of the Advanced Research Projects Agency-Energy (ARPA-E) in September 2009, and confirmed by the U.S. Senate in October 2009. Dr. Majumdar resigned his position in May 2012.

Present Position
Dr. Majumdar is Director of Energy Initiatives at Google.org, which develops technologies to help address global challenges and supports innovative partners through grants, investments, and in-kind resources.

Academic Experience
Prior to being confirmed as Director, Dr. Majumdar was the Associate Laboratory Director for Energy and Environment at Lawrence Berkeley National Laboratory and Professor of Mechanical Engineering and Materials Science and Engineering at the University of California, Berkeley. He served as head of the Berkeley National Laboratory's Environmental Energy Technology Division from 2007 to 2009. He has also been a faculty member at the University of California, Santa Barbara and at Arizona State University.

Education
Dr. Majumdar received his bachelor's degree in Mechanical Engineering at the Indian Institute of Technology, Bombay, in 1985 and his Ph.D. from the University of California, Berkeley in 1989.

Reflecting on Serving at ARPA-E
"This is my way of paying back to the nation. I'm an immigrant, so this is a real opportunity for me to serve my country. It's the best job I've ever had.

"My goal is to leave behind an organization with a set of core values and a talent pool that will position ARPA-E for the future. I want to build the organization which has a high level of technical excellence, which requires getting the right people."

Victor M. Mendez

Tenure
Mr. Mendez was nominated by President Obama to serve as Administrator of the Federal Highway Administration in April 2009, and confirmed by the U.S. Senate in July 2009.

State Government Experience
Prior to being confirmed as Administrator, Mr. Mendez served as Director of the Arizona Department of Transportation (ADOT) from 2001 to 2009. During his career at ADOT, he also served as Deputy Director and as a transportation engineer.

Federal Government Experience
Mr. Mendez worked as a civil engineer for the U.S. Forest Service in Oregon.

Education
Mr. Mendez earned a B.S. degree in Civil Engineering from the University of Texas at El Paso and an M.B.A. from Arizona State University.

Reflecting on Running FHWA
"I like what I do all day long. The job is a challenge but I enjoy it. We have a good leadership team and they are good to work with. If we see an issue, we deal with it. Everybody contributed to implementing the Recovery Act. We got that done."

Joseph C. Szabo

Tenure
Mr. Szabo was nominated by President Obama
to serve as Administrator of the Federal Railroad
Administration in March 2009, and confirmed
by the U.S. Senate in April 2009.

Private Sector Experience
Prior to being confirmed as Administrator, Mr.
Szabo served as State Legislative Director of the
United Transportation Union (UTU) and Vice
President of the Illinois State Federation of the
American Federation of Labor and Congress of
Industrial Organizations (AFL-CIO). He start-
ed his railroad career in 1976 with the Illinois
Central Railroad and worked in numerous

positions, including as a yard switcher, road trainman, and a commuter passenger
conductor.

State and Local Government Experience
Mr. Szabo served as Mayor of Riverdale, Illinois, a member of the South Suburban
Mayors Transportation Committee, and Vice Chairman of the Chicago Area
Transportation Study's Executive Committee. In 2002, he chaired the Governor's
Freight Rail Sub-Committee.

Education
Mr. Szabo holds a B.A. degree in Labor Relations from Governors State University.

Reflecting on Serving in the FRA
"This has been a fascinating time to be at FRA. We have awarded more than $8
billion in two years. I believe that most of my predecessors would agree that this
has probably been one of the most challenging undertakings ever for FRA: one that
fundamentally expanded the mission and scope of the agency forever.

"We not only had to enhance our own capacity, but that of other partners so we could
build the momentum which will ultimately change America's transportation landscape for the centuries to come. We were already good custodians of the taxpayers'
investment, but the high-speed program made protecting these investments more
important than ever. We are building the equivalent of the interstate highway system
and that took over 40 years to complete.

"I'm really proud of all the employees at FRA. They responded to the challenge and
have done an excellent job as we make history building a world-class rail network
for future generations. "

Chapter Seven

The Scientists

Understanding the Job of the Scientist

While nearly every federal Department funds research and development projects, there is a group of federal agencies solely dedicated to research, statistics, and analysis in specific scientific disciplines. We call these organizations the science agencies, led by individuals whom we have termed science political executives. The science political executives profiled in this chapter all share two key characteristics. First, they are highly qualified for their positions. In fact, calling them immensely qualified is not an overstatement. All have Ph.D.s in their respective fields and all have had long and distinguished careers prior to their Presidential appointments.

Second, they all have deep knowledge of their field. This deep knowledge enables them to communicate effectively both within and outside their organization. In addition, several brought deep knowledge about their organization to their positions as well. All five executives profiled had served in government previously, with Patrick Gallagher, Director of NIST, Marcia McNutt, Director of USGS, and Kathryn Sullivan, Deputy Administrator at NOAA, having prior experience in the agencies that they are now leading.

It is also important to note that science political executives tend to be among the few political appointees in their agencies. In the case of Gallagher, McNutt, and Richard Newell, Administrator of EIA, they are the only political appointee in the organization. In the case of Rebecca

The Scientists

Rebecca M. Blank, page 155

Under Secretary for Economic Affairs, Economics and Statistics Administration (ESA), Department of Commerce

Patrick D. Gallagher, page 157

Director, National Institute of Standards and Technology (NIST) and Under Secretary of Commerce for Standards and Technology, Department of Commerce

Marcia K. McNutt, page 159

Director, U.S. Geological Survey (USGS), Department of the Interior

Richard G. Newell, page 161

Administrator, U.S. Energy Information Administration (EIA), Department of Energy

Kathryn D. Sullivan, page 163

Deputy Administrator and Assistant Secretary of Commerce for Environmental Observation and Prediction, National Oceanic and Atmospheric Administration, Department of Commerce

Blank, former Commerce Under Secretary for Economic Affairs, there were only two other political appointees in her organization.

Key Components of the Job of the Scientist

The science political executives we interviewed all faced similar management challenges. In addition to their ongoing management roles, all define their positions as including the following:

- Guarding the scientific integrity of their organization
- Interfacing with the political leadership of their organization
- Making their organization relevant to government decision-making
- Strengthening their institution
- Reaching out to external stakeholders

Guarding the Scientific Integrity of Their Organization

All five of the individuals profiled emphasize the importance of scientific integrity. They all tell us that there is no margin of error in this role. Marcia McNutt says, "You need a strong firewall between USGS and the political chain of command. There is tension between keeping our peer-reviewed scientific studies independent until they are ready to be released. We share these scientific studies with the political appointees. I need to keep them informed and give them a heads-up at the appropriate time." Richard Newell comments, "I have to be sensitive not to blindside any of our political people on EIA reports." While needed by all political executives, good judgment and a sensitive political antenna are crucial to the success of a science political executive in order to maintain their credibility in both the scientific and political communities in which they travel.

After discussing their concern about potential conflicts between the scientific integrity of their organization and politics, none of the science political executives interviewed report any instances of political interference during their tenure. "I've been surprised," says McNutt, "at how rarely politics have intervened. We were involved in the Recovery Act. I didn't receive any requests for specific projects. We were doing what was right."

While government's science civil servants clearly recognize that politics is a component of life in government, there is great sensitivity to "too much politics." Gallagher recalls, "In Administrations of recent years, the position of NIST Director seemed somewhat more political than in the past—which it had never been before. That was a little unsettling to folks here, so they are glad now to be back in the days when a career person was selected for the Presidential appointment as Director."

Interfacing with the Political Leadership of Their Organization

Given that Gallagher, McNutt, and Newell are the sole political appointees in their organizations, this responsibility adds an additional complexity to their position. "I'm the only appointee here," says McNutt, "which has been difficult at times. There are meetings to which only I can go. My career Deputy can't replace me at these meetings." The role also requires the science political executive to know the Administration and their Secretary's agenda and to determine how their organization can help move that agenda along. In many cases, this requires the science political executive to make key connections to other political executives and to "work the process." McNutt says that she spent more than 60 percent of her time working closely with the Office of the Secretary and other political appointees in the Department of the Interior.

The job of the science political executive is also to know when there is a problem in the organization. The executive must then determine whether that problem needs to be brought to the attention of the Department's political team. Rebecca Blank describes her experience with the 2010 Census: "We have a good team on this. Nancy Potok, Deputy Under Secretary at ESA, has done the day-to-day oversight, so I've spent less time on this than I had imagined. I am brought in when there is a problem to deal with."

Making Their Organization Relevant to Government Decision-Making

All the science political executives profiled made great efforts to increase the relevance of their organization. In her position near the top of the Department of Commerce, Rebecca Blank spent much of her time talking with key individuals in the White House, the Council of Economic Advisors, and the National Economic Council to better understand their economic information needs. As a result of Blank's interactions with policy makers, the White House asked her organization to produce several key studies for them.

While wanting their organizations to be policy-relevant, science political executives walk a fine line between wanting to be relevant and helpful and not distorting their historic mission. This tension was clearly seen in Patrick Gallagher's participation in the Administration's review of cybersecurity and the development of new policies in this area. "I was concerned that the issue of cybersecurity might change the role of NIST," says Gallagher. "We have a clear role to play on the technology side of the issue. We did not, however, want to be put in the position of setting policy rules. That isn't the role of NIST. We need to continue to do what we do best. I worry about mission creep. I understand what my organization can add and I know our capabilities. Key is understanding your role."

Like the other science political executives profiled in this chapter, Newell sought to encourage greater use of EIA data by the Department while avoiding any hint of politicizing the data. "I want EIA to be viewed as independent," says Newell, "and we want to be a place where the Department can seek advice. I want EIA to do more analysis and help the Department more. We don't advocate, we analyze. I want us to provide input into policy making and provide higher quality analysis … It is important to note that our vision statement says that we are independent. We want to be impartial, but not irrelevant."

Strengthening the Institution

At their core, the science organizations in government are about people. While many of the science agencies have world-class equipment and facilities, we were told many times throughout our interviews about the importance of people.

Selecting Science Political Executives

We found that science political executives believe that the academic and non-profit sectors prepared them well for their present position. The common thread between universities, non-profits, and government science agencies is that all tend to be collegial and somewhat "flatter" than most organizations. In describing his transition from academic life to government, Richard Newell says, "I used the skills I gained in academia and non-profits to bring people together. My agency isn't like the private sector where I can just tell people what to do. Here, I have to use my interpersonal skills." Industry research and development laboratories often have the same collegial atmosphere, as do universities; these are institutions from which science political executives have been recruited in the past.

Sullivan believes that her experience running a non-profit organization prepared her well for her return to government. Sullivan says, "Running a non-profit was a good experience. It required focus and discipline, sound strategy and crisp execution, robust internal and external communications. We have to motivate people to invest precious time and money to visit a science museum. We built a new building during my tenure, which forced every facet of our operations to change. Our staff had to do things that they had never done before and do familiar things in altogether different ways. We had to invest on the front end and build new business processes. I had to make sure that we were having the right conversations—bringing all pertinent expertise and perspectives to bear—on each of these challenges during this transformation."

But most of all, science political executives need to be highly regarded and respected scientists with strong professional careers. The credential for receiving a Presidential appointment as an executive leading a government science agency is time spent in their discipline, not time spent on the campaign trail. In short, no amateurs need apply for a political appointment as an executive of a science agency.

"The Energy Information Administration is all about its people—federal employees and contractors," says Newell. "It is a people organization. We have 370 federal employees with about 200 contractors. We need to keep them and attract new people. I'm pleased that people in our community are asking me about whether there are any new positions at EIA."

Patrick Gallagher is very clear about his deep commitment to the institution: "I want to create an environment conducive for our scientists. We have world class scientists here. Our job is all about attracting people—hiring and then retaining them. Retaining people is always a challenge because they can make three or four times more money anywhere else, either in the academic community or industry. Not only am I impressed that NIST has three Nobel Prize winners here, I'm more impressed that all three have stayed."

One aspect of strengthening the institution is putting the agency on sound financial footing and receiving funding from Congress. Kathryn Sullivan, Deputy Administrator, NOAA, describes her experience working on the NOAA satellite programs: "Our joint satellite program had been progressing technically, but we were operating on a continuing resolution that provided less than half the funding needed to sustain that progress in FY 11. We had to move the needle. I met with stakeholders inside and out of government ... This is a long ballgame. We are putting our satellite programs on firm footing. These are seminal programs which must be fielded on schedule. We had to strengthen our analytical capabilities, scrub our requirements and cost figures. We also needed to communicate much more, get NOAA on some key radar screens again."

Reaching Out to External Stakeholders

Kathryn Sullivan described the importance of external stakeholders in her role as Acting Administrator of NOAA. Sullivan told the *Washington Post,* "Now that I'm in the lead seat, I understand more clearly the dynamics and importance of stakeholder engagement and the degree to which, in an agency like NOAA, there are many entities that feel they fully share the agency's passion and purpose and have an expectation of being accorded some kind of participation in the decision-making. The day I took the helm as Acting Administrator, I had our folks pull together a list of our most valued stakeholders, and I penned a short, handwritten note to each introducing myself, commenting how honored I was to be tapped as Acting, and assuring them that I knew of our partnership and their concerns.

"I got back e-mails and personal notes appreciating the fact that a NOAA Administrator, Acting or not, would reach out—not driven by an issue or a need— just to say 'I'm here. I know you're there. It matters to me that we're connected and that you know I care about that connection.'" (Fox)

Science political executives serve as the main liaison to their relevant scientific organization. Rebecca Blank recalls, "There are a number of groups who care about the Bureau of Economic Analysis and the Census Bureau, such as the American Statistical Association. I speak to those groups." Shortly after her confirmation as Director of the United States Geological Survey, Marcia McNutt spoke to the American Geological Association.

Scientists in Action

Rebecca M. Blank at the Economics and Statistics Administration, Department of Commerce

Rebecca Blank served as one of five Under Secretaries in the Department of Commerce. Each of the Under Secretaries is responsible for a group of line agencies that report to them. Each Under Secretary reports to the Secretary and Deputy Secretary of the Department. In the case of Blank, her office—the Economics and Statistics Administration (ESA)—oversees the U.S. Census Bureau, the Bureau of Economic Analysis, and the Office of the Chief Economist. In addition, ESA has its own staff of economists and experts who produce in-depth reports, fact sheets, and briefings on policy issues and current economic events.

Like some of the other political executives profiled in the book, Blank found a somewhat sleepy organization in ESA when she arrived. "I was impressed with the career civil service. They are always right there to help you. They have excellent technical skills—first rate. They get you the information you need. We have 16 Ph.D. economists on staff and they had not been utilized very well in recent years." Unlike some agencies, where the new political executive found a workforce with either the wrong set or an inadequate set of skills, Blank found a highly skilled workforce in place. The challenge facing Blank was to more effectively deploy that expert staff. Her job as Under Secretary consisted of three other major challenges:

- Overseeing the data agencies reporting to ESA. As it turned out, Blank's tenure as Under Secretary coincided with the 2010 Census.
- Participating in establishing data policies for the government's statistical agencies. There are nearly 100 federal agencies with statistical programs. Working with these agencies, the Office of Management and Budget, and the academic statistical community, the Commerce Under Secretary for Economic Affairs is a key player in setting national statistical policy.
- Undertaking policy-relevant studies that will produce useful information for the White House on Administration priority issues.

At the top of Blank's must-succeed list was the 2010 Census. The 2010 Census was on the Government Accountability Office high-risk list when Blank arrived at Commerce. "It's the biggest civilian hiring project in government—we hire about 850,000 Census takers. The Census had a lot of problems getting ready for the 2010 Census, including the cancellation of a contract to develop hand-held computers to conduct the Census. I'll be involved in overseeing management issues related to the Census, including the problems we already know about."

In reflecting back on her experience overseeing the Census, Blank says, "It was one of the most interesting things I have ever been involved in. All the pieces came together. It has been interesting from three perspectives: the management issues surrounding mobilizing for the Census, substantive issues regarding data collection, and the political overlay. I am proud of how well the Census Bureau handled the planning, execution, and follow-up of the 2010 Census. We were visiting almost 150 million households, so you can imagine the opportunities for problems. We had over 500 regional offices, one in every Congressional district. There were problems, as expected with undertakings of this size, but no major disasters. The news coverage of the Census changed significantly from the 2000 Census. For that Census, you could bring in a group of seven reporters and brief them. Today, there are numerous bloggers out there, including some of our own census takers. So there was more coverage and more interest than in the past."

Blank and the ESA staff learned from previous Censuses the importance of responding to misinformation or misleading stories about the Census. "We scheduled regular meetings with the public affairs office to go over any newsworthy events," recalls Blank. "We worked as a rapid response team. We had all the right people in the room. As a consequence, there were not as many inaccurate stories as might have been anticipated."

Like the other four science political executives profiled in this chapter, Blank's job is to manage the interface with political leaders in the Department. Upon arrival, Blank found intense interest in the Census from the Secretary and his staff. "I had meetings during my first week here on the Census with the Secretary and seven or eight other key decision-makers. We had a lot of the fifth-floor people (the Secretary's staff) in those meetings. There were a lot of different players involved in the oversight on the Census within our own Department—the General Counsel, Legislative Affairs, the Chief of Staff, Census Bureau staff, and others. You had to get everybody on board. And you then had to respond to questions from the Hill."

In addition to managing the interface with political leaders, all the science political executives profiled devote significant time and energy to making science (in Blank's case, economics) both communicable and relevant to top Administration officials. "Our job is to communicate to the political staff, none of whom are economists," says Blank. "We need to explain economics to them. We undertook economic briefings for the Secretary and his senior staff. The economy was obviously very important to them."

In reflecting on her accomplishments to date, Blank says, "We increased the visibility of ESA in the White House. The job and the agency had been relatively low visibility in the past." The increased visibility in the White House and other parts of the Administration were a consequence of Blank's finding opportunities in which economic analysis could contribute to policy making in the Administration.

Patrick D. Gallagher at the National Institute of Standards and Technology, Department of Commerce

There were really two beginnings for Patrick Gallagher. The first occurred in September 2008 when he was appointed Deputy Director while the Director position remained vacant. After carrying out the duties of Director for 13 months, he was nomi-

nated to be Director in October 2009 and confirmed by the United States Senate in November 2009. While he led the agency as Deputy Director, Gallagher recalls, "I didn't want to do the traditional caretaker role, but I also didn't want to make major decisions which might be binding on the new Director. But there were things that we could do. I knew that the next Director would need a management agenda," so Gallagher set the stage for organizational change by improving management in areas such as safety. "A new Director would want the organization to be organized and effective," says Gallagher. After being confirmed as the next NIST Director, he set out to create a plan for realigning the organizational structure of the agency.

The second beginning occurred after confirmation. "There was a greater sense of urgency about business after I got confirmed," says Gallagher. "There were more commitments, more media attention, and an increased level of activity. The confirmation impacted how I would spend my time and how I would manage."

The historical origins of the current National Institute of Standards and Technology (NIST) date back to the writing of the Constitution of the United States, which assigned the federal government responsibility "to fix the standard of weights and measures" for the nation. The National Bureau of Standards was formed in 1901. In 1988, the Bureau was renamed the National Institute of Standards and Technology. In addition to its historical measurement role, the mission of NIST is to promote U.S. innovation and industrial competitiveness by advancing measurement science, standards, and technology. In Fiscal Year 2010, the agency budget was approximately $1 billion, consisting of about $850 million in appropriated funds, $50 million in service fees, and $100 million in funding from other federal agencies. NIST employs 2,900 scientists, engineers, technicians, and support and administrative personnel. In addition, NIST hosts about 2,600 associates and facility users from academia, industry, and other government agencies.

When Gallagher was appointed Deputy Director in September 2008, NIST faced the following issues common to many government science agencies:

- It had a historically low profile.
- Its mission was not always clear to the Administration's political leadership and the agency's relevance was frequently questioned.
- It had not been reorganized in over 20 years, since the 1988 legislation which renamed the agency and added several functions.
- It was facing the continued challenge of recruiting and retaining a world-class workforce.

Based on his previous 15 years as a career scientist at NIST, Gallagher had a clear sense of where he thought the organization needed to go. "I knew that the agency had to be better organized and more effective," reflects Gallagher. "I wanted to improve the stability of NIST. I thought it was unstable with a single Presidential appointee and a single Deputy Director. The previous NIST management structure had upwards of 18 line organizations all reporting to the Director or Deputy Director. In addition, NIST is like a national laboratory in many ways, but it wasn't organized that way. The Director of NIST was like a weak mayor. It wasn't working. We needed to remap the organization and we needed to improve customer service."

Implementing the reorganization required approval by the Department of Commerce and Congressional appropriations committees. The reorganization was a top priority for Gallagher during his first year in office. "The organization was supportive of the change," he says. "It had been talked about for years and there was general recognition that the time had come to make the change. In the private sector, you can just come up with a plan, announce it, and then do it. Government is different. You need to invite participation. I shared our reorganization plan and met with NIST managers to discuss the reorganization. I invited everybody to comment on the plan. Things moved pretty quickly after this. I did learn the importance of engaging people on reorganizations. Nobody likes to be surprised. My rule was no surprises and we engaged people on it, including Congress which was very supportive."

The reorganization was not just an "add-on" activity for Gallagher. It was central to his strategy to change the culture of NIST and to strengthen the organization to survive in the 21st century. Because of his interest in management, Gallagher made a decision early in his scientific career that he wanted to move into management, which resulted in his serving four years as Director of the NIST Center for Neutron Research. "I really do enjoy my management activities. My reorganization initiative did help the organization. It amplified my message about the need to change the organization. Through my management activities, I am trying to make NIST a world-class destination for scientists. Being a world-class place for scientists involves a whole set of issues and activities. The reorganization was never just about organizational structure or who reports to whom. It wasn't about boxes. It was about getting the organization better aligned. We wanted to get the right people and align them in the new organization. Alignment was our larger goal. We need to reset the agency."

The increased mission focus and reorganization was clearly related to Gallagher's goal to make NIST a good place to work and to enhance the organization's external image, both within the Administration and the research community. "NIST is a very special place," states Gallagher. "Researchers at NIST like their work and their mission. I wanted to restore the old sense of mission that the National Bureau of Standards had. Our efforts have brought more visibility to the organization. I'm pleased with the Administration's interest in NIST. That happened faster than I thought. They were eager to place increased expectations and enhanced responsibilities on us. This is a change from the past when we had to explain our relevance to an Administration."

Marcia K. McNutt at the U.S. Geological Survey, Department of the Interior

The early days of a political executive are often difficult. Marcia McNutt's experience was no different. "It's the old story about finding your parking spot," recalls McNutt. "I came to the U.S. Geological Survey (USGS) from an Institute where we had 230  employees to an organization with nearly 9,000 employees. You can get lost in this building. It must have been designed by the CIA. You need friends to find your way around here."

The U.S. Geological Survey was created in 1879. The legislative mandate of USGS was to classify public lands, examine geological structure, and assess the energy, mineral, water, and biology resources and products within and outside the United States. Like the National Institute of Standards and Technology (NIST) discussed on page 157, USGS has in recent years moved away from being an agency organized around academic disciplines to an agency organized around problems. Today, the agency is organized around five key areas in which natural science can make a substantial contribution: climate and land use change; core science systems; ecosystems; energy and minerals, and environmental health; natural hazards; and water. USGS has over 8,000 employees and an annual budget of approximately $1 billion. The USGS campus is located in Reston, Virginia.

Like many leaders of government science agencies profiled in this chapter, McNutt faced three major challenges upon arrival at the USGS:

- **Financial resources:** "I was impressed with how USGS does a great amount of activity with a small amount of resources," said McNutt. "The agency has been sliced and diced very thin for several decades. The agency keeps on giving to the point that I don't know how much more I can give back to the Department."

- **People:** "The senior staff," states McNutt, "consists of very high performers. Forty percent are now eligible for retirement. I am concerned that we will be losing some good talent. We aren't doing very well on diversity. I'm not seeing an increase in the numbers that I'd like to see. We just don't have much diversity among our earth scientists and biologists. They just aren't there, which goes to the pipeline issue and reaching people when they are in school."
- **Status:** "I wanted to raise the status and prestige of the USGS," says McNutt. "My impression is that agencies that are self-standing, like the National Science Foundation and the National Aeronautics and Space Administration, receive somewhat more attention than agencies like USGS, NIST, and the National Oceanic and Atmospheric Administration, which are within Departments. Secretary Salazar does have an interest in USGS. In the past, USGS has often received little attention by departmental leadership. I want to increase the role of USGS in bringing science into decision-making."

The challenges described above are long-term and ongoing challenges faced by all directors of USGS and most heads of science agencies. In addition to these ongoing challenges, there were new challenges that were unexpected. While USGS is prepared to respond to a certain number of natural disasters annually, there were an unusually high number of incidents during Dr. McNutt's first two years at USGS. Well-known recent natural disasters included the Haiti earthquake in January 2010, the Iceland volcano in March 2010, and the Japanese earthquake of March 2011.

USGS's effective response to the increased number of natural disasters had positive impacts on the agency. McNutt states, "I think we increased the stature of the agency, increased our visibility and our name recognition. We received much attention in 2010 and were on the front pages of many newspapers. We made a diverse contribution in 2010. We were involved in responses to the earthquakes and volcanoes. It showed our diverse expertise in many areas. I think all the increased attention also helped inside the agency. It showed the relevance of the agency and it started people within the agency to think about things that we can do that they never imagined before."

Six months into her tenure, the unexpected happened. The Deepwater Horizon disaster occurred in April 2010, killing 11 men and triggering an environmental crisis. The gushing of crude oil into the Gulf of Mexico became an ongoing national story throughout the spring and summer of 2010. "I went to Houston to work with BP in May and didn't return to Reston full time until September," recalls McNutt. "Secretary Salazar wanted to place his top agency heads in places where the Department of the Interior had a major interest and a role in the recovery. The head of the National Park Service went to Mobile, Alabama to be involved in the cleanup, with a focus on Park Service lands. The head of Fish and Wildlife Service went to Louisiana to help out there."

"My job in Houston was to work with both the Coast Guard and the Department of Energy," describes McNutt. "I coordinated a group to work with

BP. My role evolved over time as we worked with BP on what was known as the top kill to halt the gushing. By July, it became more a joint enterprise with BP and the Coast Guard making decisions. My Deputy Director, Suzette Kimball, was running the agency while I was gone. She knew how to run it. I did come up once or twice but my main focus was on the oil spill. I worked 17 hours a day, seven days a week."

On reflecting on her oil spill experience, McNutt says, "It was really quite an experience—a very wild ride—and I'm grateful that I got to participate and make a contribution. But it is something that I would not want to do again. After my work on the oil spill, I don't think I will do anything again that will have the same amount of impact. We got the relief well completed on September 16th. But thanks to the capping stack, the well was shut in after 87 days instead of the 100 days originally predicted." In describing her role and stay in Houston, Joel Achenbach writes in *A Hole at the Bottom of the Sea*:

> On the evening of May 6, U.S. Geological Survey director Marcia McNutt arrived, accompanying Salazar. For the secretary of the interior, this would be a … visit of the BP war room operation, but McNutt would not be so lucky. She happened to know a lot about taking hardware into the deep sea, having served as director of the Monterey Bay Aquarium Research Institute (MBARI), widely viewed as the NASA of deep-sea research. Anyone knowing about deep water was suddenly needed on the front lines of the battle. Salazar took off and left McNutt in Houston, and she set up shop in a windowless six-by-ten foot office. She had packed only a carry-on bag for her Gulf Coast trip (Achenbach).

In July, writes Achenbach, McNutt could "only dream of being back in her spacious office at the agency's headquarters in Reston, Virginia. She was still ensconced in her windowless office in the Houston headquarters of a company that, with its cowboy culture, struck her as a throwback to an earlier era" (Achenbach). McNutt did return to Reston and resumed running USGS in September 2010.

Richard G. Newell at the U.S. Energy Information Administration, Department of Energy

Richard Newell arrived at the U. S. Energy Information Administration (EIA) with a plan to learn the organization before making any changes. U.S. Energy Information Administration "My first day was on a Monday morning after I was confirmed on a Friday," recalls Newell. "I had already planned to drive up since I knew my confirmation was coming. I didn't come in with an agenda. If I had, I think that would have turned people off. You have to learn about the agency and organization before you try to make changes. I took my time to learn and understand the agency."

There were several prior iterations to the current EIA. In 1974, the Federal Energy Administration (FEA) was created with a mandate to collect, assemble, evaluate, and analyze energy information. Today, EIA has 370 Federal employees and an annual budget of nearly $100 million. It has a comprehensive data collection program that covers the full spectrum of energy sources, end uses, and energy flows. Its products include a daily "Today in Energy," weekly reports on petroleum and natural gas storage and coal production, monthly electric power reviews, and long-term U.S. and international energy outlooks. The EIA website averages approximately 2.1 million visits per month.

Newell's early days were spent defining the challenge he faced at EIA. Newell recalls, "I had a positive impression of the agency. I thought EIA did good analysis and I had used their information previously. I thought the agency was deep in expertise. EIA undertook surveys which I thought were very important." The agency's agenda was also very clear to Newell. "We do three primary activities: collect data, analyze data, and disseminate it," he says.

While Newell had a very positive impression of the agency from both his personal experience as a consumer of EIA data and his early assessment of the agency after his arrival, he concluded that the agency would benefit from management improvements and potentially a reorganization. Newell says, "When I arrived, I saw a lack of coordination within the organization. There was too much stovepiping. I saw inefficiency in the agency and Department structure. In addition, there had been a long gap between my arrival and the departure of the previous Administrator so there were a lot of issues that had been put on hold until I arrived."

Newell also assessed the agency's website. "I thought the website could use improving," says Newell. "None of these problems were fully visible to outsiders. The website was perfectly usable. But it is critical because we use the website as our primary dissemination vehicle. I observed that we were also operating in stovepipes in how we ran the agency's website. Each office within EIA had their separate web operations. I decided we needed to focus on the look and feel and usability of the website. I wanted the agency to reexamine what kinds of software and programming they were using."

Based on his assessment of the agency, Newell reached several key conclusions about the organization and began to take steps in response to each of these challenges. First, he concluded that the agency's strategic plan wasn't going to work with the agency's current organization. "I started thinking and talking about what a new organization might look like," recalls Newell. "I talked to my Deputy Administrator, a career civil servant, who had years of experience in the agency. He thought the idea of a reorganization was good.

"I started thinking and talking to people about what a new organization might look like. The career staff thought it was feasible and would be helpful. I reached out to all the senior managers in the agency. I knew a number of the senior staff here which helped. I treated them with respect. Everybody realized that this needed to happen. If the senior staff had not bought in, it would have been really difficult to pull off the reorganization."

In describing his role in pushing the reorganization of EIA, Newell says, "My role was critical. If I had not been driving the change, I don't think it would have happened. If you don't get involved, an initiative will just chug along. So we proceeded with the reorganization. We went from eight direct reports to me to four. We created a new structure that has four Assistant Administrators, each focused on a main EIA functional area—statistics, analysis, communications, and resources and technology management. It was a well-thought-out reorganization. It was not motivated to get rid of anybody. It was all about a better structure." Previously the agency had been organized around type of energy source, such as oil and gas; coal, nuclear, electric, and alternate fuels; and energy markets.

Concurrently with proceeding to develop a plan to reorganize the agency, Newell also set out to improve other aspects of the agency's management. "I thought we needed to improve our budget tools," says Newell. "We didn't have the right codes and classification systems. Getting information sorted out was very difficult." Another problem was tracking information in and out of the Administrator's office. "The systems simply were not working when I first arrived and were not up to my expectations," he recalls. "We identified some new tools which could track incoming and outgoing information and correspondence." At the same time, the organization needed to beef up its procurement operations and replace its old procurement vehicle with a new one which would both save money and be more efficient. "I ended up spending more time on management than I had anticipated. I thought it was important to do," he says.

Kathryn D. Sullivan at the National Oceanic and Atmospheric Administration, Department of Commerce

After her confirmation, Dr. Sullivan worked with the National Oceanic and Atmospheric Administration (NOAA) staff to develop a detailed 90-day start-up plan. Recalls Sullivan, "I wanted to hit the ground running and become familiar with our operations and people as quickly as possible. I had countless briefings and made a point of getting out to meet with people in regions. I  had been appointed to a newly created position, and felt it was important for our people to get to know me." NOAA is one of the oldest agencies in government, dating back to the 19th century. The United States Coast and Geodetic Survey was formed in 1807, the roots of the National Weather Service go back to 1817, and the Bureau of Commercial Fisheries was formed in 1871. In 1970, these agencies came together to form the National Oceanic and Atmospheric Administration in the Department of Commerce.

Major components of NOAA now include the National Weather Service; the National Environmental Satellite, Data, and Information Service; the National Marine Fisheries Service; the National Ocean Service; and the Office of Oceanic Atmospheric Research. NOAA has an annual budget of over $5 billion and over 12,000 employees.

When Sullivan arrived in 2010, NOAA faced a series of major challenges. In describing these challenges, Sullivan says, "We were facing some significant programmatic challenges and the prospect of a long stretch of flat or declining budgets. We had two big satellite procurements underway when I arrived, one of which was still working through a significant reorganization. The mission of NOAA had not changed, but the pressure points were now different."

Sullivan recalls, "The budget formulation process had changed substantially; we have a very different planning and program analysis office. My primary goals for the first year were to establish the new Assistant Secretary role and stabilize our satellite portfolio. The environmental observation and prediction responsibilities of my office cut across all of NOAA. One of my challenges is to ensure that walls don't rise between these enterprise capacities and our mission areas."

In defining her job responsibilities, Sullivan says, "In setting my priorities, one question I always ask myself is, 'What are things that only the person in this job can do?' I play an important integrative role. It is my job to make sure we take the holistic view and to foster the connections that help us work as 'One NOAA.' When we do this, the whole of NOAA is truly greater than the sum of its parts."

Sullivan assumed strategic leadership for the two complicated satellite procurements. "Our joint satellite program had been progressing technically, but we were operating on a continuing resolution that provided less than half the funding needed to sustain that progress in FY11. We had to move the needle. I met with stakeholders inside and out of government. We have generally good relationships with our Congressional committees, especially on weather satellite issues, which still enjoy strong bipartisan support."

In working on the satellite programs, Sullivan says, "This is a long ballgame. We are putting our satellite programs on firm footing. These are seminal programs which must be fielded on schedule. We had to strengthen our analytical capabilities, scrub our requirements and cost figures. We also needed to communicate much more, get NOAA on some key radar screens again. There was plenty to do."

Another major activity of Dr. Sullivan's was to reach out to stakeholders beyond the Hill. "We are engaging our academic and industry partners and scientific associations and general audiences across the country," says Sullivan. "We need to tell them what we are working on. We have found that professional organizations are good aggregators. They understand many of our issues and connect us to important constituencies. We are also getting out to the general public."

Like many of the political executives profiled in this book, Sullivan's background prepared her well for the NOAA Deputy Administrator position. While understanding NASA was helpful to her, Sullivan also found her non-governmental experience very useful. She says, "Running a non-profit was a good experience. It required focus and discipline, sound strategy and crisp execution, robust internal and external communications. We have to motivate people to invest precious time and money to visit a science museum. We built a new building during my tenure, which forced every facet of our operations to change. Our staff had to do things that they had never done before and do familiar things in altogether different ways. We had to invest on the front end and build new business processes. I had to make sure that we were having the right conversations—bringing all pertinent expertise and perspectives to bear—on each of these challenges during this transformation."

Appendix to Chapter 7
Profiles of Scientists Interviewed

Rebecca M. Blank

Tenure
Dr. Blank was nominated by President Obama to serve as the Under Secretary for Economic Affairs at the Department of Commerce in April 2009, and confirmed by the U.S. Senate in May 2009.

Dr. Blank served as Acting Secretary of the Department of Commerce from June 2012 to June 2013. She served as Acting Secretary of Commerce also from August 2011 to October 2011. She was confirmed as Deputy Secretary of Commerce in March 2012, after having served as Acting Deputy Secretary for most of 2011.

Present Position
Dr. Blank is Chancellor of the University of Wisconsin–Madison.

Academic Experience
Prior to being confirmed as Under Secretary, Dr. Blank was the Robert S. Kerr Senior Fellow in Economic Studies at the Brookings Institution from 2008 to 2009. From 1999 to 2008, she was Dean of the Gerald R. Ford School of Public Policy at the University of Michigan. She also served as co-director of the University of Michigan's National Poverty Center. From 1989 to 1999, Dr. Blank was a Professor of Economics at Northwestern University and Director of the Northwestern University/University of Chicago Joint Center for Poverty Research. Dr. Blank has also taught at Princeton University and the Massachusetts Institute of Technology.

Federal Government Experience
From 1997 to 1999, Dr. Blank served as a Member of the Council of Economic Advisers. She served as a Senior Staff Economist on the Council from 1989 to 1990.

Education
Dr. Blank received her B.A. in Economics from the University of Minnesota in 1976 and her Ph.D. in Economics from Massachusetts Institute of Technology in 1983.

Reflecting on the Future of ESA
"Looking ahead, I think money is going to be a problem for our agencies in the years ahead. I see a flat budget with no increases. Keeping level will be an accomplishment. It will be hard to make anything new happen. If you have a great idea, something else will have to be cut to pay for the effort … It will be a different environment."

Patrick D. Gallagher

Tenure

Dr. Gallagher was nominated by President Obama to serve as Director of the U.S. Department of Commerce's National Institute of Standards and Technology (NIST) in September 2009, and confirmed by the U.S. Senate in November 2009. He also serves as Under Secretary of Commerce for Standards and Technology and as Co-Chair of the Standards Subcommittee under the White House National Science and Technology Council.

Present Position

Dr. Gallagher was named Acting Deputy Secretary of the Department of Commerce in June 2013.

Federal Government Experience

Prior to being confirmed as Director, Dr. Gallagher was Deputy Director of NIST. Dr. Gallagher joined NIST as an instrumental scientist in 1993. In 2004, he was selected to be the Director of the NIST Center for Neutron Research. Gallagher also served as the NIST agency representative to the National Science and Technology Council (NSTC). He also chaired the Interagency Working Group on Neutron and Light Source Facilities under the Office of Science and Technology Policy.

Education

Dr. Gallagher studied physics and philosophy at Benedictine College in Atchison, Kansas. He received his Ph.D. in Physics at the University of Pittsburgh in 1991. Gallagher did post-doctoral research at Boston University.

Reflecting on the Future of NIST

"I've never managed in such a changing environment. Two years ago, everything was on the upswing. Our budget was increasing and innovation was receiving a lot of attention. That turned out to be a snapshot in time. It's hard to set direction when there is so much uncertainty."

Marcia K. McNutt

Tenure

Dr. McNutt was nominated by President Obama to serve as the Director of the United States Geological Survey (USGS) and Science Advisor to the United States Secretary of the Interior in August 2009, and confirmed by the U.S. Senate in October 2009. Dr. McNutt resigned her position in January 2013.

Present Position

Dr. McNutt is Editor-in-Chief of the journal *Science*.

Non-Profit Sector Experience

Prior to being confirmed as Director of the USGS, Dr. McNutt served as President and Chief Executive Officer of the Monterey Bay Aquarium Research Institute in Moss Landing, California from 1997 to 2009.

Academic Experience

Dr. McNutt joined the faculty at Massachusetts Institute of Technology in 1982, becoming the Griswold Professor of Geophysics and serving as Director of the Joint Program in Oceanography & Applied Ocean Science & Engineering. She also was a Professor of Marine Geophysics at both Stanford University and at the University of California, Santa Cruz.

Federal Government Experience

Dr. McNutt worked at USGS in Menlo Park, California in the area of earthquake prediction.

Education

Dr. McNutt received a B.A. in Physics, *summa cum laude,* Phi Beta Kappa, from Colorado College in Colorado Springs. As a National Science Foundation Graduate Fellow, she studied geophysics at Scripps Institution of Oceanography in La Jolla, California, where she received a Ph.D. in Earth Sciences in 1978.

Reflecting on the Future of USGS

"We haven't made much progress on diversity at the agency level. This is a tough problem. This is about the future of the organization. We also have retirements coming. This is not a good situation.

"Budgets are going to be tight. I'm going to have to fight for USGS. This isn't going to be much fun. I think science is important, but we will have to work to prove it to the Office of Management and Budget."

Richard G. Newell

Tenure
Dr. Newell was nominated by President Obama to serve as the Administrator of the U.S. Energy Information Administration in May 2009, and confirmed by the U.S. Senate in July 2009. Dr. Newell resigned his position in June 2011.

Present Position
Dr. Newell is the Gendell Associate Professor of Energy and Environmental Economics and Director, Duke University Energy Initiative, Nicholas School of the Environment, Duke University.

Academic Experience
Prior to being confirmed as Administrator of EIA, Dr. Newell was the Gendell Associate Professor of Energy and Environmental Economics at the Nicholas School of the Environment, Duke University. He was also an Affiliated Professor of Business Administration and Corporate Sustainability at the Fuqua School of Business, Duke University. He joined the Duke faculty in 2007. He was also a Teaching Fellow at Harvard University.

Federal Government Experience
From 2005 to 2006, Dr. Newell served as the Senior Economist for energy and environment on the Council of Economic Advisers.

Non-Profit Sector Experience
From 1997 to 2006, Dr. Newell was a Fellow and Senior Fellow at Resources for the Future.

Private Sector Experience
Early in his career, he was a Senior Associate at ICF Incorporated.

Education
Dr. Newell received a B.S. in Materials Engineering and a B.A. in Philosophy from Rutgers University. He received an M.P.A. from Princeton University's Woodrow Wilson School of Public and International Affairs, and a Ph.D. from Harvard University in Environmental and Resource Economics.

Reflecting on Running EIA
"You have to walk a thin line between managing too much (micromanaging) and not managing enough. You have to know when to dig into detail and when not to dig in. But sometimes you have to dig in. You need to get your hands dirty and be willing to ask a lot of questions. You can't just go through the motions. You have to get into the details and 'go into the weeds.'"

Kathryn D. Sullivan

Tenure
Dr. Sullivan was nominated by President Obama to serve as Deputy Administrator of the National Oceanic and Atmospheric Administration in December 2010, and confirmed by the U.S. Senate in April 2011.

Present Position
Dr. Sullivan is Acting Under Secretary of Commerce for Oceans and Atmosphere and Acting Administrator of the National Oceanic and Atmospheric Administration (NOAA). She was nominated by President Obama to serve as Under Secretary and Administrator in August 2013, after having served as Acting Under Secretary and Acting Administrator since February 2013.

Academic/Non-Profit Experience
Prior to being confirmed as Deputy Administrator, Dr. Sullivan served as the inaugural Director of the Battelle Center for Mathematics and Science Education Policy at Ohio State University's John Glenn School of Public Affairs. From 1996 to 2005, she served as the Chief Executive Officer of the Center of Science and Industry (COSI) in Columbus, Ohio.

Federal Government Experience
In 1993, Dr. Sullivan was appointed NOAA's chief scientist. Prior to joining NOAA, she spent 15 years in the NASA astronaut corps as one of the first six women to be selected for such a position. She flew three shuttle missions, including the Hubble Space Telescope's deployment, and holds the honor of being the first American woman to ever walk in space.

Education
Dr. Sullivan received her B.S. in Earth Sciences from the University of California, Santa Cruz, and a Ph.D. in Geology from Dalhousie University in Canada in 1978.

Reflecting on the Future of NOAA and Science
"I am concerned about the impact that tight budgets will have on the balance of science, service, and stewardship that is vital to NOAA's mission effectiveness. The necessary growth in satellite procurement accounts, coupled with the tight fiscal constraints facing the country, poses a real risk to this balance. It also jeopardizes our ability to invest in the scientific research that produces the new ideas and talents needed to ensure the agency's long-term viability."

Chapter Eight

The Collaborators

Understanding the Job of the Collaborator

While we believe that all political executives need collaborative skills, there are some political executives whose job requires a high degree of collaboration. In our interviews, we discovered a group of political executives whom we call the collaborators. These collaborators are found in three types of agencies:

Small agencies with limited funding and staff. Because their funding and staffing levels are limited, these political executives need to figure out how to leverage federal funds by creating partnerships with state and local government, the private sector, and non-profit organizations. Prime examples of this type of agency are the Minority Business Development Agency at the Department of Commerce, which has the mission of providing support to minority businesses; the Veterans' Employment and Training Service at the Department of Labor, whose mission is to assist and prepare veterans to find jobs; and the Substance Abuse and Mental Health Administration, an agency dedicated to reducing the impact of substance abuse and mental illness on America's communities. All three agencies use their limited funding to find creative ways to further their agency's mission.

Agencies whose mission requires collaborative and partnership activities with groups outside of government. An example of this type of agency is the U.S. Fish and Wildlife Service (FWS). Because the vast majority of fish and wildlife

The Collaborators

Daniel M. Ashe, page 175

Director, U.S. Fish and Wildlife Service Department of the Interior

John Berry, page 176

Director, Office of Personnel Management (OPM)

David A. Hinson, page 177

National Director, Minority Business Development Agency (MBDA), Department of Commerce

Pamela Hyde, page 179

Administrator, Substance Abuse and Mental Health Services Administration (SAMHSA), Department of Health and Human Services

Raymond M. Jefferson, page 180

Assistant Secretary of the Veterans' Employment and Training Service (VETS), Department of Labor

Mary K. Wakefield, page 181

Administrator, Health Resources and Services Administration (HRSA), Department of Health and Human Services (HHS)

habitat is on non-federal lands, FWS has created a variety of partnership programs to foster aquatic conservation and assist voluntary habitat conservation and restoration.

Another example of this type of agency is the Health Resources and Services Administration (HRSA), which works with, through its grants programs, over 3,000 partners in state and local government agencies, non-profit organizations, hospitals, clinics, colleges and universities, and other organizations to provide health care to those with limited access.

Central management agencies, with responsibility for working across government. A prime example of this type of agency is the Office of Personnel Management. While OPM is responsible for the direct delivery of some services (retirement and health benefits), the policy part of the agency requires collaboration across government.

The Small Agency Collaborator

David Hinson at MBDA and Ray Jefferson at VETS adopted similar strategies in working toward achieving their missions. Hinson recalls, "I spent a lot of time during my first year on the road building relationships. You need to build good relationships with corporate America. Building these relationships is crucial." In describing his strategy for VETS, Jefferson says, "We want to create partnerships ... to find employment opportunities for veterans." Both Hinson and Jefferson developed working relationships with the Chamber of Commerce, among many other organizations, in support of their different missions: assisting minority businesses and assisting veterans to find employment opportunities.

In addition to their work with the private sector and non-profit organizations, Hinson and Jefferson spent a significant part of their time working with other government agencies after taking on their positions. Both MBDA and VETS were created to serve as "spurs" and leaders in government for their respective missions. Hinson and Jefferson had to carve out roles and activities in which their agencies could contribute in a crowded field of numerous agencies, all of whom have some "piece of the action" in their policy area.

For Jefferson, the veterans' field was indeed crowded. Other government agencies involved with veterans include the Office of Personnel Management (involved in the hiring of veterans within government), the Department of Veterans Affairs (involving in providing benefits to veterans via the Veterans Benefits Administration), and the Department of Defense (with its myriad offices related to veterans). There has long been a discussion as to whether VETS should be moved to the Department of Veterans Affairs or remain in the Department of Labor. In navigating between these various other government agencies, Jefferson recalls, "Sometimes I feel that I am conducting shuttle diplomacy."

At the Substance Abuse and Mental Health Administration, Pamela Hyde faced a similar challenge. Hyde states, "Lots of other agencies do part of what we do. Regarding substance abuse and mental illness, there is hardly anything we do that somebody else is not also doing." Thus, the challenge facing all small agency collaborators is developing effective working relationships with other federal agencies. These agency heads need to maximize their potential impact by enlisting other federal agencies in the accomplishment of their goals.

The Partner Collaborator

The mission of FWS is "working with others to conserve, protect, and enhance fish, wildlife, plants, and their habitats for the continuing benefit of the American people." This mission is accomplished through a wide variety of partnerships. FWS notes that throughout its history, the agency has been committed to a collaborative approach to conservation. The agency has created partnerships with local municipalities, private landowners, school groups, corporations, state governments, federal agencies, and numerous other groups and organizations.

Like other collaborative agencies which need to create partnerships with organizations outside of the federal government, the FWS uses a variety of mechanisms to achieve its partnership activities, such as grants and cooperative agreements, memoranda of understanding, donations, and statutory partnerships.

In describing his outreach activities, Daniel Ashe, Director of the U.S. Fish and Wildlife Service, says, "We are now working to improve our partnerships with other organizations. We want to strengthen our relationships with professional communities. We reached out to our legacy partners. We wanted to know what they wanted and what they expected. We found that they wanted to be part of our team. They wanted a more consistent relationship. They are significant communities. We now have a more diverse set of communities with whom we interact. We need to develop more mechanisms for participation."

The Central Management Agency Collaborator

While John Berry might have been able to give orders (when he chose to do so) within the Office of Personnel Management, his influence across the government was based on his collaboration skills. In describing the unique challenge of getting interagency clearance on many of his initiatives and policies, Berry says, "This is a responsibility that most other agencies do not have to undergo. We have to get approval from OMB and then also get approval by agencies. We need 26 agencies to say 'yes.' Any of them can say 'no.'" Berry worked hard to get input from his colleagues across government in the development of new policies and initiatives. By the time a document is ready for the clearance process, Berry has often touched base with all the key actors in Departments across government.

The interagency collaborative work is crucial to the success of OMB in its role as policy leader. Berry elaborates, "I work closely with the Chief Human Capital Officer's Council and the President's Management Council, as well as the Cabinet." In addition, it is crucial that OPM develop a close, working relationship with the Office of Management and Budget. Berry describes that relationship: "I wanted to develop a good relationship with OMB, which I have done. I work closely with the White House on many initiatives, such as our activities on improving work life and veterans' hiring."

These collaborative skills are also clearly needed in government-wide leaders, such as the heads of the General Services Administration, or White House units, such as the Council on Environmental Quality. All have responsibility for shepherding government-wide initiatives. While all can use the power of their office to get desired results on occasion, most of their time is spent cajoling and sharing information with others across government regarding shared goals.

Collaborators in Action

Daniel M. Ashe at the U.S. Fish and Wildlife Service

Like many agencies across government, the U.S. Fish and Wildlife Service (FWS) faces tightening budgets in the years ahead. Today, FWS has nearly 10,000 employees across the United States and a budget of $2.4 billion. In describing the future, Ashe compares the agency's current position to triage at a field hospital. "If we let ourselves be consumed with a crusade to save everything," says Ashe, "then we'll save nothing.

"We have to work with our partners to identify and focus on the most strategically important species and actions in order to minimize our extinction losses and achieve the greatest conservation benefits for every dollar we spend."

As a collaborator, Ashe concluded that one of his primary goals as FWS Director was to use science and strategic partnerships to improve the agency's ability to deliver conservation. "The resource challenges we face are too big and too complicated for us or any other entity to tackle alone. But by using science to improve our collective understanding of what's happening on the landscape, we can align our efforts with those of state and federal agencies, conservation organizations, and private landowners. If we do this, we can leverage our resources and have a much greater impact.

"We are very reliant on great partners to help us accomplish our mission. First among these partners are the state wildlife agencies, which have been so critical to conservation. We also have great working relationships with many organizations like Ducks Unlimited, the Nature Conservancy, Defenders of Wildlife, Trout Unlimited, and dozens of others. They can raise important funding and reach out to landowners and other partners in ways that we sometimes can't. They can also provide enormous contributions to research, land acquisition and protection, and other activities that help us do our jobs more effectively."

Similar to the other collaborative agencies discussed in this chapter, FWS is also working closely with the states. FWS is now developing a network of Landscape Conservation Cooperatives across the nation designed to coordinate biological planning, conservation design and delivery, monitoring, and research at a landscape scale.

In addition to the above programs, FWS celebrated the 25th anniversary of the Partners for Fish and Wildlife (PFW) program in 2012. The Partners program has gained national recognition as a vanguard in the new era of cooperative conservation based on the premise that fish and wildlife conservation is a responsibility shared by citizens and the government. The program is using cutting-edge restoration and enhancement techniques, along with deploying proven methods of communication and partnership building (Filsinger and Milmoe).

Improving FWS' ability to communicate is another key component of successful conservation, especially in today's media-saturated environment. "If you look at our history, the employees who've truly had an impact on society—such as Rachel Carson, Olaus Murie, and Ding Darling—have been excellent communicators. Each of them realized that to have an impact beyond the agency, they needed to reach the public in a way that was visceral and real. We don't always live up to those standards, but we've placed a renewed emphasis on communicating with the public in recent years."

John Berry at the Office of Personnel Management

John Berry is classified as a collaborator because of the importance of successful collaboration to both his and the Office of Personnel Management's (OPM) success. While OPM is responsible for the direct delivery of services, much of its remaining and ongoing agenda involves gaining the support of agencies across government and the Office of Management and Budget. OPM  has a budget of over $2 billion and over 5,000 employees and is responsible for the federal government's 1.9 million civilian employees nationwide. It performs a wide range of activities, including setting government personnel policy, delivering retirement payments, running the federal government's health benefits program, and managing federal investigative services.

In describing his collaboration role, Berry says, "I wanted to develop a good relationship with OMB, which I have done. I work closely with OMB on all our initiatives. I've also engaged the White House on many initiatives, such as our activities on improving work life and veterans' hiring. We worked hard on building our relationship with the White House."

Unlike most other federal agencies, OPM faces the unique challenge of getting interagency clearance on many of its activities. "This is a responsibility," says Berry, "that most other agencies do not have to undergo. We have to get approval from OMB and then also get approval by agencies. We need 26 agencies to say yes. Any of them can say no." In addition, Berry says, "I work closely with the Chief Human Capital Officer's Council and the President's Management Council, as well as the Cabinet. So I get a lot of feedback and people do tell me what they are thinking." It is clear that collaborating with other agencies is a key to OPM's success in its role as a central management agency.

Berry found that he needed to spend time on strengthening the institution while also fulfilling OPM's operational mission and collaborative initiatives. After working with the existing OPM organization for several months, Berry came to the conclusion that OPM needed to be reorganized. Berry says, "It's the last thing I wanted to do, but I think we needed to do it. We needed to fix the agency and I owed it to the organization to do it. I just couldn't look away from our organizational problems." He appointed a career OPM executive to lead the reorganization initiative.

In reflecting on the reorganization, Berry says, "Looking at our old organization chart, you see how difficult it was to communicate what we do. It was self-evident that it needed fixing. We also needed to create some new organizational capability. I wanted the reorganization to be clean, simple, and fill our capability gaps."

David A. Hinson at the Minority Business Development Agency, Department of Commerce

Before arriving at the Minority Business Development Agency (MBDA), David Hinson read everything he could find about the agency and developed a strategic plan that he could begin executing upon arrival. Hinson  recalls, "I realized early on that the success of MBDA was contingent upon the ability of the agency to build a new level of strategic partnerships and collaborative relationships both outside and inside government. With this in mind, I was driven to move quickly to build the relationships necessary to achieve great success." Hinson's strategy was necessitated by the fact that MBDA is one of the smallest agencies in the Department of Commerce, with a budget of $30 million and staff of about 100. MBDA's mission is to assist minority firms to gain access to capital, contracts, and new markets.

A key action by Hinson was his decision to improve the agency's relationships with its stakeholders across the country. Hinson recounts, "There had been a decade of poor relationships with stakeholders. So I hit the road. I spent a lot of time during my first year on the road building relationships. You need to build good relationships with corporate America. Building these relationships is critical. You can't work in a box. You need to work with your stakeholders and you need to continue to build more partnerships. You have to work with cities and states and you have to build relationships with the Chamber of Commerce."

The goal of these outreach efforts is to get MBDA into the mainstream of the nation's economy. "I've been building relationships and working on access to capital," says Hinson. "We want to enter into new markets. We also want to get minority businesses out of minority business status. Once minority businesses get bigger, they get access to capital. We are increasing our strategic partnerships and devoting more effort to outreach." As part of the agency's outreach to stakeholders, Hinson formed a National Advisory Council for Minority Business Enterprises. The Advisory Council is the first council focused on promoting the minority business community since the early 1970s. The Advisory Council includes high-level private sector executives. A key MBDA goal under Hinson has been to increase private sector involvement in minority businesses.

Hinson concluded that he had to build new relationships with Congress. "I needed to develop a legislative strategy for Capitol Hill. We had no legislative strategy in place when I arrived and we had no staff devoted to working with Congress. I wanted to start articulating our value proposition." As part of this outreach, Hinson testified more times before Congress than any other MBDA national director in the agency's history.

Just as he developed a strategy to work more closely with Congress, Hinson also developed an outreach effort to work with key agencies across government that have expertise in business development: the Overseas Private Investment Corporation, the Export-Import Bank of the United States, the United States Agency for International Development, and the Small Business Administration. "We want the support of these agencies and have begun piloting programs with them. We are seeking to increase our interagency collaboration and participation in government-wide task forces."

Hinson also increased his outreach initiatives to other agencies within Commerce: the Bureau of Industry and Security, the International Trade Administration, and the United States Patent and Trademark Office, to find opportunities to work together and support one another in their efforts to reach out to minority-owned businesses. Hinson says, "We are being more assertive in our relationships within the Department." Hinson also worked with Commerce's National Telecommunications and Information Administration (NTIA) in its implementation of the Recovery Act's broadband initiative.

Pamela Hyde at the Substance Abuse and Mental Health Services Administration, Department of Health and Human Services

The Substance Abuse and Mental Health Services Administration (SAMHSA) is one of the smallest operating divisions within the Department of Health and Human Services. It has a budget of $3.6 billion, with a  staff of a little over 600. SAMHSA leads public health efforts to advance the behavioral health of the nation. SAMHSA's mission is to reduce the impact of substance abuse and mental illness on America's communities. Because of its budget, SAMHSA has to be innovative and seek partnerships with organizations both inside and outside of government. "We have to work in non-traditional ways," says Administrator Hyde. "Our budget is a drop in the bucket of health care spending. SAMHSA is like a pebble in a large stone quarry. "

Thus, Pamela Hyde had to quickly confront the challenge facing all collaborators—how do you make a difference with a small budget and a limited number of grants to be distributed across the nation? It quickly became apparent to Hyde that the organization would need to work more closely with state governments. "I've worked at the state, city, and county levels. States are now driving the health agenda of the nation," reflects Hyde. "States are also now reorganizing by putting mental health and substance abuse programs together again. So our focus must now be on the states because of this particular time in history."

As a consequence of Hyde's decision to place greater focus on the states, SAMHSA reorganized to create 10 regional administrators. "We are now organized around states," says Hyde. "We have regional groupings and technical centers. People in the states now know who to go to at the regional level. The White House is also very interested in states. Our challenge is how to bring states along. We need to work on how it all aligns. We could have continued as we have done in the past. Behavioral health now covers a large set of issues, with many different funding streams. I have seen this shift over time."

In addition to working more closely with states, Hyde must also work with other federal agencies. She says, "Lots of other agencies do part of what we do. Regarding substance abuse and mental illness, there is hardly anything we do that somebody else is not also doing. The Centers for Disease Control and Prevention and the Administration for Children and Families have similar programs. For instance, we all have grants programs for childhood trauma. SAMHSA works closely with the National Institutes of Mental Health (which was once together with SAMHSA in a predecessor organization). We have a strong relationship with NIMH. Initiatives that are started as research at NIMH are handed off to us to implement in the field.

"We also need to work closely with the Centers for Medicare and Medicaid Services," notes Hyde. "CMS sets the guidelines for insurance for behavioral health treatment, so we have to work with them on those guidelines." In addition, SAMHSA works with the Department of Veterans Affairs and the Department of Defense on ensuring that behavioral health services are accessible to military families and veterans (one of SAMHSA's eight strategic initiatives).

In addition to federal, state, and local agencies, SAMHSA seeks partnerships with non-profit and private sector organizations. One such partnership is between the SAMHSA-funded National Suicide Prevention Lifeline and Facebook. A new Facebook service allows users to report suicidal comments they see posted online by a friend, who then receives an e-mail encouraging them to call the Lifeline.

A major component of the collaborator's position is to raise the visibility of their agency's mission. In reflecting on her tenure at SAMHSA, Hyde states, "We have gotten our name around. I am happy that behavioral health is getting more well known by people inside and outside of Washington."

Raymond M. Jefferson at the Veterans' Employment and Training Service, Department of Labor

Like the other collaborators profiled in this chapter, Raymond Jefferson found himself leading one of the smallest agencies in the Department of Labor with a budget of over $250 million and over 200 employees. The Congressional intent for the agency was to establish  a leadership position in the Department of Labor for services related to veterans, including job and job training counseling programs, employment placement programs, and job training placement service programs.

Jefferson determined that one of his key strategies in implementing his program was to develop key relationships both within the federal government and across the private sector. Because of the Veterans' Employment and Training Service's (VETS) relatively small budget, it was crucial for Jefferson to create partnerships and to leverage the programs of VETS with activities in other agencies and in the private sector. As an example, one of the major goals that Jefferson set out for VETS was increasing awareness about veteran unemployment. This goal led to collaborations with *Fortune, Forbes, Business Week,* and *GI Jobs* to increase attention to unemployed veterans.

Another key outreach initiative by Jefferson was to the private sector. "We have been meeting with the Chamber of Commerce, the Business Roundtable, the Young Presidents Organization, Business Executives for National Security, and CEOs of Fortune 500 companies," says Jefferson. "We want to create partnerships and to work with their staff to find employment opportunities for veterans."

In addition to reaching out to the private sector, Jefferson was also busy meeting with representatives from other federal Departments, including the Department of Defense, the Office of Personnel Management, and the Department of Veterans

Affairs. "Sometimes I feel," recounts Jefferson, "that I am conducting shuttle di-plomacy. We brought together agencies to work on developing an interagency, public-private, online National Platform and Program for veteran employment. This is a major initiative that would be the one-stop solution that the private sec-tor and all employers would use to hire veterans and veterans would use to find employment. Nothing like it had been attempted before, and it has the potential to solve the high rate of veterans' unemployment—a true game-changer. We needed to get the involvement and support of other agencies to participate in this impor-tant initiative. We reached out to get White House involvement and they were very supportive."

Mary K. Wakefield at the Health Resources and Services Administration, Department of Health and Human Services

The Health Resources and Services Administration (HRSA) is the primary federal agency for improving ac-cess to health care services for people who are uninsured, isolated, or medically vulnerable. While larger than SAMHSA, HRSA is one of the smaller agencies within HHS. It has a budget of over $8 billion and a staff of over 1,800 employees.

Like other collaborators profiled, Dr. Wakefield faced the challenge of in-creasing awareness of her agency. "Some in Congress didn't seem to know much about the breadth and reach of HRSA's programs," recalls Wakefield. "I wanted to make sure that they knew about our agency and all of our programs and the extent to which we had activity underway in their state. I wanted them to be informed about HRSA's assets in their states and in service to their underserved and vulner-able populations. We needed to do a better job telling people, including Congress, what we do."

Dr. Wakefield also found that she needed to work closely with her fellow political executives, since other HHS agencies provide complementary services to the populations served by HRSA. "Secretary Sebelius and Deputy Secretary Corr made a major point about us working together. I found everybody to be coopera-tive and approachable. We share our problems and have open exchanges. There is an esprit de corps among us. We look out for each other and let each other know about problems."

Unlike the production agencies, which primarily deliver services directly to the public, collaborative agencies relay on an intricate network of partners out-side of government. HRSA is a prime example of a government grant-making agency. In describing her agency, Wakefield states that HRSA provides grants to over 3,000 partners in state and local agencies, non-profit organizations, hospi-tals, clinics, colleges and universities, and other organizations. HRSA Community

Health Center networks deliver primary and preventive care at some 8,500 sites to over 20 million mostly low-income patients each year. The Bureau of Maternal and Child Health provides block grants to states to support care to improve the health of women before, during, and after pregnancy and support infants through adolescents, particularly those with special health needs.

A key component of Administrator Wakefield's job is to effectively leverage federal dollars to accomplish national health objectives. A prime example of leveraging federal dollars is HRSA's $4 million grant to the University of Minnesota to create a Coordinating Center for Interprofessional Education and Collaborative Practice. The National Center for Interprofessional Practice and Education supports research, education, data collection, and analysis on the use of well-functioning, well-coordinated teams to provide better patient and family outcomes. In addition to the $4 million federal grant, HRSA worked together with four private philanthropies that committed an additional $8.6 million to support Center projects. Thus, a $4 million grant grew to a $12.6 million project.

While much of Wakefield's time was spent on working with HRSA's network of grantees and implementing the Affordable Care Act, Wakefield was surprised at the time required to work on strengthening the agency itself. Wakefield recalls, "I had to look at the infrastructure of our organization and how well it supported meeting our mission to improve access to quality care. This involved carefully reviewing and adjusting our deployment of people and resources, from realigning the agency's organizational structure to investing in training and information technology. For example, too often we were still processing paperwork the old way and agency hiring was slow."

In reflecting on her accomplishments at HRSA, Wakefield says, "I think it is strengthening the organization. We now have a much stronger organization. I must admit, this took far more of my time than I anticipated but meeting program and policy expectations is contingent on a high performing organization. It is what leaders must do when they find weak features in their organizational infrastructure."

Appendix to Chapter 8
Profiles of Collaborators Interviewed

Daniel M. Ashe

Tenure

Mr. Ashe was nominated by President Obama to serve as Director of the U.S. Fish and Wildlife Service (FWS) in December 2010, and confirmed by the U.S. Senate in June 2011.

Federal Government Experience

Prior to being confirmed as Director, Mr. Ashe held a variety of key career positions within FWS, including Deputy Director for Policy, Science Advisor to the Director of FWS, Chief of the National Wildlife Refuge System, and Assistant Director for External Affairs. From 1982 to 1995, he served as a member of the professional staff of the former Committee on Merchant Marine and Fisheries in the U.S. House of Representatives. Ashe is a second-generation FWS employee. His father was a 37-year career employee, retiring in 1990 as Deputy Regional Director for the Northeast Region.

Education

Mr. Ashe received his B.A. degree in Biological Sciences from Florida State University, and a Masters of Marine Affairs from the Institute for Marine Studies at the University of Washington.

Reflecting on Leading the U.S Fish and Wildlife Service

"You need to understand the agency. If you want to get things done here, somebody once told me that you cannot use a command-and-control approach. You need to engage the organization and get employees invested in your vision for the future. They don't respond to command-and-control. The people here really care about the mission of the agency. They are very supportive if you can show them how they fit in with where you want to go."

John Berry

Tenure
Mr. Berry was nominated by President Obama to serve as Director of the U.S. Office of Personnel Management (OPM) in March 2009, and confirmed by the U.S. Senate in April 2009. Mr. Berry announced his departure from OPM in April 2013 after completion of his four-year term.

Present Position
Mr. Berry is serving as Ambassador of the United States to Australia after confirmation by the U.S Senate in August 2013.

Photo: Tony Powell

Federal Government Experience
Prior to being confirmed as Director of OPM, Mr. Berry was the Director of the National Zoo in Washington, D.C. from 2005 to 2009. From 1997 to 2000, Mr. Berry served as Assistant Secretary for Policy, Management and Budget at the Department of the Interior. Mr. Berry also served in the Department of the Treasury and the Smithsonian Institution. Prior to his executive branch service, Mr. Berry served for nearly 10 years on the staff of Representative Steny Hoyer.

Non-Profit Sector Experience
From 2000 to 2005, Mr. Berry served as the Director of the National Fish and Wildlife Foundation.

State and Local Government Experience
Earlier in his career, Mr. Berry worked for the Montgomery County government. He also served as Staff Director of the Maryland Senate Finance Committee.

Education
Mr. Berry graduated *summa cum laude* from the University of Maryland with a Bachelor's degree in Government and Politics in 1980. In 1981, he earned a Master's degree in Public Administration from Syracuse University.

Reflecting on Serving in OPM
In 2010, Berry told *Government Executive* magazine, "I'm having a ball. The opportunity to do good in government service is incredible—and humbling. And I'm working real hard to try to get as much good done as I can, knowing that the clock is ticking … Because I've got such a great team, I sleep well at night, and I'm pretty confident we're going to get some good points on the board" (Rosenberg).

In reflecting on his time at OPM, Berry describes one of his highlights, "We had a national conference on workplace life at the White House with private-sector leaders. I got to introduce the President. That was really neat for a boy from Montgomery County, Maryland."

David A. Hinson

Tenure
Mr. Hinson was appointed by Secretary of Commerce Gary Locke as National Director of the Minority Business Development Agency in July 2009.

Private Sector Experience
Prior to joining the Department of Commerce, Mr. Hinson was President and CEO of Wealth Management Network, Inc., a financial advisory company. Mr. Hinson managed a 10-state sales region as Director of Advisory Services and Managing Director of Business Development for Envestnet Asset Management, a publicly traded, $70 billion financial advisory firm. Mr. Hinson has also held a variety of positions at Bank of America, Morgan Stanley & Company, First Chicago (now JP Morgan Chase) and the Village Foundation.

Education
Mr. Hinson received an M.B.A. in Finance from The University of Pennsylvania Wharton School, and a Bachelor's degree in Insurance and Finance with honors from Howard University.

Reflecting on Serving at MBDA
"We have increased the stature of the organization. More people are paying attention to us now. I think the image of MBDA has improved. We are trying to get everybody engaged internally and are engaging more stakeholders and government agencies. We have a job to do—expanding the United States economy and creating more jobs. We want to do more. I believe we can go from $2.9 billion in minority business exports to $6 billion.

"It's been a great experience. I think we have moved the needle. I'm happy to be here. I think we have added value."

Pamela S. Hyde

Tenure
Ms. Hyde was nominated by President Obama to serve as Administrator, Substance Abuse and Mental Health Services Administration (SAMHSA) in October 2009, and confirmed by the U.S. Senate in November 2009.

State Government Experience
Prior to her appointment as Administrator of SAMHSA, Ms. Hyde was Secretary of the New Mexico Human Services Department from 2003 to 2009. She also served as Director of the Job and Family Services Department and Director of the Department of Mental Health for the state of Ohio.

Private Sector Experience
Ms. Hyde served as President of the Community Partnership for Behavioral Health Care in Maricopa County, Arizona.

Local Government Experience
Ms. Hyde served as Director, Department of Housing and Human Services for the city of Seattle, Washington.

Federal Government Experience
Ms. Hyde served as a VISTA Volunteer in southeast Ohio, and as a consultant to the Department of Justice.

Education
Ms. Hyde received her J.D. degree from the University of Michigan Law School and her B.A. degree from Southwest Missouri State University.

Reflecting on Serving in Government
"I would encourage others to serve in government. I would say, 'Do it.' Government is a special place. Like in any other organizations, you have to take advantage of opportunities. And you have to be persistent. You will win some and lose some. You just need to keep trying."

Raymond M. (Ray) Jefferson

Tenure
Mr. Jefferson was nominated by President Obama to be Assistant Secretary of the Veterans' Employment and Training Service in June 2009, and confirmed by the U.S. Senate in August 2009. Mr. Jefferson resigned his position at the Department of Labor in July 2011.

Present Position
Mr. Jefferson is an entrepreneur now based in Singapore.

Private Sector Experience
Prior to being confirmed as Assistant Secretary, Mr. Jefferson served as a Leadership Consultant with McKinsey & Company in Singapore.

State Government Experience
Mr. Jefferson served as the Deputy Director for the State of Hawaii's Department of Business, Economic Development and Tourism.

Federal Government Experience
Mr. Jefferson was selected as a White House Fellow and worked as a Special Assistant to the U.S. Secretary of Commerce. He served as an Army Officer with the infantry, Rangers, and Special Forces, with leadership positions in the U.S. Presidential Honor Guard, 3rd Ranger Battalion, and 1st Special Forces Group.

Education
Mr. Jefferson graduated from the U.S. Military Academy at West Point with a major in leadership. Mr. Jefferson attended Harvard's Kennedy School of Government, earning an M.P.A. in Strategic Management with Distinction as a Littauer Fellow. He also has an M.B.A. from Harvard Business School.

Reflecting on Serving in VETS
"I've enjoyed being part of an organization that is passionate about their mission. I view our mission as a noble calling. Our team has brought energy and skill to our mission. Our goals are to assist and prepare veterans and service members to obtain meaningful careers, maximize their employment opportunities, and protect their employment rights.

"Being part of this team has been a great experience and very meaningful. It's been a robust and rich experience for me."

Mary K. Wakefield

Tenure
Dr. Wakefield was named by President Obama to serve as Administrator of the Health Resources and Services Administration in February 2009.

Academic Experience
Prior to being appointed as Administrator, Dr. Wakefield was Associate Dean for Rural Health at the School of Medicine and Health at the University of North Dakota, where she was also a tenured professor and Director of the Center for Rural Health. She also served as the Director of the Center for Health Policy, Research and Ethics at George Mason University. She began her health care career as a registered nurse.

Federal Government Experience
From 1987 to 1992, Dr. Wakefield served as Chief of Staff to Senator Quentin Burdick. From 1993 to 1996, she served as Chief of Staff to Senator Kent Conrad. She has also served on a number of federal advisory committees.

Education
Dr. Wakefield has a Bachelor of Science degree in nursing from the University of Mary in Bismarck, North Dakota, and master's and doctoral degrees in nursing from the University of Texas at Austin.

Reflecting on Serving in HRSA
"It is a privilege to work with the leaders and staff at HRSA. Too often, rank and file federal employees are the subject of sweeping criticism. The people I work with have an incredible commitment to mission, they work very hard to get to yes. Human resources are the government's most important asset and I highly value their contributions. It's important for me to show them appreciation."

Appendix

Dates of Interviews

Dates of Interviews

Jonathan S. Adelstein, Administrator, Rural Utilities Service, Department of Agriculture
April 8, 2010; October 15, 2010; April 7, 2011

Daniel M. Ashe, Director, U.S. Fish & Wildlife Service, Department of the Interior
April 4, 2012

John Berry, Director, Office of Personnel Management
July 30, 2009; June 21, 2010; March 15, 2011

Rebecca M. Blank, Under Secretary for Economic Affairs, Economics and Statistics Administration, Department of Commerce
December 4, 2009; June 1, 2010; March 9, 2011

Rafael Borras, Under Secretary for Management, Department of Homeland Security
April 25, 2012

Michael R. Bromwich, Director, Bureau of Ocean Energy Management, Regulation and Enforcement, Department of the Interior
November 30, 2010; June 28, 2011

William V. Corr, Deputy Secretary, Department of Health and Human Services
March 26, 2012

Patrick D. Gallagher, Director, National Institute of Standards and Technology and Under Secretary of Commerce for Standards and Technology, Department of Commerce
January 15, 2010; July 26, 2010; May 13, 2011

W. Scott Gould, Deputy Secretary, Department of Veterans Affairs
October 8, 2009; June 4, 2010; March 22, 2011

Margaret A. Hamburg, Commissioner, Food and Drug Administration
June 13, 2013

Seth D. Harris, Deputy Secretary, Department of Labor
December 22, 2009; June 25, 2010; April 11, 2011

David J. Hayes, Deputy Secretary, Department of the Interior
March 23, 2012

Allison A. Hickey, Under Secretary for Benefits, Department of Veterans Affairs
March 7, 2012; August 14, 2012

David A. Hinson, National Director, Minority Business Development Agency, Department of Commerce
June 25, 2010; December 20, 2010; June 29, 2011

Dennis F. Hightower, Deputy Secretary, Department of Commerce
November 11, 2009; July 6, 2010

Pamela S. Hyde, Administrator, Substance Abuse and Mental Health Services Administration, Department of Health and Human Services
July 8, 2013

Raymond M. Jefferson, Assistant Secretary of the Veterans' Employment and Training Service, Department of Labor
June 16, 2010; December 3, 2010; July 5, 2011

Maurice Jones, Deputy Secretary, Department of Housing and Urban Development
May 31, 2013

David J. Kappos, Under Secretary of Commerce for Intellectual Property and Director, United States Patent and Trademark Office, Department of Commerce
March 30, 2010; August 25, 2010, April 26, 2011

Joseph A. Main, Assistant Secretary of Labor for Mine Safety and Health, Department of Labor
March 9, 2010; September 1, 2010; May 24, 2011

Arun Majumdar, Director, Advanced Research Projects Agency-Energy, Department of Energy
June 10, 2010; January 7, 2011; July 6, 2011

Allison M. Macfarlane, Chairman, United States Nuclear Regulatory Commission
April 5, 2013

Alejandro Mayorkas, Director, U.S. Citizenship and Immigration Services
March 27, 2013

Marcia K. McNutt, Director, U.S. Geological Survey, Department of the Interior
March 30, 2010; September 16, 2010; March 24, 2011

Victor M. Mendez, Administrator, Federal Highway Administration, Department of Transportation
December 8, 2009; June 22, 2010; March 16, 2011

Kathleen A. Merrigan, Deputy Secretary, Department of Agriculture
November 4, 2009; May 25, 2010; March 8, 2011

Anthony W. Miller, Deputy Secretary, Department of Education
January 13, 2009; July 8, 2010; March 23, 2011

John T. Morton, Director, United States Immigration and Customs Enforcement, Department of Homeland Security
June 5, 2013

Richard G. Newell, Administrator, U.S. Energy Information Administration, Department of Energy
April 12, 2010; November 3, 2010; April 20, 2011

Thomas R. Nides, Deputy Secretary for Management and Resources, Department of State
March 7, 2012

Robert A. Petzel, Under Secretary for Health, Department of Veterans Affairs
June 14, 2013

John S. Pistole, Administrator, Transportation Security Administration,
    Department of Homeland Security
    May 10, 2012
Daniel B. Poneman, Deputy Secretary, Department of Energy
    February 25, 2010; August 3, 2010; May 18, 2011
James W. Runcie, Chief Operating Officer, Office of Federal Student Aid,
    Department of Eduction
    April 17, 2013
David H. Stevens, Assistant Secretary for Housing and Commissioner, Federal
    Housing Administration, Department of Housing and Urban Development
    December 16, 2009; June 22, 2010; March 21, 2011
David L. Strickland, Administrator, National Highway Traffic Safety
    Administration, Department of Transportation
    June 21, 2010; December 1, 2010; June 15, 2011
Kathryn D. Sullivan, Deputy Administrator and Assistant Secretary of
    Commerce for Environmental Observation and Prediction, National
    Oceanic and Atmospheric Administration, Department of Commerce
    April 4, 2010
Joseph C. Szabo, Administrator, Federal Railroad Administration, Department
    of Transportation
    June 21, 2010; December 16, 2010; July 6, 2011
William J. Taggart, Chief Operating Officer, Office of Federal Student Aid,
    Department of Education
    February 24, 2010; August 2, 2010; March 31, 2011
Inez Moore Tenenbaum, Chairman, Consumer Product Safety Commission
    November 13, 2009; June 3, 2010; April 7, 2011
Mary K. Wakefield, Administrator, Health Resources and Services
    Administration, Department of Health and Human Services
    April 22, 2013
Jon Wellinghoff, Chairman, Federal Energy Regulatory Commission
    May 31, 2013

References

Achenbach, Joel. *A Hole at the Bottom of the Sea: The Race to Kill the BP Oil Gusher.* New York: Simon & Schuster, 2011.

Bair, Sheila. *Bull by the Horns: Fighting To Save Main Street from Wall Street and Wall Street from Itself.* New York: Free Press, 2012.

Broder, John M. "The Regulator: Answering a Call, Slowly." *New York Times,* April 20, 2011.

Clark, Charles. "State Department Executive: No 'Fantasy World' about Budget." *Government Executive* website, March 15, 2012.

Coons, Chris. "Statement from Senator Coons on Resignation of ARPA-E Director." May 9, 2012.

Department of Homeland Security, "Rafael Borras Confirmation Hearing to be Under Secretary for Management, U.S. Department of Homeland Security." April 7, 2011.

Department of State, 2011. "A Unified Security Budget for the United States," Remarks by Thomas Nides to the Center for American Progress. August 31, 2011.

Department of State, 2012a. "Rightsizing U.S. Mission Iraq." Special Briefing: Thomas Nides via Teleconference, February 8, 2012.

Department of State, 2012b. "Remarks to the Global Business Conference." Remarks by Thomas Nides, February 21, 2012.

DeSeve, G. Edward. *Speeding Up the Learning Curve: Observations from a Survey of Seasoned Political Appointees.* IBM Center for The Business of Government, 2009.

Filsinger, Matthew and Milmoe, Joe. "Restore & Enhance." *Fish & Wildlife News,* Summer 2012.

Fox, Tom. "The Federal Coach." *Washington Post,* September 6, 2013.

Government Accountability Office (GAOa). "GAO High Risk and Other Major Government Challenges: Department of Veterans Affairs." www.gao.gov/highrisk/agency/vad/.

Government Accountability Office (GAOb). "GAO High Risk and Other Major Government Challenges: Strategic Human Capital Management." http://www.gao.gov/highrisk/risks/efficiency-effectiveness/strategic_human_management.php.

Government Accountability Office (GAOc). "GAO's High Risk List: Implementing and Transforming the Department of Homeland Security." February 2011, GAO-11-278.

Government Accountability Office (GAOd). "Continued Progress Made Improving and Integrating Management Areas, but More Work Remains." March 1, 2012, GAO-12-365T.

Lawrence, Paul R., and Mark A. Abramson (2010a). *Analysis: Getting Appointees Up to Speed.* GovernmentExecutive.com, February 17, 2010.

Lawrence, Paul R., and Mark A. Abramson (2010b). *Speeding up Government: Responding to the Continuing Challenge.* Federal News Radio website, May 18, 2010.

Lederman, Doug. "So Far So Good." *Inside Higher Ed*, October 25, 2010.

Nixon, Ron. "Consumer Safety Chief Leaves a Small Agency with Bigger Powers," *New York Times,* November 30, 2013.

Partnership for Public Service. *Ready to Govern: Improving the Presidential Transition.* January 2010.

Peters, Katherine McIntire. "Wasteland: Decades of Poor Management at the Energy Department Threatens Public Health and National Security." *Government Executive*, December 2010.

Pistole, John S. Statement of John S. Pistole before the United States House of Representatives, Committee on Homeland Security, Subcommittee on Transportation Security, June 7, 2012.

Rein, Lisa. "The Rights Man for the Job." *Washington Post,* September 19, 2012.

Rosenberg, Alyssa. "Charged for Change: OPM Director John Berry Taps Positive Energy to Push Through Telework, Hiring, and Pay Reforms." *Government Executive*, March 2010.

Rossotti, Charles O. *Many Unhappy Returns: One Man's Quest to Turn Around the Most Unpopular Organization in America.* Boston: Harvard Business School Press, 2005.

Springer, Linda. "Building Relationships: Three Conversations to Have Right Away," in Paul Lawrence and Mark Abramson, *Paths to Making a Difference: Leading in Government (Revised Edition).* Lanham: Rowman and Littlefield Publishers, 2013.

Sullivan, Kathryn D. Written Statement by Kathryn D. Sullivan before the United States House of Representatives, Committee on Science, Space and Technology, Subcommittees on Energy and Environment and Investigations and Oversight, June 27, 2012.

Wilson, James Q. *Bureaucracy: What Government Agencies Do and Why They Do It.* New York: Basic Books, 1989.

About the Authors

Paul R. Lawrence is a Principal in the Advisory Services practice of Ernst & Young LLP, and a leader in its Federal Government Consulting Practice. He served as the Partner-in-Charge of the Ernst & Young "Initiative on Leadership," which resulted in the publication of this book.

Mr. Lawrence has more than 25 years of experience working closely with government leaders. Prior to joining Ernst & Young LLP, Mr. Lawrence was a Vice President with Accenture, an Executive Director with the MITRE Corporation, a Vice President with IBM Business Consulting Services, and a Partner at PricewaterhouseCoopers.

He has written extensively on technology, management, and government. He is the co-author of *Paths to Making a Difference: Leading in Government* and the co-editor of *Transforming Organizations* and *Learning the Ropes: Insights for Political Appointees*. He has testified before Congress and several state legislatures. He serves on the Board of Advisors to the Economic Program at the University of Massachusetts and has served on the Board of Advisors of the Thomas Jefferson Public Policy Program at The College of William and Mary. He was twice selected by *Federal Computer Week* as one of the top 100 public service business leaders. He is a Fellow of the National Academy of Public Administration.

Mr. Lawrence earned his Master of Arts and Ph.D. in Economics from Virginia Tech. He earned his Bachelor of Arts degree in Economics from the University of Massachusetts, Amherst, graduating Phi Beta Kappa.

Mark A. Abramson is President of Leadership Inc. He served as Project Director of the EY "Initiative on Leadership."

During his career, Mr. Abramson has served as Executive Director of the IBM Center for The Business of Government, President of the Council for Excellence in Government, and a Senior Program Evaluator in the Office of the Assistant Secretary for Planning and Evaluation in the Department of Health and Human Services. While at the Council for Excellence in Government, Mr. Abramson was instrumental in launching *The Prune Book* series in 1988, which profiled the toughest jobs in government.

Throughout his career, Mr. Abramson has published numerous books and articles. He is the co-author of *Paths to Making a Difference: Leading in Government* and co-editor of *The Operator's Manual for the New Administration, Getting It Done: A Guide for Government Executives,* and *Learning the Ropes: Insights for Political Appointees.* Mr. Abramson serves as editor of the *IBM Center for The Business of Government Book Series,* published by Rowman & Littlefield Publishers. He is also the author or editor of 16 books and has published more than 100 articles on public management. From 2005 to 2008, he served on the editorial board of the *Public Administration Review* as Case Study Editor. He has also served as a Contributing Editor to *Government Executive* and as a member of the Board of Editors and Forum Editor for *The Public Manager.*

Mr. Abramson was elected a Fellow of the National Academy of Public Administration and is past President of the National Capital Area Chapter (NCAC) of the American Society for Public Administration. He received a Master of Arts degree in political science from the Maxwell School of Citizenship and Public Affairs at Syracuse University and a Bachelor of Arts degree from Florida State University.

About EY

EY | Assurance | Tax | Transactions | Advisory

About EY

EY is a global leader in assurance, tax, transaction and advisory services. The insights and quality services we deliver help build trust and confidence in the capital markets and in economies the world over. We develop outstanding leaders who team to deliver on our promises to all of our stakeholders. In so doing, we play a critical role in building a better working world for our people, for our clients and for our communities.

EY refers to the global organization, and may refer to one or more, of the member firms of Ernst & Young Global Limited, each of which is a separate legal entity. Ernst & Young Global Limited, a UK company limited by guarantee, does not provide services to clients. For more information about our organization, please visit ey.com.

Ernst & Young LLP is a client-serving member firm of Ernst & Young Global Limited operating in the US.

SCORE no. BT0364